Privatization and Market Development

Privatization and Market Development

Global Movements in Public Policy Ideas

Edited by

Graeme Hodge

Director, Centre for Regulatory Studies, Faculty of Law, Monash University, Australia

MONASH STUDIES IN GLOBAL MOVEMENTS

Edward Elgar

Cheltenham, UK • Northampton, MA, USA

Published by
Edward Elgar Publishing Limited
Glensanda House
Montpellier Parade
Cheltenham
Glos GL50 1UA
UK

Edward Elgar Publishing, Inc.
William Pratt House
9 Dewey Court
Northampton
Massachusetts 01060
USA

A catalogue record for this book
is available from the British Library

Library of Congress Cataloguing in Publication Data

Privatization and market development : global movements in public policy
ideas / edited by Graeme Hodge.
    p. cm.—(Monash studies in global movements series)
    Includes bibliographical references and index.
    1. Privatization. 2. Economic policy. I. Hodge, Graeme A. II. Series.
    HD3850.P733 2006
    338.9′25—dc22   2006011711

ISBN-13: 978 1 84376 935 4
ISBN-10: 1 84376 935 2

Typeset by Cambrian Typesetters, Camberley, Surrey
Printed and bound in Great Britain by MPG Books Ltd, Bodmin, Cornwall

Contents

Figures

Tables

Contributors

Dr Alesya Bogaevskaya

Alesya Bogaevskaya, Ph.D., is a doctoral student at the Center for Public Administration and Policy, School of Public and International Affairs, Virginia Polytechnic Institute and State University, USA. She received her Ph.D. in Sociology from Moscow State University in 1995. She has served as Assistant Professor at the Maritime State Academy, Vladivostok, Russia (1996–1998) and as Chair of the Department of Social Management at the Far Eastern State University, Vladivostok, Russia (1999–2002). In 2002–2003 she was a Fulbright Scholar in the United States. Her research interests are in regulation, privatization, and comparative human capital development policy in the United States and the European Union.

Ms Diana Bowman

Diana Bowman is a Research Fellow in the Centre for Regulatory Studies, Faculty of Law at Monash University, Australia, and a visiting lecturer in sports law at Victoria University. She has published in the areas of public accountability, contracting out government services, public–private partnerships, energy regulation and regulating medical practices. Her current doctoral studies at Monash University have investigated the regulation of new technologies such as nanotechnology and have covered several frontiers including product safety, intellectual property, international law and public policy.

Professor Paul Cook

Paul Cook is Professor of Economics and Development Policy and Head of the Institute for Development Policy and Management (IDPM) at the University of Manchester, UK. He is also Director of the Centre on Regulation and Competition in the Institute. He has previously held teaching positions in universities in Canada and the United States, and has published widely in the areas of privatization and public enterprise reform and development policy.

Associate Professor Larkin Dudley

Larkin Dudley, Ph.D., is Associate Professor/Chair, Center for Public Adminis-tration and Policy, School of Public and International Affairs, Virginia Polytechnic Institute and State University, USA. Dr. Dudley is a graduate of the University of Georgia (B.A., M.A.) and Virginia Tech (Ph.D.).

Dudley teaches and does research in the areas of public–private relationships, public policy, deliberative democracy, and public management. She is the winner of a CAUS teaching award and has been at Virginia Polytechnic Institute and State University since 1974. She has also pursued interests in women and world development, legislation and lobbying, and the application of law in organizations. At Virginia Polytechnic Institute and State University, she has served as Visiting Assistant Professor, Political Science (1990–1991); Academic Advisor, University Academic Advising Center (1990–1991); and Research Associate, Institute for Public Management, College of Architecture and Urban Studies (1987–1989).

Dr Fabrizio Gilardi

Fabrizio Gilardi, Ph.D., is a lecturer in political science at the University of Lausanne, Switzerland. His research interests include regulation, comparative political economy, welfare state policy and politics, political delegation, and policy diffusion processes. His work has been published in the *Journal of Theoretical Politics*, the *Journal of European Public Policy*, the *Annals of the American Academy of Political and Social Science*, *Politische Vierteljahresschrift*, and the *Swiss Political Science Review*. He has also co-edited a volume on delegation in contemporary democracies (Routledge, 2006).

Dr George Gilligan

Dr George Gilligan lives in Melbourne, Australia, where he is Senior Research Fellow in the Department of Business Law and Taxation at Monash University. He has taught at the University of Cambridge, Exeter University and Middlesex University in the UK, and La Trobe University, the University of Melbourne and Monash University in Australia. His research interests centre on regulatory theory and practice, especially in relation to the financial services sector; white-collar crime; organized crime; and corruption. He has published extensively in these areas and conducted numerous field research projects examining the praxis of regulation.

Professor Carsten Greve

Carsten Greve is Professor in public–private cooperation and public management at the International Center for Business and Politics, Copenhagen Business School in Denmark. He has previously held posts at Aalborg University and the University of Copenhagen. His main research interests are privatization, contracting out, regulatory reform, public–private partnerships and public management reform in a comparative perspective. Recent publications include *The Challenge of Public–Private Partnerships: Learning from International Experience* (edited with Graeme Hodge) (Edward Elgar, 2005), and *Contracts as Reinvented Institutions in the Public Sector* (with Niels

Ejersbo) (Praeger, 2005). He currently directs a research project on 'PPPs – policymaking and regulation'.

Professor Graeme Hodge

Graeme Hodge is Professor of Law and Director of the Centre for Regulatory Studies, Faculty of Law at Monash University, Australia. A leading international analyst on privatization, outsourcing and public–private partnerships he has served as a Special Adviser to several Parliamentary Committees and Inquiries. He has published in management, social and economic policy, public administration, law, governance and regulation. His most recent publication was *The Challenge of Public–Private Partnerships: Learning from International Experience* (edited with Carsten Greve) (Edward Elgar, 2005). He has acted as a consultant on governance matters in Australasia, Indonesia, Philippines and China.

Professor Jacint Jordana

Jacint Jordana is Professor of Political Science at the Department of Political and Social Sciences in the Universitat Pompeu Fabra (Barcelona, Spain). His main research area is focused on the analysis of public policies, with special emphasis being laid on regulatory policy and regulatory governance. Recent publications include the article 'Policy networks and market opening: telecommunications liberalization in Spain' (with D. Sancho, *European Journal of Political Research* 2005), *The Politics of Regulation* (edited with D. Levi-Faur, Edward Elgar, 2004) and *The Rise of Regulatory Capitalism: The Global Diffusion of a New Order* (edited with D. Levi-Faur, *Annals of the American Academy of Political and Social Science*, 2005). He is currently the director of the Barcelona Institute for International Studies (IBEI).

Dr David Levi-Faur

David Levi-Faur is a Senior Lecturer at the University of Haifa. He has held research positions in the University of Oxford, the Australian National University and the University of Manchester and visiting positions in the London School of Economics, the University of Amsterdam, University of Utrecht and University of California (Berkeley). He is currently working on a book manuscript *Regulating Capitalism: Governance and the Global Spread of Regulatory Agencies*, to be published by Princeton University Press. His recent work includes special issues of the *Annals of the American Academy of Political and Social Sciences* ('The global diffusion of regulatory capitalism', co-edited with Jacint Jordana) and *Governance* ('Varieties of regulatory capitalism').

Professor David Parker

David Parker is Research Professor in Privatisation and Regulation at the Cranfield School of Management, Cranfield University, UK and Co-director of the Regulation Research Programme at the Centre on Regulation and Competition at the University of Manchester, UK. He has written extensively on privatization and economic regulation and is a member of the UK's Competition Commission and an Economic Advisor to the Office of Utilities Regulation in Jamaica. He has acted as a consultant on privatization and economic regulation in a range of countries and is currently writing the Government's official history of privatization in the UK.

Acknowledgements

The Editor would like to thank the authors for their contributions, engagement and encouragement throughout this project; Diana Bowman at the Centre for Regulatory Studies, Monash University for her editorial assistance and project management skills, patience and diplomacy; Elaya Mutabazi, for her editorial assistance; the Monash Institute for the Study of Global Movements for project funding; staff at Edward Elgar; and finally Stephanie, Anthony, Christopher and Michael for their love and family support.

1. Introduction

Graeme Hodge

The spread of the privatization ethos has been remarkable. At a simplistic level, it began as a political initiative under Margaret Thatcher in the United Kingdom and became a global movement. But this enterprise sales policy was always one part of a bigger story. This book traces how the strength of the privatization idea has grown in application, and how it has spread around the world to become a central dimension to public policy concerns.

At the broadest level, privatization is a philosophical stance. It is a statement as to the existence of an economy founded on a market of privately owned companies and firms, as distinct from a centrally controlled economic engine based on public ownership. The demise of most centrally controlled economies over the past two decades showed that the latter idea seemed to work far better in theory than practice. Whilst in concept the idea was to generate wealth for the common good, in practice it fell far short on almost every test of effectiveness. The ideas underpinning the privatization stance, whether they are economic, philosophical, political, cultural or even religious, have as their essence a belief that the engine of economic growth is fundamentally private.

IDEAS AND LESSONS IN THE PRIVATIZATION DEBATE

This privatization belief, perhaps understandably, has been one side of what has been termed 'the privatization war' over the past few centuries (Hodge, 2002). The privatization war has been raging on at least three fronts. First, it is a part of a philosophical battle between individualism in preference to collectivism. The collective good as a priority over one's own individual private interests is the lifeblood in the role of government. All public policy decisions are about determining how best to serve the interests of citizens and the public, rather than solely private interests. The second front of the privatization war has been on the territory of service delivery, and the question of whether the public or the private sector is best placed to deliver government services. On the one side, privatization reformers attack with claims of inefficiency and service incompetence from government bureaucracies. Critics of privatization return fire with observations of cutting corners to increase profits and unethical corporate behaviour. The third fighting front for the privatization war exists through the eternal struggle of capital interests against civility in society and human rights. This territory witnesses ongoing battles between the powerful and sometimes shadowy influence of capital owners with a voracious desire for higher rates of investment return on the one hand, and the welfare of human beings, their human rights and governing for social cohesion on the other. All three fighting fronts exist within the battleground of political and social change.

The lessons to date from the battlefield of privatization have been many. Our collective experience suggests that the privatization rhetoric offered by political and investment actors does differ from the empirical realities of citizens and consumers living on the battlefield. The single overarching lesson for governments around the globe has clearly been for far greater care to be taken when adopting privatization policies. Privatization can be a useful policy servant, but it can also be a poor ideological master.

Our experience suggests that privatization policies have usually seen strong winners and losers. This implies that, as well as care in decision making, policy debates should be open and thorough. Empirical studies suggest that whilst there are often economic gains with the sale of public enterprises, for instance, these tend to be relatively modest on average, and fall short of grandiose political promises made (Martin and Parker, 1997; Hodge, 2000; Cook and Kirkpatrick, 2003). Contracting-out public services as well has provided some gains in efficiency, but again these have been modest on average, and far short of the political panaceas promised.

Looking above the various techniques towards the national level of policy, it is evident that strong communities nowadays need both strong government and a strong private sector. The dominance of one over the other inevitably leads to poorer communities in terms of liveability. Returning to a theme from history, that of 'the mixed economy', it is apparent that the critical issue is that of balance rather than supremacy of one sector over the other. Clearly, strong communities need wealth in order for resources to be available for public policy purposes as well as private purposes. But equally, private markets do not naturally serve the public interest – they require good governance and regulation in order for market games to be played according to fair and effective rules for all. Reflecting on our earlier comment regarding the power of the private sector engine to drive economic growth, we might add that it is the public sector's governing role which ought properly steer the engine towards societal goals.

Looking back, privatization was always as much about power and influence in times of change, as it was about economics. In this respect, and perhaps paradoxically, privatization initiatives have always required greater attention to improving public accountability if governments are to avoid the hostility of citizens intent on continuing to receive essential services at reasonable cost and quality. The learning here has been that we now need stronger and more capable government as a result. The rise of the 're-regulated state' is the physical manifestation of this learning.

THE PRIVATIZATION POLICY FAMILY

So, whilst the privatization movement was most commonly identified initially as the sale of enterprises in the UK, it has now developed into a broad family of techniques. These number several dozen and now have global relevance, covering multiple activities from denationalizing, load-shedding, subsidizing the private production of goods, deregulation/liberalization through to the introduction of user charges (Hodge, 2000:15). These days, we might posit the strongest threads of the privatization movement to be:

* Enterprise sales
* Contracting-out of government services
* Public–private partnerships, and
* Private sector development strategy.

Critically, this family of privatization ideas has been bolstered by the philosophies and techniques of the New Public Management (NPM) movement. There has been much debate over the past decade on just what constitutes NPM, but it is broadly conceived as the greater use of private sector techniques in a government of reduced size and scope, restructured bureaucracies and the introduction of competition through internal markets and contracted-out services, and the stronger use of performance management and auditing techniques (Minogue, 2004). It is hardly surprising therefore that this movement has been mutually supportive of privatization policies. Of particular importance, though, have been two thrusts. First has been the progressive contractualization of government service delivery arrangements. Contracts have themselves risen from simply being a tighter arrangement through which commercial services such as cleaning and maintenance can be delivered, to becoming a governing mechanism for several coming decades in the case of public–private partnerships. Second, there has been an increasing focus on better performance measurement in all areas of government. The performance measurement and management literature has had a long history over the past half-century, and the promise of performance-based contracts in government has represented a recent holy grail to some proponents.[1]

In this age of the privatized state, there is also now a renewed emphasis on better understanding the major dimensions of competition, ownership and regulation, with a renewed desire to separate out the effects of each of these dimensions more clearly in our debates. And above these concerns, we have also rediscovered, albeit belatedly, the need for stronger governance as the underpinning political and institutional foundation of a vibrant market and society.

THIS BOOK

The aim of this book is to inform readers interested in assessing privatization and market development on a global scale in an accessible manner and to outline some of the more important understandings on how these ideas have moved around the globe. Following the ideas of writers such as Rogers (1995), Stone (2000) or Bennett (1997), there is a need to better understand the processes by which ideas have spread, and practices and policies have diffused. Bennett's references to 'ripple effects', and Stone's challenge to better understand lesson drawing, policy transfer and international diffusion all provide sensible foundations on which to build stronger empirical understandings of the phenomenon of global privatization policy. The transfer of privatization policies around the globe, according to Bennett (1997) might potentially involve penetration, harmonization, elite networking and policy communities or emulation (Bennett, 1997). Each of these mechanisms is likely to have different implications.

The book therefore brings together a range of contributions with two purposes. First, it aims to trace how the privatization idea has grown in application, and how it has spread to become a central policy idea – many would say 'solution' to governance concerns. Second, it aims to bridge the divide between developed economies and developing economies and provide space for reflection and thought on the importance of these policy ideas. This book is oriented to public policy readers.

Book Structure

In terms of structure, there are two broad thrusts to the book. The first thrust focuses on each of four components of privatization; enterprise sales, contracting-out government services, public–private partnerships and private sector development strategy. Key ideas to be followed up here are numerous, to my mind. Some of the critical questions for us to consider include:

* What is the policy idea, and what has it now become?
* How has the idea spread, why and through whom?

- How effective has the policy idea been based on empirical evidence to date?
- How can the effectiveness of this idea be improved now?

In terms of the global spread of policy ideas, we might also consider questions such as the roles of the international institutions, including the World Bank, International Monetary Fund and the OECD. And, as well, we ought assess which lessons are being learned internationally now, and which are not.

The second thrust of the book investigates a few of the myriad of market development issues influential as markets develop. We look primarily at three areas.

The first observation is that 'change in government' has today become a global business. In other words, reforming the public sector has intrinsic value not only in the sense of the search for better management and capability, but such business financial transactions have also begun to play a part of the economic engine of the economy itself. Indeed, with some privatizations such as the sale of public enterprises, success is now judged as much on the size of the financial transaction, as it is on the effectiveness of reform outcomes. But to what degree are governments now dependent on business advice and leadership, and should governments be reducing their dependence on buying such business reform policy advice?

One of the most notable characteristics of the past two decades has been the rise of the re-regulated state as efficiency in the production of essential services and competitive market structures have both been pursued. This is the second focal point for our discussions on market development. There appears to have been a global diffusion of common regulatory practices and institutional frameworks. But how have governments themselves applied such regulatory notions, how have these ideas spread and, importantly, to what degree has such re-regulation been successful from experience to date?

Thirdly, the international level of markets has been lubricated by the global availability of finance. And governing such global markets has become an increasingly important dimension to today's privatized world. But what are the multilateral mechanisms being adopted for governance here, and where have these policy ideas come from? How have these ideas spread, and how effective are they in meeting the needs of global citizens?

CONCLUSIONS

If there is one single theme throughout this book, it is that the global movement of privatization and market development ideas has been a central factor in business over the past two decades. It is also likely that this movement will continue with strength over future decades. If some of the elements underpinning this global movement are better illuminated through this book, we will have succeeded. If we can, as well as understanding this phenomenon, also learn to better control its excesses and encourage its benefits to a global citizenry, this book will have more than earned its place on library shelves.

NOTES

1. The increasing managerialization of government has seen an emphasis on purchasing defined services. This has been a part of a broader performance measurement movement under way over the past century. From the influential observations of Frederick Taylor on the nature of production work efficiency numerous advances in measuring performance included zero-based budgeting, programme budgeting, programme priority and planning, performance indicators and performance budgeting, to name a few. Each reform promoted greater specification, more measurement and greater control over the production agent. The simple underlying belief here was that better specification through contracts promotes better performance.

REFERENCES

Bennett, C.J. (1997), 'Understanding ripple effects: the cross-national adoption of policy instruments for bureaucratic accountability', *Governance: An International Journal of Policy and Administration*, **10** (3), 213–33.

Cook, P. and C. Kirkpatrick (2003), 'Assessing the impact of privatisation in developing countries', in David Parker and David Saal (eds), *International Handbook on Privatization*, Cheltenham, UK and Northampton, MA, USA: Edward Elgar, pp. 209–19.

Hodge, G. (2002), 'Privatisation: lessons from the war', *Alternative Law Journal*, **27** (4), 177–83.

Hodge, G.A. (2000), *Privatisation: An International Review of Performance*, Boulder, CO: Westview Press.

Martin, S. and D. Parker (1997), *The Impact of Privatisation: Ownership and Corporate Performance in the UK*, London: Routledge.

Minogue, M. (2004), 'Public management and regulatory governance: problems of policy transfer to developing countries', in Paul Cook, Colin Kirkpatrick, Martin Minogue and David Parker (eds), *Leading Issues in Competition, Regulation and Development*, Cheltenham, UK and Northampton, MA, USA: Edward Elgar, pp. 165–81.

Rogers, E. (1995), *Diffusion of Innovations*, 4th edn, New York: Free Press.

Stone, D. (2000), *Learning Lessons, Policy Transfer and the International Diffusion of Policy Ideas*: University of Warkwick Centre for the Study of Globalisation and Regionalisation.

PART I

Privatization components

2. Enterprise sales: Thatcher leads the charge

David Parker

INTRODUCTION

The origins of the term 'privatization' are unclear. It seems to have surfaced during the late 1970s and various persons or bodies are credited with coining it, including the management writer Drucker (1969). Like all economic ideas it flourished because of the economic and political trends of the period. The 1970s saw the end of the post-war years of almost continuous economic growth, low unemployment and subdued inflation. The 'oil shocks' of 1973/74 and 1978/79 led to 'stagflation' in the Western world, rising unemployment and industry closures. Unsurprisingly, a search began for an economic remedy. This was so particularly in the UK, which, at the time was often referred to as 'the sick man of Europe'. During the 1950s and 1960s, the UK economy had expanded but at an appreciably slower rate than elsewhere in western Europe. For example, whereas the UK had the seventh-highest labour productivity in 1950 measured by real GDP to hours worked, by 1973 the UK was in thirteenth place (Crafts, 2002:46). The result was that GDP per capita in the UK in 1979 had fallen behind that of a number of countries in Europe including Austria, France, Germany, Italy, Belgium, Denmark, Netherlands, Norway, Switzerland, Luxembourg and Sweden (House of Commons, 1998). The UK's share of world trade in manufactures fell from 25.4 per cent in 1950 to 9.1 per cent in 1973 (Crafts, 2002:58). In 1975 the UK's inflation rate peaked at 24.2 per cent and by 1980 was still at 17.9 per cent. Meanwhile unemployment had risen to nearly 1.7 million and labour unrest had grown sharply. Between 1974 and 1979 an average of almost 11.7 million working days were lost each year through strikes, compared with 3.9 million a decade earlier, and general government expenditure had grown from 38.8 per cent in 1972 to 42.5 per cent by 1979 (Saunders, 1993:22; Artis, 1996). As Nigel Lawson, who served as Chancellor of the Exchequer from June 1983 to October 1989, has commented, 'By the time Margaret Thatcher became Prime Minister, the British economy was trapped in the cycle of low growth and high inflation, which economists called "stagflation"; and mainstream Keynesianism was intellectually and politically bankrupt of solutions to it' (Lawson, 1992:29 30).

It was in this climate of economic crisis that Margaret Thatcher led the Conservative Party to electoral victory in May 1979. During the 1980s, Thatcher's government introduced a radical departure from the economics of the 'post-war consensus', attacking trade union powers, public expenditure budgets, tax levels and the grip of the nationalized industries on the supply of critical services such as telecommunications, electricity and water (Thatcher, 1993). Between 1979 and 2001, total privatization receipts in the UK totalled around $US115 billion. The UK led in terms of the scale of privatization in western Europe until well into the 1990s. During the 1990s other countries, emulating the UK's experience, introduced major privatization programmes, such as Portugal, Spain, Italy and France. For example, as a share of GDP Portugal's programme was the largest in the 1990s with proceeds equivalent to 25 per cent of GDP, compared with a much smaller 7 per cent in the UK (Clifton et al., 2003:97). Figure 2.1 details the value of UK privatization sales in each year between 1979 and 2000; since 2000 receipts have been minimal. It can be seen that privatization peaked in value terms in the UK in the late

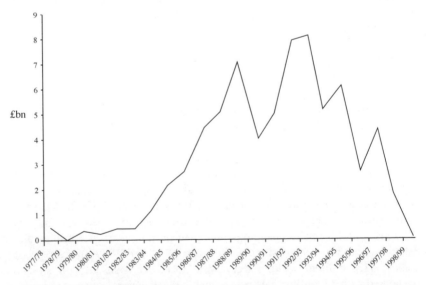

Note: Figures exclude council housing receipts and receipts of subsidiaries retained by the parent. Since 2000 privatization receipts have been negligible

Sources: HM Treasury, *The Financial Statement and Budget Report* (various); Parker (2004)

Figure 2.1   Privatization proceeds, 1979–2000

Table 2.1   Major privatizations in the UK

	Date of sale	Method of sale
British Petroleum	November 1979	Offer for sale
	September 1983	Sale by tender
	November 1987	Offer for sale
British Aerospace	February 1981	Offer for sale
	May 1985	Offer for sale
Cable & Wireless	October 1981	Offer for sale
	December 1983	Offer for sale
	December 1985	Offer for sale
Amersham International	February 1982	Offer for sale
National Freight Corporation	February 1982	Private sale
Britoil	November 1982	Sale by tender
	August 1985	Offer for sale
Associated British Port Holdings	February 1983	Offer for sale
	April 1984	Sale by tender
Enterprise Oil	June 1984	Sale by tender
Jaguar	July 1984	Offer for sale
British Telecommunications	December 1984	Offer for sale
	December 1991	Offer for sale
	July 1993	Offer for sale
British Shipbuilders and Naval Dockyards	May 1985 onwards	Private sales
National Bus Company	August 1986 to June 1987 – followed by sales of local authority bus companies	Private sales
British Gas	December 1986	Offer for sale
Rover Group	January 1987 to 1988	Private sales
British Airways	February 1987	Offer for sale
Rolls-Royce	May 1987	Offer for sale
BAA (British Airports Authority)	July 1987	Offer for sale & sale by tender
British Steel	December 1988	Offer for sale
Anglian Water	December 1989	Offer for sale
Northumbrian Water	December 1989	Offer for sale
North West Water	December 1989	Offer for sale
Severn Trent	December 1989	Offer for sale
Southern Water	December 1989	Offer for sale

Table 2.1   continued

	Date of sale	Method of sale
South West Water	December 1989	Offer for sale
Thames Water	December 1989	Offer for sale
Welsh Water	December 1989	Offer for sale
Wessex Water	December 1989	Offer for sale
Yorkshire Water	December 1989	Offer for sale
Eastern Electricity	December 1990	Offer for sale
East Midlands Electricity	December 1990	Offer for sale
London Electricity	December 1990	Offer for sale
Manweb	December 1990	Offer for sale
Midlands Electricity	December 1990	Offer for sale
Northern Electric	December 1990	Offer for sale
NORWEB	December 1990	Offer for sale
SEEBOARD	December 1990	Offer for sale
Southern Electric	December 1990	Offer for sale
South Wales Electricity	December 1990	Offer for sale
South Western Electricity	December 1990	Offer for sale
Yorkshire Electricity	December 1990	Offer for sale
National Power	March 1991	Offer for sale
PowerGen	March 1995	Offer for sale
Scottish Hydro-Electric	June 1991	Offer for sale
Scottish Power	June 1991	Offer for sale
Trust Ports	1992–97 (various dates)	Private sales
Northern Ireland Electricity	June 1993	Offer for sale & private sales
British Coal	December 1994	Private sales
Railtrack	May 1996	Offer for sale
British Energy	July 1996	Offer for sale
AEA Technology	September 1996	Private sales
Train Operating Companies	Various dates in 1996/7	Private sales/ franchises
National Air Traffic Services	July 2001	Private sale

Notes: Where more than one date is given the shares were sold in tranches. Under an offer for sale the assets are sold at a price fixed ahead of the sale. Under a sale by tender the price is set according to the demand for shares and the supply of shares available.

1980s and the very early 1990s with the sale of the water and sewerage and electricity industries. Table 2.1 gives details of some of the main privatizations in the UK, including their dates and the method of sale.

This chapter firstly considers privatization as a policy idea. How did privatization enter the political agenda in the UK, what are its economic foundations and why did it spread as an idea internationally? During the 1990s privatization was policy in many countries around the world and global privatization receipts were almost $US937 billion (OECD, 2001:44). Secondly, the chapter looks at some of the effects of privatization and the gainers and losers. Finally, the chapter concludes by making some comments on when privatization is likely to have its biggest net benefits.

PRIVATIZATION: THEORY IN SEARCH OF A POLICY

In some senses 'privatization' was not a new idea in the late 1970s. In the early 1950s in the UK, a Conservative administration 'denationalized' a few industries, notably steel and road freight, and in the early 1970s another Conservative government sold off state-owned travel agents and pubs. Equally, West Germany had what we would now refer to as a 'privatization programme' in the early 1960s (Esser, 1998:107), as did Taiwan in 1964 (Parker, 2002a:156). Other countries had also disposed of state assets to the private sector from time to time, just as they had acquired other assets during industrial or banking crises (Parker, 1998). However, what was different from the late 1970s was the development of privatization as a *core* component of government policy in a number of countries, which was consistently pursued over a period of time. This change in sentiment towards policy, to reduce the role of the state in the economy, was promoted by the development of economic theories in favour of private over state enterprise. Opposition to state ownership in economic writings was not new; but this opposition became arguably more coherent and less obviously ideological than in the past. While the Conservative Party opposed the nationalizations introduced in the UK by the 1945–51 Labour governments, it had done so without a distinct body of economic theory to justify its stance. This theory existed by 1980 and had gained support in university social science faculties and in policy-oriented think tanks on both sides of the Atlantic, although the theories also met with some determined opposition on both theoretical and empirical grounds (Hastings and Levie, 1983; Dunsire et al., 1988; Udehn, 1996)

In neoclassical economics, the dominant paradigm in economics for the entire twentieth century, ownership does not feature as an important variable. The market models of perfect competition, imperfect competition, oligopoly and monopoly are concerned with the number of firms operating in the market and their market shares – reflecting a 'structure-conduct-performance' view of the competitive process (Bain, 1956). They are not concerned with the ownership of firms, per se. The implication seems to be that state-owned firms are subject to the same product market constraints on management behaviour as privately owned firms. Hence, while a monopoly state-owned organization might be expected to produce less efficiently than a competitive privately owned firm, it does so because of the lack of competition and not because of the form of ownership. Equally, a private sector monopoly and a state-owned monopoly face the same lack of competitive pressures to operate efficiently. However, this does not necessarily mean that they will produce the same level of outputs at the same prices. Indeed, the argument for state ownership of the so-called 'natural monopoly' industries, such as electricity distribution and water and sewerage services, lay in the state-owned body pursuing the public interest, while the private sector monopolist maximized profits. Therefore, the presumption was that the state-owned monopoly would supply a larger output at lower prices than the profit-maximizing monopolist, thereby raising social welfare.

Only in the 'Austrian' and Marxist traditions of economics was there an emphasis on the importance of ownership. Whereas Marxist economists tended to welcome state ownership (in more recent times with a greater emphasis on worker collectives and similar; Brown, 1984), the so-called Austrian economists adopted a critical approach to state provision (Littlechild, 1978; Shand, 1984). Austrians opposed the concentration of economic power within the state. Hayek, in particular, warned that governments lacked the information to allocate resources efficiently. He criticized both state planning of the economy and state provision (Hayek, 1948). However, the Austrian tradition in economics remained marginalized in economics faculties by the dominance of neoclassical economics. In neoclassical economics information is assumed to be either perfect or subject to some reasonably well-defined probability distribution (Stigler, 1961). In addition, the rise of Keynesian macroeconomics after the Second World War seemed to legitimize high levels of state intervention in the economy to facilitate macroeconomic planning.

The economic 'stagflation' of the 1970s saw the coming to prominence of two important themes within economics that challenged this dominant paradigm and the notion that 'ownership does not matter'. The first was the development of theories of property rights, a theme which lies on the border between law and economics. Property rights theorists, such as Alchian and Demsetz (1972) and Furubotn and Pejovich (1972), concentrated upon management incentives to behave efficiently and minimize costs and maximize productivity under different property rights regimes. Their conclusion was that managers in state-owned enterprises had inferior incentives to allocate resources efficiently than their counterparts in the private sector. In the private sector, the argument went, managers face constant pressure from a competitive capital market to maximize profits. By contrast, managers in the state sector face no similar pressure. During the 1980s, this approach to the study of economic performance under different forms of ownership expanded into a detailed study of principal–agent relationships under different forms of ownership (see, for example, Fama and Jensen, 1983; Bös, 1991). As a result, today this body of literature is commonly referred to as 'principal–agent' rather than 'property rights' theory.

The second theme that developed within economics in the 1970s involved studies on the interrelationship between economics and politics, which are sometimes labelled 'the economics of politics', 'the Virginia school' (reflecting its origins at the University of Virginia) or 'public choice' theory. This body of theory is concerned with the actual rather than assumed behaviour of politicians and state employees. Instead of expecting politicians and state officials to pursue the public interest in some disinterested or Platonic sense, this literature argues that politicians and state managers, like employees in the private sector, can be expected to pursue their own interests or utility in their decision making (Buchanan, 1972; Tullock, 1976). Utility-maximizing politicians are likely to concentrate on championing policies that maximize votes and political funding, to retain office, while civil servants will be primarily interested in maximizing their budgets (Niskanen, 1971). Larger departmental budgets reduce the threat of redundancy, increase promotion and salary prospects, and enable larger administrative empires to be built. This literature, therefore, anticipates a Leviathan state; an ever-expanding, resource-destroying organism that ultimately impoverishes the economy.

The combination of the principal–agent and economics of politics literatures created a heady brew of intellectual endeavour, which gradually undermined support for state ownership during the 1970s and 1980s. In 1986 John Kay and David Thompson published, with some justification, an article in the *Economic Journal* entitled 'Privatization: a policy in search of a rationale'. But arguably, the title of the paper exaggerated the position: by the mid-1980s privatization had a developing rationale – to improve economic efficiency by changing principal–agent relationships and ending state sector self-seeking behaviour. Nigel Lawson, Chancellor of the Exchequer during the planning of many of the UK's most important privatizations, attacks in his memoirs those economists who criticized the government's privatizations for their emphasis on ownership rather than competition: 'It reflects the standard mainstream economists' party line that it is only competition that matters not ownership. This ignores both the theoretical importance of property rights and the practical experience of countries moving away from centrally controlled economies' (Lawson, 1992:239). A similar sentiment appears in Mrs Thatcher's memoirs: 'The state should not be in business . . . state-owned businesses can never function as proper businesses. The fact that the state is ultimately accountable for them to Parliament rather than management to the shareholders means that they cannot be. The spur is just not there' (Thatcher, 1993:677). Both statements reflect a debt to principal–agent and public choice theories. For the Conservative governments of the 1980s, privatization was a central part of a wider economic programme focused on public spending cuts, tax reductions and market liberalization policies, aimed at 'rolling back the state' (Thatcher, 1993:677).

In October 1977 the Conservatives' policies were set out in a document called *The Right Approach to the Economy*, which developed what were to become familiar themes of the subsequent Conservative government about the need to 'set the people free' (Keegan, 1984:99). To prevent an outbreak of internal strife the document attempted to balance views from the different wings of the party; nevertheless it signposted the future. Later Mrs Thatcher was to disparagingly label the more liberal wing of her party 'the wets' and a number of 'the wets' were eased out of ministerial positions.

During the second half of the 1970s, under Mrs Thatcher's leadership (Mrs Thatcher became leader of the Conservative Party in February 1975), the party had undergone a period of policy introspection that had led to a new conservatism. The Conservative government of 1970 to 1974 had fallen in the face of a strike by Britain's coal miners; the coal industry was state owned. Also, plans in 1970 for tax and government spending cuts had largely failed to materialize. The introspection from 1975 involved a fundamental reconsideration of policy and policy objectives. Leading figures within the Conservative Party, including Mrs Thatcher but also in particular Sir Geoffrey Howe, Sir Keith Joseph, Nicholas Ridley and Nigel Lawson, are known to have attended meetings of free market think tanks in London during this period. Especially important in helping to shape the Conservative Party's policies were the Institute of Economic Affairs (IEA) (Keegan, 1984:38) and the Adam Smith Institute (ASI). Both bodies championed the new literature on property rights and the economics of politics while the IEA, in particular, also published on Austrian economics (Littlechild, 1978). In addition, the Conservative Party's own Centre for Policy Studies, founded by Sir Keith Joseph in 1974, was influential in channelling these ideas into policy proposals.

It is, of course, always difficult to assess the impact of lobbying groups including think tanks on economic policy. Nevertheless, it seems reasonable to assume that the work of bodies such as the IEA and ASI played a significant role during the late 1970s in shifting thinking within the Conservative Party, and also within industry and the media, to favour private over state enterprise. In addition, both bodies continued to be influential in political, industrial and media circles during the 1980s, although probably less so in the 1990s. By the 1990s many of the free market proposals put forward by such groups, such as tax cuts and privatization of power and water and sewerage, were already policy. In 1997 the election of a Labour government, after 18 years of Conservative administration, seemed to reflect a desire within the electorate for more investment in public services such as health and education – although not necessarily for the higher taxes to pay for such spending!

THE EVOLVING PRIVATIZATION AGENDA

In spite of the influence of new economic thinking on the importance of ownership, the Conservative government from May 1979 was elected on a manifesto that paid only passing attention to 'denationalization'. There was nothing in this manifesto to suggest that a major programme of privatizations would occur over the following years. The manifesto made a few references only to the possibility of selling off the nationalized industries, naming the state-owned shipbuilding and aerospace industries as candidates. These industries had only recently been nationalized and this commitment to denationalize should merely be seen as a response to promises made by the Conservative front bench during the completion of the nationalizations in 1977. Apart from these references, the manifesto signalled the sale of the state's road freight business, which was languishing in a body called the National Freight Corporation (NFC) (Conservative Party, 1979:8).[1] NFC had almost gone bankrupt in 1975 and even the Labour administration at the time had reputedly considered radical solutions, including its dismemberment. This proposed 'privatization' was also, therefore, unremarkable. In other words, the election of the Conservative government in 1979 did not herald years of concentrated state sell-offs, even though the new government was intent on cutting government. As Sir Ian Gilmour, a government minister, commented on the mood at this time, 'even the most ideological Thatcherites had not advocated denationalizing the natural monopolies' (Gilmour, 1993:120).

The first privatization by the new government, in October 1979, involved selling some of the state's remaining shareholdings in British Petroleum (BP). The state's shareholdings in this company dated back to the outbreak of the First World War when the state attempted to protect the country (and more specifically the Royal Navy) from insufficient oil supplies. A cash-strapped Labour government in 1977 had already unearthed these shares and begun to sell them. The new Conservative government simply continued an existing policy.

The next privatization was of British Aerospace. As already mentioned this was a new state industry and the Conservatives were politically committed to its sell-off. In February 1981 British Aerospace was successfully floated on the stock market. Shares valued at £150 million were sold and the sale was 3.5

times over-subscribed. Investors achieved a short-term, 'stagging' gain when the share price went from 150p to 171p by the end of the first day's trading in the shares in the London stock market (Price Waterhouse, 1987:18). The ability to sell state assets successfully in the City was vital to the take-off of privatization as policy. In October 1981, almost two and a half years into the Conservative government, the first of the privatizations not specifically flagged in the election manifesto of 1979 was introduced: the sale of 49 per cent of the issued share capital of Cable & Wireless. This time there were 5.6 times more shares demanded by investors than on offer (Price Waterhouse, 1987:53). This was quickly followed by the sale of Amersham International, a high-technology company using radioactive materials to manufacture specialist products. This event marked an important stage in the development of policy in the UK because the successful sale established that privatization could both raise revenue for government and attract investors in growing numbers – on this occasion the issue was a massive 24 times over-subscribed. The same month also saw the promised sale of NFC, which due to its uncertain financial future was disposed of through a management buy-out (supported by banks), although some ordinary employees also purchased shares.

The privatization of NFC proved highly successful, contrary to City expectations at the time. The business was turned around under more or less the same management as under state ownership, but now incentivized by the prospects of personal gain. The value of NFC rose enormously during the 1980s so that when the company was eventually listed in the stock market, in 1989, those managers and employees astute enough to buy shares in February 1982 and hold on to them achieved spectacular capital gains. The average employee shareholding of £600 had become worth around £60 000. However, the use of management and employee buy-outs was not favoured for later privatizations of entire corporations; instead they featured when corporations were split up for sale, for example for some shipyards,[2] bus companies and coal mines. For sales of entire enterprises the government preferred the option of an Initial Public Offering (IPO), in the form of 'offers for sale' and 'sales by tender', or 'private (trade) sales', under which assets were purchased by existing companies. The preference for IPOs reflected the way that public flotations, particularly offers for sale, attracted small investors.[3] For example, the privatization of British Telecom in 1984 attracted 2.3 million small investors and the sale of British Gas in 1986 around 4.4 million – in both cases small investors were seduced by vouchers against their telephone and gas bills, respectively, by loyalty bonuses for holding on to their shares, as well as the prospect of a large capital gain. Instead of privatization proving to be publicly unpopular, there were signs that it could be a vote winner or at least not a notable vote loser. In February 1983, a number of state-owned ports were sold in the shape of Associated British Ports.

When the Thatcher government won a resounding endorsement from voters in the June 1983 general election, the Conservatives' majority in the House of Commons rose from 44 to 144, the largest gained by any party since 1945, a number of state-owned firms had already been privatized.[4] However, while privatization featured more prominently than it had in the 1979 manifesto – 'We shall transfer more state-owned businesses to independent ownership' (Conservative Party, 1983:7) – the economics editor of *The Observer* newspaper, William Keegan, in a popular critique of Thatcherism published a year later, has only one reference to the policy in his index (Keegan, 1984:127). At this time Thatcherism was associated with tax and public spending cuts rather than widespread denationalization. Also, it is important to note that all of the enterprises so far sold operated in competitive markets. For example, NFC never had more than around 7 per cent of the UK freight market and British Aerospace, Cable & Wireless and Amersham International faced foreign competition. ABP had competition from other UK ports and for European cargoes from ports on the Continent, especially Rotterdam. To date none of the major state monopolies had succumbed to privatization.

Following the election, the new Conservative administration began to finalize plans for the sale of British Telecom (BT), a proposal first published the previous autumn. The government's initial plans for BT had involved retaining the corporation in the state sector but allowing it more freedom to borrow commercially, through so-called 'Buzby bonds' (named after a cartoon character used in BT advertising, called Buzby). Only after the Treasury raised serious concerns about allowing BT the freedom to borrow with a de facto government guarantee of its loans did the privatization option win through. In November 1984 the first of the large state monopolies, BT, was successfully sold. The sale involved the largest IPO in the history of the UK stock market up until that time. There were real concerns about the willingness of the City to absorb such a large share issue, valued at around £3.9 billion and this encouraged the government to pursue an active marketing programme to attract the small investor. In the event, small investors bought shares in unprecedented numbers and immediately benefited from a sharp capital appreciation. The potential 'stagging' gain after the first day of stock market trading in BT shares was 96 per cent.[5] It was the BT flotation that finally confirmed within government that privatization was not only possible for even the largest of state enterprises, but also that it was unlikely to be a serious vote loser.

Up until 1983 arguably it is an exaggeration to talk about 'the UK privatization programme'. Prior to BT there was no programme, as such, but rather an evolving number of privatizations with each case seemingly looked at on its own individual merits. From 1984 there is more evidence of a concerted policy within government of lining up state-owned businesses as candidates for sale, as evidenced in the Conservatives' election manifesto.[6] Even so, at no time did a UK government in the 1980s and 1990s publish a detailed privatization plan setting out a timetable for the sale of industries over the coming years, as occurred later in a number of countries, such as Taiwan (Parker, 2002a). Moreover, it is not even clear that such a plan existed within government. It is probably accurate to describe British privatizations throughout the 1980s and 1990s as partially planned and partially opportunistic. While the Thatcher and Lawson memoirs attest to the belief that privatization would improve economic performance, it appears that government budgetary needs were an important driver of the timing of at least some sell-offs.

That privatization in the UK was driven in part by the Conservatives' fiscal policy is controversial, but it seems clear that state sell-offs did provide a welcome boost to the Exchequer. On balance, it seems that the policy on privatization, as it evolved in the 1980s, resulted from a combination of economic principles, immediate budgetary needs and ideology. At the same time the policy was complicated by differing and shifting objectives.

The Conservative government had been elected in 1979 to reduce taxation. The economic recession of 1979–81 delayed the new government's start on tax cutting, and indeed in 1980 taxes rose to fund a soaring welfare budget. However, afterwards tax cuts were introduced, although taking the government's record overall, the total tax cuts achieved proved modest. Between 1981 and 1989, as a percentage of GDP in the UK, tax revenues fell only from 43.6 per cent to 42.9 per cent (Burton and Parker, 1991). In this climate of difficulty in cutting actual government spending (as against spending *plans*), receipts from the sale of state assets provided useful supplementary funding to enable the Chancellor of the Exchequer to cut taxes. Nevertheless, in relation to the size of state spending, the budgetary contribution from privatization was always marginal, although useful.

The manner in which the policy of privatization evolved during the 1980s meant that various policy objectives were emphasized from time to time. In addition to raising government funding and improving economic efficiency, the desire to reduce trade union militancy – state industries were heavily unionized – also played a role. So did encouraging public investment in private sector companies. This objective was consistent with the Conservatives' encouragement of private enterprise and their hope that shareholders would be more likely to vote Conservative. These different policy objectives inevitably led to some policy conflict (Vickers and Yarrow, 1988:187). In particular, raising economic efficiency was likely to be best achieved if state industries were transferred into competitive markets. But the highest price for state industries would be obtained where the industries were more or less guaranteed high profits, and this would occur where the industries remained monopoly suppliers and with lenient state regulatory regimes. The sale of BT in 1984 and the sale of British Gas in 1986 both involved only a limited introduction of competition initially. This led to criticisms of these privatizations. Therefore, in 1990/91 when the electricity industry was privatized, it was first 'unbundled' and electricity generation, transmission and distribution were separately sold off. Competition was introduced immediately into electricity generation and a phased introduction of competition into electricity supply was announced, beginning with large users. By June 1999 all customers in England, Wales and Scotland had obtained access to competing electricity suppliers and prices had fallen sharply (Littlechild, 2000:29–30). Also during the 1990s new measures were introduced to accelerate the development of competition in telecommunications and gas supply. However, the privatization of water and sewerage services, in 1989, involved the sale of ten existing state-owned corporations and each retained a regional monopoly especially in sewerage services.

Environmental concerns and the technology of water services provision means that it has proved very difficult to introduce effective competition into the water industry anywhere in the world. However, the water monopolies in England and Wales could have been sold off under franchises, with periodic competition for the franchise; although when such a model was later adopted for Britain's railways, in the mid-1990s, it hardly proved to be a shining success. Britain's railways were privatized between 1995 and 1997 during which the monopoly British Rail was divided into around 100 operating concerns. The result has been a lawyer's delight with contracts between train operating companies, the infrastructure owner (initially Railtrack, placed in receivership in 2001, and now Network Rail), rail maintenance and rolling stock companies, replacing vertical integration. After some signs of improving services, costs have risen sharply and service reliability has deteriorated. The cost of running trains per kilometre in Britain averaged between £15 and £17.50 (in 2001/02 prices) for much of the period from the early 1960s to the late 1980s. It fell below this level during most of the 1990s, both in the years of state and private ownership. Since 2000 the figure has jumped sharply, to £21.70 (Smith, 2004).[7] Today rail privatization has few friends in the UK.

In summary, privatization policy in the UK was not especially well thought out *ex ante* and there is no sense of an overriding privatization plan. One consequence of this was shifting policy objectives and changing policy focuses, not least the growing attention to introducing competition in public utilities. Another result was an opportunistic rush to dispose of state industries before the return of a socialist administration, well illustrated by the botched privatization of rail in the mid-1990s. Lady Thatcher (1993:676–677) reflects this imperative in her memoirs:

> Just as nationalization was at the heart of the collectivist programme by which the Labour Government sought to remodel British society, so privatization is at the

centre of any programme of reclaiming territory for freedom. Whatever arguments there may — and should – be about means of sale, the competitive structures or the regulatory frameworks adopted in different cases, this fundamental purpose of privatization must not be overlooked. That consideration was of practical relevance. For it meant that in some cases it was a choice between having the ideal circumstances for privatization, which might take years to achieve, and going for a sale within a particular politically determined timescale, the second was the preferable option.

The apparent success of privatization in the UK, reflected in evidence of higher productivity and profitability post-sale, meant that the UK became a model for privatizations internationally. The collapse of the Berlin Wall in 1989 signalled the transformation of central and eastern Europe from centralized planning to market economies. As part of this process, mass privatization programmes were introduced, which led to the transfer to the private sector of most or all of the state-owned industries (Filatotchev, 2003). Elsewhere, in the developing world, from the late 1980s the World Bank and the International Monetary Fund (IMF) began to link funding, including 'structural adjustment loans', to economic reform programmes including privatizations (World Bank, 1995). 'Conditionality' became the key to obtaining loans and grants from international donor agencies, heralding a period of state sell-offs, sometimes in the face of lukewarm local support. As part of this process, the British think tanks that had championed privatization in the UK in the 1970s and 1980s, notably the IEA and ASI, were active in promoting privatization in the transition and developing countries through publications and, especially in the case of the ASI, through training courses. In this endeavour they were joined by North American free market organizations such as the Fraser Institute, the Heritage Foundation and the Cato Institute.

Another catalyst for privatization internationally, in addition to the UK example and donor agency pressure, was growing evidence of 'government failure'. The most obvious example of this existed in central and eastern Europe, where comparative GDP per capita figures languished well below western European levels by the late 1980s. For example, when East and West Germany united in October 1990, the East was found to have an average real income per head of only around 57 per cent of the level earned in the West (Hunt, 2000). There was also mounting evidence of state failure in the form of government waste and corruption across the developing world. Indeed, it is this failure that convinced the World Bank to switch to promoting privatization during the late 1980s, after largely giving up trying to reform state industries (World Bank, 1995). However, it is interesting to note that while there are many examples of state failure, the empirical evidence on the effects of privatization is more mixed than is often assumed. Space prevents a detailed discussion of the evidence, but it is summarized in detail for developed countries in

Martin and Parker (1997) and for developing countries in Parker and Kirkpatrick (2005a). This is not to say that privatization failed to lead to performance improvements in the form of both increased allocative and technical efficiency – it did so in many cases. Rather it is to stress that privatization has not proved a panacea for economic problems in either developed or developing economies. Also, it is now increasingly recognized that the success of privatization requires supporting institutional reforms, including the promotion of competition, the protection of private property rights, and effective regulation where there is market failure (Parker and Kirkpatrick, 2005b).

Finally, privatization sales helped to widen share ownership and from time to time this was mentioned as an important goal of privatization. By 1991 the proportion of adults in the UK holding shares directly (as against through pension funds and other institutional savings) had risen from 7 per cent in 1979 to around 25 per cent. However, whilst this was seen as conducive to sustaining 'a property-owning democracy' in Conservative circles, it did not reverse the relentless rise in the proportion of total shares in the UK held by the financial institutions. The proportion of shares held by small investors fell from 30 per cent to 20 per cent during the 1980s, despite privatizations. Moreover, the 25 per cent of adults that held shares due to being enticed to take part in privatization issues usually continued to hold no other shares. Only 17 per cent of the population held shares in more than four firms in the early 1990s (HM Treasury, 1991). Looking back, it is difficult to conclude that privatization had much long-term effect on the structure of private ownership in the UK. In addition, there has been criticism that government mishandled a number of the privatization sales by selling the shares too cheaply, as reflected in the large 'stagging' gains. At least in part this criticism seems valid. Although it is always difficult to price new share issues accurately and standard practice is to factor in some potential stagging gains to attract investors to IPOs, the capital gains registered for a number of the privatizations seems excessive especially in the early years of privatization. Later the government took some steps to limit the potential stagging gains, with mixed success. After allowing for transaction costs, the typical stag made a net profit from privatization issues in excess of 10 per cent on 15 occasions during the 1980s and in 11 cases in excess of over 20 per cent (Ernst & Young, 1994:15–16). In so far as shares were priced too low, there was income redistribution from taxpayers to investors.

GAINERS AND LOSERS

Clearly, nobody seems to have done especially well out of the privatization of the railways. Taxpayers and customers have seen little improvement and some shareholders have lost money. But what about the other privatizations – what is the experience here?

Assessing the social welfare effects of dozens of privatizations collectively is impossibly complex. So what follows are some general observations, starting with the effect on customers.

Customers

In competitive privatized industries such as road freight customers have continued to benefit from a choice of suppliers. In the former monopoly public utilities of gas, electricity and telecommunications, consumers now benefit from a rich range of suppliers and, as to be expected, prices have fallen and services have improved. For example, by 1999 industrial electricity customers had benefited from price reductions in real terms of 25 per cent to 34 per cent, compared with prices at privatization. The real reduction for domestic consumers was around 26 per cent. At the same time, the regulator has set the electricity companies demanding 'Standards of Performance' with penalty payments if the standards are not met. Service quality has improved (Littlechild, 2000:32–33). Prices in water and sewerage have risen sharply in real terms since privatization, by over 40 per cent for unmetered supplies,[8] reflecting high levels of investment to make good the previous neglect of the water and sewerage infrastructure and stricter EU environmental and water quality directives. But in telecommunications and gas supply, as in electricity, prices have fallen sharply at the same time as services have improved. Therefore, it seems that consumers have benefited since privatization in these industries. Even in water and sewerage, without the efficiency gains achieved under privatization the rise in charges would have been even higher if the same investment level had been undertaken. What is less clear is the extent to which the real price reductions achieved outside of the water sector have been *due* to privatization or to other factors, notably changes in world prices for key inputs, such as oil and natural gas in electricity generation, or technological change, especially in the case of telecommunications. Fuel prices and telephone charges have dropped all over the world, including in countries with continuing high levels of state ownership, such as France. Assessing the counterfactual, or what would have happened in the absence of privatization, is notoriously difficult.

What is clear is that some customer groups have benefited a lot more than others from price changes. In particular, large users of power have achieved sharp price reductions as the privatized companies have related individual charges more closely to marginal costs. In the main, the losers in this process have been small-volume users and especially those with pre-payment meters – those with prepayment meters are often in poorer income groups with bad credit ratings (Hancock and Waddams Price, 1995; Waddams Price and Young, 2003). The result seems to be that privatization may have led to some regressive redistribution of income between consumers. This is perhaps not surprising given that state ownership was associated with providing cross-subsidized, 'national', services.

Workers

The impact of privatization on workers in the industries has been mixed. There is some evidence of a decline in unionization and improved industrial relations in privatized firms (Pendleton and Winterton, 1993), but this mirrors national trends. In terms of wages, while average earnings in the industries may not have been materially affected by privatization, wage differentials do seem to have widened (Parker and Martin, 1996). But again, this has been occurring across the UK economy and not simply in privatized companies.

Table 2.2 provides details of employment levels in a number of UK privatized industries at privatization and a few years later. It is clear that there have been large job losses in a number of industries, especially the public utilities. This is reflected in the large gains in labour productivity in these industries (Parker and Martin, 1996).

Table 2.2   Examples of employment changes in UK privatized companies in the first few years after privatization

	Employment at privatization	Employment in (year)	
Associated British Ports	10 200	2 300	(1994)
British Aerospace	77 500	56 400	(1994)
British Airports Authority	7 400	8 200	(1995)
British Airways	40 400	53 060	(1995)
British Gas	88 500	36 600	(1996)
British Steel	55 200	39 800	(1995)
British Telecom (BT)	238 000	129 600	(1996/97)
National Freight Corp.	23 900	34 000	(1994)
National Power	15 700	4 500	(1996/97)
PowerGen	8 840	3 400	(1996/97)
Regional Electricity Cos	82 300	47 000	(1996/97)
Rolls-Royce	41 900	43 500	(1994)
Water and Sewerage Cos	40 000	28 400	(1996/97)

Source: Annual Reports and Accounts; Martin and Parker, 1997:157.

Managers

More obvious gainers in privatized businesses have been the top management. This results from deflated senior salaries in nationalized concerns and from the introduction of performance-related pay, individually negotiated salaries, stock options, bonuses and the like after privatization (Cragg and Dyck, 1999). So sharp was the upward movement in senior management pay following some privatizations (see Curwen, 1994, for some examples) that the media introduced a 'fat cats' campaign against major beneficiaries and particularly Cedric Brown at British Gas. The current Labour government has encouraged industry regulators to oversee management pay to prevent excesses, but it seems that the regulators have been reluctant to get involved in decisions on the appropriate level of management pay.

Investors

Profitability rose in a number of firms following privatization and shareholders (and government through higher tax revenues paid from these profits) were the immediate gainers. Investors also gained when the share price rose quickly in the stock market due to the under-pricing of share issues. In an attempt to secure a successful share flotation and avoid a politically embarrassing failure shares were priced low, especially in the early years, as already mentioned. Also, the government was keen in a number of the high-profile privatizations, such as BT, British Gas, water and electricity, to attract the small investor. Equally, however, successive governments seem to have had difficulty in estimating the real value of the underlying assets of the businesses being sold.

The result has been some large windfall gains to investors, assisted by the 'bull market' that existed in UK shares through much of the 1980s and 1990s. For example, the return to investors in the water and sewerage companies averaged 24 per cent per annum over the first five years after privatization and 33 per cent per annum over the same period for the regional electricity companies (Parker, 1997).[9] However, the gains in some privatizations were much lower, especially when second or third tranches of shares were issued reflecting the greater difficulty in correctly estimating the market clearing price for an IPO. The large shareholder gains provided an opportunity for the incoming Labour government after 1997 to introduce a 'windfall profits tax' on the privatized utilities, amounting to £5.2 billion. This effectively clawed back some of the shareholder gains, but only from those (unlucky) persons still holding shares in the affected companies at the time that the tax was levied. For many of the privatizations, small shareholders, in particular, had sold their shares and taken their gains well before 1997. In sum, privatization in the UK led to income and wealth redistribution and, while the effects deserve fuller study, the gainers included those who were most able to invest in the industries at the time of their privatization, which were not the poor (Florio, 2002; Florio and Grasseni, 2003). However, given that the number of shares each small investor was allowed to buy at each privatization issue was capped, the amount of the capital gain per issue was normally only a few hundred pounds per head.

Banks, Lawyers and Consultancies

Privatization created employment and profits in the City, about that there is no doubt. Each privatization led to work for banks in valuing the assets, arranging the sale and underwriting the share issues. Lawyers obtained lucrative employment drafting all of the necessary contracts and other legal documentation. Management consultancies benefited in terms of obtaining work in privatized companies, such as arranging retraining and 'change management' programmes, and in other countries as privatization spread internationally. To the best of my knowledge no one has attempted to put a figure on the total earnings from privatization in the City from all of the privatization work, although no one questions that it has been substantial.[10]

WHEN PRIVATIZATION IS LIKELY TO HAVE ITS GREATEST BENEFITS

Privatization is like the curate's egg, good in parts. It has enabled industry management to break away from stifling state bureaucracy, which slowed down new investment and distorted commercial decision making. It has enabled governments to raise funding that could be used to finance government expenditures or tax cuts, depending upon the political preference. It has enabled companies to access new, private capital and facilitated large, overdue, investment schemes, notably in water services. In some countries it has also facilitated the development of capital markets. In a number of countries the shares of privatized companies dominate, most obviously in central and eastern Europe, although privatization has also been important in this respect in some Western countries, too (Parker, 1998; Boutchkova and Megginson, 2000).

But at the same time, privatization has been unequal in its distribution of benefits – there have been gainers and losers. Moreover, not all privatizations have been a success. In the UK privatization did not stop, indeed it may well have accelerated, the collapse of the shipbuilding and coal mining industries. British Steel has continued to struggle financially despite privatization, as did Jaguar before its takeover by Ford, and in recent years British Airways seems to have lost competitive ground to a number of international airlines. The National Air Traffic System (NATS) had to be financially bailed out almost immediately after it was part privatized through a PPP (public–private partnership) in 2001 (Shaoul, 2003). British Energy, the nuclear electricity generator privatized in July 1996, would almost certainly have gone into receivership recently without government financial assistance; and Railtrack, owner of the railway track, signalling and main-line stations after privatization, was forced into administration in October 2001, after the government refused the company further financial subsidies. There are similar examples of privatization failures and, at best, only partial successes in other countries (see, for example, Parker and Kirkpatrick (2005a), for the developing country experience).

If we return to the economic ideas that helped trigger the development of privatization as policy, we are able to get a better understanding of when privatization is most likely to be successful, and when it is not. The property rights literature later incorporated into principal–agent theory stresses the importance of a competitive capital market. It is shareholders buying and selling shares, actions reflected in share prices that indirectly police management behaviour. Where there is a serious loss of shareholder confidence then the share price can be expected to fall, in severe cases triggering a hostile takeover bid by new management. This view of capital markets and principal–agent relationships in capitalist industry is commensurate with the way capital markets operate in North America and the UK. However, most capital markets around the world are much smaller-scale operations with much fewer shares quoted, and where families, bank groups and oligarchies commonly have controlling interests in the issued shares. In these conditions, it is far from obvious that principal–agent theory, with its emphasis on the role of competitive capital markets, is helpful. In other words, part of the economics that drove privatization in the UK, and influenced the IMF, World Bank and other international agencies (especially those based in the US) to embrace privatization, may not transfer well to the very different circumstances that apply in transition and developing countries. The country readings in Parker (1998) on privatization in the EU demonstrate that the competitive capital market model is attenuated in large parts of western Europe too.

The other part of the relevant economics, the 'economics of politics' or 'public choice' theory, may also be divorced from reality. While self-seeking behaviour no doubt goes on within governments, it is to be expected that the conduct of politicians and civil servants will vary from country to country depending upon local attitudes to probity, honesty, corruption and cronyism. A number of African countries, for example, have an unenviable reputation in these respects, while the Australian and Swiss civil services are held in high standing. In other words, arguably the tenets of the 'economics of politics' are too broad a brush to provide a useful critique of decision making within governments. However, there is another objection to this body of ideas as a justification for privatization and that lies in the *process* by which privatizations occur. In principle, privatization should have its greatest benefits economically where governments are at their most inefficient and corrupt because this is presumably when state industries will be at their most inefficient. But it seems to stretch credibility to believe that these very same governments will privatize efficiently. In fact, there is growing evidence of badly planned privatizations and sales of state assets to cronies and outright corruption in the privatization process in many parts of the world (Craig, 2000; Parker and Kirkpatrick, 2005b). This experience is probably the cause of many of the disappointing privatizations.

A number of economists have argued that privatization will have its greatest benefits in terms of raising economic efficiency where firms are sold into competitive markets. This reflects the focus within neoclassical economics on product market competition rather than ownership. That this is the case is also borne out in the increasing number of studies of privatization in the developed and developing worlds. For example, in the UK large gains in productivity were achieved in BT and British Gas, but mainly after significant competition was introduced, which was a few years after privatization. For developing countries recent studies of privatizations in telecommunications (Wallsten, 2001) and electricity generation (Zhang, Parker and Kirkpatrick, 2002) have demonstrated that privatization alone has little obvious effect on economic performance. Only where competition or effective state regulation is also introduced does performance respond to the ownership change.

In the absence of effective product market competition, the nature of state regulation after privatization becomes important. In the UK the privatization of the 'natural monopolies' led to the establishment of a series of regulatory offices at the industry level, quasi-independent of government departments (namely, Oftel, Ofgas, Offer, Ofwat, ORR, Ofgem, SRA and Ofcom). Although state regulation raises certain objections because the decisions of regulators can distort prices, outputs, employment, investment and service quality (Parker, 2002b), so that economists see regulation as 'second best' to competition, these regulatory offices have certainly played an important part in stimulating efficiency gains in the privatized, monopoly industries in the UK. For instance, productivity and costs of production did not alter much in the privatized water and sewerage industry until regulatory intervention in April 1995 in the form of much tougher price caps (Saal and Parker, 2000, 2001).

Figure 2.2 summarizes the circumstances when privatization is most likely to lead to economic efficiency gains and when it is most likely to disappoint. In essence, where product competition is poor, state regulation is necessary

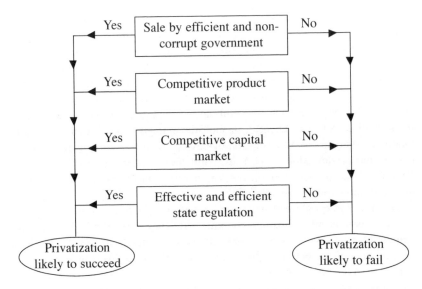

Figure 2.2   Summarizing when privatization is likely to have the greatest economic benefits

but non-existent, ineffective or, worse, inept; governments privatize ineffi-ciently and cronyism and corruption dominate; and where there is no compet-itive capital market following privatization, then all of these indicators suggest that privatization will fail, in the sense of achieving the expected economic efficiencies. By contrast, privatization by efficient and non-corrupt governments, in competitive product markets or with effective and efficient state regulatory bodies, and where there will be ongoing scrutiny of manage-ment behaviour by a competitive capital market, has its best chance of raising economic performance.

SPREADING THE WORD

The UK's privatization experiment was soon copied by other countries. From as early as around 1983 the UK government received delegations from other governments keen to learn more about the UK's experience. France had intro-duced a major programme of nationalization in the early 1980s, but reversed this policy from the mid-'80s. A right of centre government in France privatized 14 large industrial and financial enterprises. Other European countries also began to adopt privatization programmes. In the 1990s all European countries introduced some privatization with Italy, Portugal, Spain and France having particularly active programmes (for details see Parker, 1998). Unsurprisingly, the largest programmes of privatization occurred in the transition economies of central and eastern Europe, where again the UK was held up as a model.

Outside of Europe privatization was soon a central policy of the international donor agencies notably the World Bank (Parker and Kirkpatrick, 2005a). Consultancies from the UK became very active in designing privatizations including helping to draft the necessary legislation, for example for privatizations in South Africa, Uganda and Malawi. The regulatory bodies established to oversee the operation of newly privatized utilities in telecommunications, energy and transport were often modelled on regulatory agencies in the UK. The 'price cap' method of regulating prices in privatized monopolies has been exported from the UK to countries around the globe (Parker and Kirkpatrick, 2005b).

It is quite possible that privatization would have occurred internationally without the UK's experience. However, there can be no doubting that the UK model proved to be inspirational in changing attitudes towards the selling off of state enterprises.

CONCLUSIONS

This chapter has considered why privatization developed as policy especially in the UK, who have been the main gainers and losers from the policy, and the circumstances under which privatization is most likely to be successful. The study has identified an evolving and opportunistic programme of privatizations in the UK, driven by a number of changing and sometimes conflicting policy objectives, but with an intellectual underpinning drawn from principal–agent theory and the 'economics of politics' literatures. We have also seen that privatization does have an impact on income and wealth distribution. In the UK the senior managers of privatized firms, when they retained their jobs, have been obvious gainers, through large salary increases to reflect top salaries in the private sector. Workers as a group have been both gainers and losers and it is more difficult to generalize the outcome. However, it seems that low-skilled employees are the most likely to have lost out, reflecting non-market pay under public ownership, and there have been some sharp reductions in overall employment in a number of the privatized firms. Consumers have generally gained in terms of prices and services, especially where they were previously dependent on a state-owned monopoly. Finally, the City had done well with investors more frequently achieving large capital gains on their privatization shares than losing out through subsequent share price movements during the bull market of the 1980s and 1990s, and banks and consultancies obtaining lucrative contracts.

The chapter has also attempted to summarize when privatization is most likely to be successful in achieving economic efficiencies. Where there is little competition for consumers, an ineffective capital market and inefficient or corrupt government, then privatization is likely to disappoint. Unfortunately, at least some of these conditions exist in many developing and transition economies and not all developed, industrialized countries have the ideal conditions for successful privatization. It is not surprising, therefore, that there is growing empirical evidence of privatization failures. Such failures have recently caused the World Bank to switch its policy focus from privatization to creating the conditions for effective state regulation. It is a beguiling possibility that the privatizations of the 1980s and 1990s will ultimately be best known for not having led to less but rather to more effective government.

NOTES

1. The manifesto also mentioned relaxing licensing regulations to allow new private bus operations.
2. British Shipbuilders was disposed of through private sales. Naval dockyards were privatized through contracting out their management.
3. Under an offer for sale the assets are sold at a price fixed ahead of the sale. Under a sale by tender the price is set according to the demand for shares and the supply of shares available. Offers for sale therefore provide the biggest prospect of a stagging gain.
4. By this time the government had also embarked on a high-profile policy of selling council (state) housing to tenants at below market values.
5. The shares were sold at 130p per share but only 50p was initially payable. At the end of the first day's trading the share price stood at 93p. In the London stock market a 'stag' is someone who buys a share at flotation with a view to selling it quickly at a profit.
6. The manifesto referred to the sale of BT, Rolls-Royce, British Airways, 'substantial parts of British Steel, of British Shipbuilders and of British Leyland, and as many as possible of British Airports', and the introduction of private capital into the National Bus Company. It also referred to introducing private capital into gas and electricity and the sale of the state's remaining offshore oil interests (Conservative Party, 1983:7). These privatizations were introduced in the following years.
7. Increased spending of track repair and maintenance following a series of rail accidents accounts for some of this increase.
8. About 80 per cent of domestic consumers obtain unmetered water, paying a fixed charge for the supply.
9. This return is calculated as an internal rate of return and is in real terms (see Parker (1997) for details).
10. There are some examples for particular privatizations in Ernst & Young (1994:10–14).

REFERENCES

Alchian, A.A. and H. Demsetz (1972), 'Production, information costs and economic organization', *American Economic Review*, **62**, 777–95.
Artis, M.J. (ed.) (1996), *The UK Economy*, 14th edn, Oxford: Oxford University Press.

Bain, J.S. (1956), *Barriers to New Competition*, Cambridge, MA: Harvard University Press.

Bös, D. (1991), *Privatization: A Theoretical Treatment*, Oxford: Clarendon Press.

Boutchkova, M.K. and W.L. Megginson (2000), 'Privatization and the rise of global capital markets', Fondazione Eni Enrico Mattei working paper no.53.

Brown, M.B. (1984), *Models in Political Economy: A Guide to the Arguments*, Harmondsworth: Penguin.

Buchanan, J.M. (1972), *Theory of Public Choice*, Ann Arbor, MI: University of Michigan Press.

Burton, J. and D. Parker (1991), 'Rolling back the state?: UK tax and government spending changes in the 1980s', *British Review of Economic Issues*, **13** (31), 29–66.

Clifton, J., F. Comín, and D.D. Fuentes (2003), *Privatisation in the European Union: Public Enterprise and Integration*, Dordrecht: Kluwer.

Conservative Party (1979), *Election Manifesto 1979*, London: Conservative Party.

Conservative Party (1983), *Election Manifesto 1983*, London: Conservative Party.

Crafts, N. (2002), *Britain's Relative Economic Performance, 1870–1999*, research monograph no. 55, London: Institute of Economic Affairs.

Cragg, M. and I.J.A. Dyck (1999), 'Management control and privatization in the UK', *RAND Journal of Economics*, **30** (3), 475–97.

Craig, J. (2000), 'Evaluating privatisation in Zambia: a tale of two processes', *Review of African Political Economy*, **27** (85), 357–66.

Curwen, P. (1994), 'Directors' pay in privatized companies', *Public Money and Management*, **14** (1), 8–9.

Drucker, P. (1969), *The Age of Discontinuity*, New York: Harper Row.

Dunsire, A., K. Hartley, D. Parker and B. Dimitriou (1988), 'Organisational status and performance: a conceptual framework for testing public choice theories', *Public Administration*, **66** (4), 363–88.

Ernst & Young (1994), *Privatization in the UK: The Facts and Figures*, compiled by Peter Curwen, London: Ernst & Young.

Esser, J. (1998), 'Privatisation in Germany: symbolism in the social market economy?', in D. Parker (ed.), *Privatisation in the European Union: Theory and Policy Perspectives*, London: Routledge.

Fama, E.F. and M.V. Jensen (1983), 'Separation of ownership and control', *Journal of Law and Economics*, **26**, 301–25.

Filatotchev, I. (2003), 'Privatization and corporate governance in transition economies: theory and concepts', in D. Parker and D. Saal (eds), *International Handbook on Privatization*, Cheltenham, UK and Northampton, MA, USA: Edward Elgar.

Florio, M. (2002), 'A state without ownership: the welfare impact of British privatisations 1979–1997', Dipartimento di Economia Politica e Aziendale, Universita degli Studi di Milano working paper no. 24.2002, Milan.

Florio, M. and M. Grasseni (2003), 'The missing shock: the macroeconomic impact of British privatisation', Dipartimento di Economia Politica e Aziendale, Universita degli Studi di Milano working paper no. 21.2003, Milan.

Furubotn, E.G. and S. Pejovich (1972), 'Property rights and economic theory: a survey of the recent literature', *Journal of Economic Literature*, **10**, 1137–62.

Gilmour, I. (1993), *Dancing with Dogma*, London: Simon & Schuster.

Hancock, C. and C. Waddams Price (1995), 'Competition in British domestic gas market: efficiency and equity', *Fiscal Studies*, **16** (3), 81–105.

Hastings, S. and H. Levie (1983), *Privatisation?*, Nottingham: Spokesman.

Hayek, F.A. von (1948), *Individualism and the Economic Order*, Chicago, IL: University of Chicago Press.

HM Treasury (1991), *Economic Briefing*, no. 2, May, London: HM Treasury.

House of Commons (1998) 'GDP per capita in OECD countries: the UK's relative position', Research Paper 98/64, June.

Hunt, J. (2000), 'Why do people still live in East Germany?', National Bureau of Economic Research working paper no. 7564, Cambridge, MA.

Kay, J.A. and D.J. Thompson (1986), 'Privatisation: a policy in search of a rationale', *Economic Journal*, **96**, 18–32.

Keegan, W. (1984), *Mrs Thatcher's Economic Experiment*, Harmondsworth: Penguin.

Lawson, N. (1992), *The View from No. 11: Memoirs of a Tory Radical*, London: Bantam Press.

Littlechild, S.C. (2000) 'Privatisation, competition and regulation', Institute of Economic Affairs occasional paper no. 110, London.

Littlechild, S.C. (1978), 'The fallacy of the mixed economy: an "Austrian" critique of recent economic thinking and policy', Institute of Economic Affairs Hobart Paper no. 80, London.

Martin, S. and D. Parker (1997), *The Impact of Privatisation: Ownership and Corporate Performance in the UK*, London: Routledge.

Niskanen, W.A. Jr. (1971), *Bureaucracy and Representative Government*, Chicago, IL: Aldine.

Organisation for Economic Co-operation and Development (OECD) (2001), 'Privatisation: recent trends', *Financial Market Trends*, 79 (June), Paris: OECD.

Parker, D. (1997), 'Price cap regulation, profitability and returns to investors in the UK regulated industries', *Utilities Policy*, **6** (4), 103–15.

Parker, D. (ed.) (1998), *Privatisation in the European Union: Theory and Policy Perspectives*, London: Routledge.

Parker, D. (2002a), 'Inertia in the implementation of a privatisation programme', in M. De Jong, K. Lalenis and V. Mamdouh (eds), *The Theory and Practice of Institutional Transplantation: Experiences with the Transfer of Policy Institutions*, Dordrecht: Kluwer.

Parker, D. (2002b), 'Economic regulation: a review of issues', *Annals of Public and Cooperative Economics*, **73** (4), 493–519.

Parker, D. (2004), 'The UK's privatisation experiment: the passage of time permits a sober assessment', Centre for Economic Studies & Ifo Institute for Economic Research working paper no. 1126, Munich.

Parker, D. and C. Kirkpatrick (2005a), 'The impact of privatization in developing countries: a review of the evidence and the policy lessons', *Journal of Development Studies*, **41** (4), 513–41.

Parker, D. and C. Kirkpatrick (2005b), 'Regulating prices and profits in utility industries in low income economies: rate of return, price cap or sliding scale regulation?', *International Journal of Public Sector Management*, **18** (3), 241–55.

Parker, D. and S. Martin (1996), 'The impact of UK privatization on employment, profits and the distribution of business income', *Public Money and Management*, **16** (1), 31–8.

Pendleton, A. and J. Winterton (eds) (1993), *Public Enterprise in Transition: Industrial Relations in State and Privatized Corporations*, London: Routledge.

Price Waterhouse (1987), *Privatisation: The Facts*, London: Price Waterhouse.

Saal, D. (2003), 'Restructuring, regulation and the liberalization of privatized utilities in the UK', in D. Parker and D. Saal (eds), *International Handbook on Privatization*, Cheltenham, UK, and Northampton, MA, USA: Edward Elgar.

Saal, D. and D. Parker (2000), 'The impact of privatisation and regulation on the water and sewerage industry in England and Wales: a translog cost function model', *Managerial and Decision Economics,* **21**, 253–68.

Saal, D. and D. Parker (2001), 'Productivity and price performance in the privatized water and sewerage companies in England and Wales', *Journal of Regulatory Economics,* **20** (1), 61–90.

Saunders, P. (1993), 'Recent trends in the size and growth of government in OECD countries', in N. Gemmell (ed.), *The Growth of the Public Sector: Theories and International Evidence,* Aldershot: Edward Elgar.

Shand, A.H. (1984), *The Capitalist Alternative: An Introduction to Neo-Austrian Economics,* Hemel Hempstead: Harvester Wheatsheaf.

Shaoul, J. (2003), 'A financial analysis of the National Air Traffic Services PPP', *Public Money and Management,* **23** (3), 185–94.

Smith, A. (2004), 'UK regulatory price review: the role of efficiency estimates', paper presented at the conference on UK Regulatory Price Review: The Role of Efficiency Estimates, London Business School, 6 July.

Stigler, G.J. (1961), 'The economics of information', *Journal of Political Economy,* June, 213–25.

Thatcher, M. (1993), *The Downing Street Years,* New York: HarperCollins.

Tullock, G. (1976), *The Vote Motive,* London: Institute of Economic Affairs.

Udehn, L. (1996), *The Limits of Public Choice: Sociological Critique of the Economic Theory of Politics,* London: Routledge.

Vickers, J. and G. Yarrow (1988), *Privatization: An Economic Analysis,* Cambridge, MA: MIT Press.

Waddams Price, C. and A. Young (2003), 'UK utility reform: distributional implications and government response', in C. Ugaz and C. Waddams Price (eds), *Utility Privatization and Regulation: A Fair Deal for Consumers?,* Cheltenham, UK and Northampton, MA, USA: Edward Elgar.

Wallsten, S.J. (2001), 'An econometric analysis of telecom competition, privatization, and regulation in Africa and Latin America', *Journal of Industrial Economics,* **49** (1), 1–19.

World Bank (1995), *Bureaucrats in Business: The Economics and Politics of Government Ownership,* Oxford: Oxford University Press for the World Bank.

Zhang, Y., D. Parker and C. Kirkpatrick (2002), 'Electricity sector reform in developing countries: an econometric assessment of the effects of privatisation, competition and regulation', Centre on Regulation and Competition working paper no. 31, University of Manchester, Manchester.

3. Contracting as policy: worldwide implications

Larkin Dudley and Alesya Bogaevskaya

INTRODUCTION

How governing bodies should provide, allocate and deliver services and goods for the public has been an issue for debate since government began. In most of the world, the pendulum has swung from the provision of some collective goods by family and clan to government. More recently, provision has swung over to the private sector through privatization. One of the means of privatizing is through contracting with private providers, both for profit and not for profit. This chapter examines contracting for public provision as policy through a discussion of the ideas supporting the practice, the distribution and implementation of contracting policy, and an evaluation of its effectiveness.

The nomenclature surrounding privatization is confusing and varies by world region and academic field. However, for this paper, we will use the following terms, somewhat consistent with an evolving consensus on definitions in the literature. Privatization is often used as the most generic term referring to any means of increasing private provision of what had been thought of as public goods and services. Although in recent years, in much of the literature, privatization has come to be equated with the total divestiture of goods or services – for example, selling off public enterprises – the term here will be used as the more generic term of which there can be many types and techniques. In relationship to public goods, contracting, contracting-out and outsourcing all refer to the process of purchasing goods or services via contractual agreements from another public organization or a private or not-for-profit organization. The term contracting-out has often been used specifically to denote the contracting process targeting the purchasing of goods and services that once were provided by government or thought to be a part of the responsibility of government to provide (Domberger, 1998). Managed competition is the term most often used for those contracting situations where government units and outside sources, usually for-profit companies, bid against each other to provide services once performed by government.

The basic policy idea behind contracting is to reduce the activity of the state and to utilize competition as a means of assuring the best price. The idea is that government should let the private (including profit and not-for-profit) sector provide services while government steers. The process is one where organizations submit bids to provide particular services to the client. Contract specifications define the market with the bidding process resembling an auction where the lowest-priced bid wins. Thus, there is competition for the market, *ex ante* competition, rather than competition in it. Compared with selling off state-owned enterprises, the government retains more control, monitors performance, imposes financial penalties and replaces the contractor in cases of outright performance failure.

Discrete contracting has always been a part of most governments, but became even more popular in the 1980s with a focus on contracting-out services that were easily measured, planned ahead of time, assumed that all contingencies were covered and focused on bounded transactions between client and patron; for example, janitorial services or snow removal. Growing alongside discrete contracting, relational contracting became the terminology for the relationships needed to cover harder to measure services. These, in turn, evolved and the contract time span lengthened as risks were taken together and relationships developed amongst professionals. Such contract arrangements were usually a part of basic research, some social service areas and policy development. Contract types of discrete and relational contracts may vary and include an emphasis on fixed price, cost plus or best value. One important variety of contracting, competitive tendering or competitive contracting, such as that under Circular A-76 in the United States, sets up competition for provision of a governmental service between the governmental agency and outside private for profit or non-profit contractors. Finally, as will be discussed below, contractualism, as exemplified in the New Zealand model, is now a reality. Contractualism refers to a very ingrained system where most governing processes, both internal and external, are provided by contractors.

CONTRACTING AS POLICY

Ancient history reveals contracting as a tool of government. Contracting out was tried as a tool of administration in Persia under the Achaemenid Empire (559–330 BC) for collecting fixed property taxes and on a mass scale for hiring Greek mercenaries to fight and complete public works (Farazmand, 2001). In ancient Greece, the government contracted out the working of government-owned land, forests and mines to individuals and firms (Megginson and Netter, 2001). More important to this chapter, however, is the recent history of events that helped to lift the practice of contracting to the policy agenda of many nations in the 1980s. With the end of the cold war, many nations found themselves in debates about the role of government. The most industrialized nations faced a loss of trust in government and corporate leaders complained that tax and regulations hurt their ability to create jobs and prosper. Former Iron Curtain countries had to re-conceptualize their ideas of governing, the role of private and public, and the role of citizens. Developing nations also were faced with pressures worldwide to modernize and to enter into global trade. Economic stagnation was pervasive in all continents, including New Zealand, where some of the most radical reforms were initiated.

Although contracting had been part of each of these governments' management tools, Australia, New Zealand, United Kingdom and United States of America emphasized the need for policy reform in the 1980s to cut the cost and size of government. These events all contributed to the growing perception that the processes of governing were problems themselves reflecting the theoretical axiom that conditions come to be defined as problems depending on who is paying attention at the time, the values and beliefs of the individuals concerned and the magnitude of change in the conditions (Kingdon, 1995).

Thus, contracting as a long-term government practice grew into a policy of preference in the last quarter of the twentieth century through its inclusion in the spate of managerial reforms which together both reinforced and reinvigorated a commercial ideology. According to Donald Kettl (2000), the reforms have been characterized by an emphasis on productivity (produce more with less tax base); marketization (use market-style incentives to change bureaucratic pathologies); service orientation (use a customer orientation to connect with citizens); decentralization (move programmes to lower levels of government or to frontline managers); policy (improve the tracking of policy, sometimes by separating policy and service delivery); and accountability (focus on outputs and outcomes, not process). When considered as policy, contracting is usually bundled with many of the practices and ideas immediately above under the rubric of government reform and is most often accompanied by a renewed emphasis on measurement and performance.

Throughout the 1980s and 1990s, scholars labelled these sets of reforms New Public Management (NPM). Hughes (2003) argues that New Public Management reform was facilitated by three distinct themes including the continuing attack on the public sector, prevalence of economic theory (including public choice theory and principal–agent theory) and globalization and competition. New Public Management purports to be designed to 'fix the problems of government' such as low public confidence in bureaucracy, waste, poor programme design and performance deficit. Efforts to explain turned to institutional economics, public choice and principal–agent ideas to provide a sounder theoretical base (Kaboolian, 1998; Eagle, 2005). Two intellectual themes grounding New Public Management are institutional economics and managerialism (Lynn, 1996). Institutional economics proposes the disaggregation of public bureaucracies and the use of competition while managerialism includes an emphasis on private sector management techniques, hands-on professional management and performance measurement (Lynn, 1996). Generally, New Public Management argues that the market, not the government, is the best allocator of resources; individuals are the best judges of their own welfare; and that private sector management techniques could be useful to improve government performance (Hodge, 2000; Hughes, 2003).

GLOBAL DIVERSITY IN ACCEPTANCE OF NEW PUBLIC MANAGEMENT IDEAS

The New Public Management reforms have been impressive because they spread globally in such a short period of time and some of the ideas behind the reforms have been remarkably similar in nations as diverse as New Zealand, United States, Mongolia and Sweden (Kettl, 2000). Scholars representing several schools of thought have tried to explain the phenomenon of the popularity of the New Public Management (Christensen and Laegreid, 2001). The widespread acceptance of these ideas includes both their appeal as solutions to technical problems and the ideological support they received from both political figures and institutions. As a technical solution, competitive tendering and contracting (CTC), also known as outsourcing, took on increasing significance under the implied assumption that CTC reduces costs and improves the quality of the service or both. Some other technical reforms included the introduction of accrual accounting, managing by outputs, utilizing a 'user-pays' regime and various forms of privatization.

In addition to the appeal of contracting out as a solution to technical problems, political acceptance and institutional approval yielded coalitions in many countries that often included both strong advocates of contracting from the industrial world and from elected politicians. The importance of international organizations should also be highlighted, such as the Organisation for Economic Co-operation and Development (OECD) where reform guidelines took hold, became ideologically dominant, and diffused all over the world. For example, OECD Public Management Services published 'The Best Practice Guidelines' in 1997 with the purpose to assist all member countries in further implementation of contracting-out mechanisms (OECD, 1997). Thus, both the need to solve common instrumental problems and the isomorphic pressure of dominating norms seem to be a part of the worldwide pattern of distribution of New Public Management, particularly in the adoption of contracting out as process and policy.

However, the roads taken by the reformers in different countries reflect the

Table 3.1   Global differences in contracting-out through the mid-1990s

Type of reformers	Countries	Scope of reforms
Initiators Anglo-American	UK, Australia, New Zealand and, to some extent, USA	– Radical reforms since early 1980s – Initiated by the national governments (top-down) approach – Neo-liberal politics – Market mechanisms – Privatization – Managerialism – Commercialization – Running governments as business
Cautious Nordic	Sweden, Norway, Finland, Denmark and the Netherlands	– Gradual reforms since early 1990s – Economic depression and financial devolution – EU integration – Local bottom-up approach – High degree of service delivery through agencies – Customization
Minimalists	*Germanic*: Germany, Austria and Switzerland *Southern European*: France, Italy, Portugal, Spain Canada	– Minimal incremental reforms since mid-1990s – Fiscal urgency – Initiated by local governments – Bottom-up approach – Customer orientation – Flexible resource management
Devolution Asian	South Korea, Thailand, Malaysia, Singapore	– Late 1990s – Partial, often derivative reforms were enforced by the national governments – Stimulated by financial crisis and needs to reduce administrative expenses – Privatization – Commercialization

Major characteristics	Source
− Performance and result-based management − Fiscal balance − Efficiency − Accountability − Accrual budgeting − Competitiveness − Strategic and hard-to-specify tasks − Best value approach	Flynn (1997, 2000), Shick (1998), Kettl (1996, 1997, 2000), McIntosh et al. (1997), Savas (1997, 2000), Pollitt and Bouckaert (2000)
− Financial balance − Customers' satisfaction − Strong sense of social responsibility − Community-based services − Competitive tendering for specific local services and some infrastructure − Greater reliance on user fees	OEDC (PUMA) (1997), Manning and Parison (2004), Klausen (1992), Premfors (1998), Alford (2002), Wollmann (2001)
− Easily specified support tasks − Local services delivery based on competition and customers' satisfaction − Traditional input budgeting − Accountability	Manning and Parison (2004), OECD (1997), Torres (2004), Pollitt and Bouckaert (2000), Rouban (1997), LaPanet and Trebilcock (1998), Kickert (1997)
− Management based on performance and results − Some semi-autonomous agencies have been established − Easily specified support tasks have been contracted out	Manning and Parison (2004), Park (2004), Kim (1998), Khan (1998), Schick (1998), MOGAHA, Korean Ministry of Government Administration and Home Affairs (2003)

Table 3.1   continued

Type of reformers	Countries	Scope of reforms
Central control Latin-American	Mexico, Chile, Brazil, Argentina	– Mid-1990s – To reduce public debt – Privatization – Central control of resources and decentralize implementation – Pro-market policies – Managerialism
Central and Eastern European	Hungary, Poland, Romania, Czech Republic, Slovenia, Lithuania, Latvia, Estonia and Russia	– Since early 1990s – Total privatization – Democratization and implementation of market mechanisms through a series of centrally designed and coordinated programmes (top-down approach) – Radical privatization with partial implementation of contracting out since mid-1990s – Initiated by the national governments in compliance with EU integration processes (except Russia) – Necessity to reduce budget deficit
Isomorphic Developing African and Asian	Zimbabwe, Ghana, Tanzania and Mongolia	– Late 1990s – Initiated by the national governments (top-down approach) – Radical privatization with extensive introduction of market mechanisms and contracting out

features of national institutional processes. Internal factors, such as the national historical-institutional context and/or the different constitutional features and political-administrative structures become salient. The main features of the polity, the form of government and the formal structure of decision making within the political-administrative system may all affect a country's capacity to realize administrative reforms. The greater the consistency between the values underlying the reforms and the values on which the existing administrative system is based, the more likely the reforms are to be successful.

Major characteristics	Source
– Contract-management – Performance-based management – Competitiveness – Substantial services have been contracted out	Manning and Parison (2004), Meacham (1999), Klingner (2000), Borzutzky (2003)
– Basic reforms in public services provision – Contracting out restricted to the easily specified support tasks and natural monopolies services – Traditional input budgeting – Lack of trade union resistance – Corruption and lack of effective competition	Manning and Parison (2004), OECD (1997), Vladesca and Redulescu (2001), Martin (1999), Oswald (2000), Blejer and Skreb (2001), Antal-Mokos (1998), Dittrich (2001)
– Contracting out easily specified supporting tasks and natural monopolies services in accordance with major donors' models – Recently, contracting out core regulatory functions to international parties	World Bank (2004), Shick (1998), Farazmand (2001, 2002), Therkildsen (2000), Nixon and Walters (1999), McCourt (2001)

Table 3.1 illustrates the variety in the scope of the reforms. The typology is based on the descriptions in the literature specifically on contracting where available and on references to contracting in the explanations of the general reforms of New Public Management. In our attempts to give a general overview, of course, the many nuances and differences within the countries and among the countries within a single grouping are lost. However, this typology does attempt to give a fuller picture of the many different approaches to contracting around the world based on current reports from the literature on

the level of reforms and the degree of implementation of contracting out. Seven groups of countries have been included.

Initiators: Anglo-American Reformers

The first group can be considered the most advanced reformers, represented by Anglo-American countries (USA, UK, New Zealand and Australia). As discussed above, NPM reforms stem from neoliberal ideology, which prioritizes market over the state and establishes a goal to run government as a business. Accordingly, many governmental services – federal and local – are contracted out to private providers, including such strategic functions as human resources management and planning. In several of these countries, there was an absence of institutional and constitutional constraints to radical, top-down, reform programme development and implementation and the presence of relatively simple state structures. New Zealand and the United Kingdom are both unitary states and Australia, although a federal state, has traditionally had a strong federal level of government. Although the federal system of the United States yielded different variants and a different pace of contracting among local, state and national agencies, the overall respect for private sector solutions in this capitalist economy made contracting appealing.

In the United States, the pace of contracting out quickened in the 1980s, dramatically expanded during the early 1990s and levelled off at the turn of the century (Colman, 1989; Ferris and Graddy, 1986; Fixler and Poole, 1987; Hatry, 1983; Rehfuss, 1989; Smith, 1987). In the USA, unabashedly the policy is that the government should not compete with the private sector, as revealed at the national level in its Circular A-76 and in similar documents or ideas at the local and state level. The protection of the right of the private sector to compete is well ingrained in American culture and could be interpreted as a right more sacred in some senses than protection of the public sector (Dudley, 1997). Selected features of the United States system will be used below to illustrate the interweaving of New Public Management ideas with traditional values.

CASE STUDY EXAMPLE – UNITED STATES CIRCULAR A-76

The principle that the general policy of the government is to rely on commercial sources to supply the products and services the government needs is best articulated in the United States in

Circular A-76. Initiated by the Bureau of the Budget under the administration of Dwight Eisenhower, Circular A-76 established federal policy regarding the performance of commercial activities. Now, guidance on contracting at the federal level is derived by agency personnel and contractors from Circular A-76, the FAIR Act, Government Performance and Results Act of 1993 and the Clinger-Cohen Act. According to the guidance, the key criterion as to whether a function must be performed by a civil servant is the exercise of sovereignty. Public employees must retain the power to tax and the power to make policy decisions for the government. Under the guidance, it is clear, for example, that agency heads exercising budgeting and policy decision power are inherently governmental, but supply room clerks, janitors and landscapers may not be. Still, the guidance leaves considerable room for agencies to make their own outsourcing decisions, to try their best to use the criteria found in the current policies and in practice to decide whether a position could possibly be exempt from the necessity to compete as part of a Circular A-76 study.

The ideas surrounding what is appropriate for other sectors to provide as commercial activities, i.e. what should be outsourced, have evolved since the Air Corps Act of 1926, an early predecessor of the idea of giving government the discretion to weigh performance, as well as price in contract awards. The issuance of the series of bulletins of the Bureau of the Budget in the 1950s, however, is seen as the direct predecessor for Circular A-76. The first of the series, Bulletin N. 55-4, was issued by the executive branch on 15 January 1955. It stated that

> It is the general policy of the administration that the Federal Government will not start or carry on any commercial activity to provide a service or product for its own use if such product or service can be procured from private enterprise through ordinary business channels. Exceptions to this policy shall be made by the head of an agency only where it is clearly demonstrated in each case that it is not in the public interest to procure such product or service from private enterprise (President's Commission on Privatization, 1988:1).

Taking this as a beginning for the dialogue in the United States, we can trace several different conceptions of contracting in the dialogue of what government should or should not contract out. They include Acknowledgment of Private Enterprise and Governments' Roles; Transition to Cost Emphasis; New Public

Management as Policy; and Courting Comprehensiveness. However, even within the nuances of different conceptions, it is important to remember that the policy has always held to the idea that reliance on private enterprise for commercial activities was the position to be privileged in the contracting-out debate with the exception of those activities or positions that were seen as inherently governmental. The definition of inherently governmental functions in the Circular is as being 'so intimately related to the public interest as to mandate performance by federal employees'. It's also crucial to realize that each conception of contracting blends into the next and that themes once apparent continue in some form into the next conception.

Acknowledgment of Private Enterprise and Governments' Roles

At the beginning of Circular A-76, the dialogue did revolve around what was more appropriately governmental and what should be commercial services. Nevertheless, the definite focus was on defining what was commercial, that is to say a privileging of the commercial in order to support private enterprise.

Transition to Cost Emphasis

In the 1970s under the Carter administration, a Cost Comparison Handbook was issued which spelled out cost comparison procedures and established competition between government and commercial concerns for the public largesse and concomitant opportunities. The shift from how the government does business to a focus on what the government needs done gave government managers incentives to review their organizations to develop more efficient procedures. The die was cast though for cost comparisons to become the major factor in deciding not only how, but sometimes what, functions would be contracted. What gave the process new life was the attention it received politically in the Carter/Ford presidential campaign.

New Public Management

The true impetus, however, for moving contracting-out from consideration as another procedure to procure services to a more important policy role came in the Reagan administration when the idea of contracting could be merged with other ideas of slenderizing the bureaucracy and cutting federal personnel. Here we see a deepening of contracting as policy and its favoured position coupled with other rhetoric, such as an emphasis on measurement and agencies meeting specific annual goals of studying areas to be contracted. This era of Reagan set the base for what later became labelled the New Public Management philosophy, including the continuing attack on the public sector, the prevalence of ideas compatible with economic theory (including public choice theory and principal–agent theory) as measures of government success and the privileging of competition, rather than co-operation, as a means towards effective government service. The Clinton administration with its focus on Reinventing Government and the performance review also gives more credibility to contracting philosophy and rounds out the New Public Management ideas by increasing a customer focus, devolution and an outcomes orientation.

Courting Comprehensiveness

Finally, the rhetoric for contracting blossoms again in the George W. Bush regime with a quite elaborate schema for identifying and measuring which positions should be commercial and which inherently governmental. In addition, a newer version of Circular A-76 combines several policies from different sources and rolls them into the Circular. In an attempt to be more comprehensive, OMB has issued more specific reason codes for determining what is inherently governmental along with plans to issue a best practices guide on how to decide which jobs are inherently governmental or commercial. The guide will in part be based on the recent work of the Chief Acquisition Officers Council subcommittee on competitive sourcing.

Among Anglo-American reformers, New Zealand represents an extreme case of 'contractual' state or 'government by contract' (Schick, 1998). Internal factors appear to have shaped the New Zealand model. Since 1988, New Zealand has implemented management reforms designed to establish or strengthen contract-like relationships between the government and ministers as purchasers of goods and services and departments and other private entities as suppliers. New Zealand government creates conditions under which hundreds of formal contracts are negotiated and enforced each year. Thus, according to Kettl (1997), New Zealand has aggressively pursued a philosophy of 'making the managers manage'. The only way to improve government performance, the reformers believed, was to change the incentives of government managers by subjecting them to market forces and contracts. Top managers were hired on fixed-term contracts, rewarded according to their performance and could theoretically be fired if their work did not measure up. Individual work- and performance-contracts replaced the rule- and process-based civil service system, but a team approach among governmental managers did include incentives to cooperate. Many departments decoupled policy making from the delivery of services. Contract agreements have even been extended to policy advice and analysis. Schick (1998) argues that this 'new contractualism' replaces the implicit or relational contracts that characterize traditional public administration and may weaken traditional values of public service and professionalism as well as carry enormous transaction costs.

Selected features of the New Zealand model were adopted by very few developed countries, for instance by Iceland (Reeves and Barrow, 2000) and Singapore (Schick, 1998). In the 1980s Australia used NPM more pragmatically than New Zealand. The Australian government, unlike New Zealand, initiated managerial reforms first and then the marketization and contracting policies. The two countries have become more similar in the 1990s through the greater emphasis Australia has put on market elements – competition, contracting out and privatization (McIntosh et al., 1997; Wettenhall, 1998). The Australian Capital Territory (Canberra) and Victoria are reported to be more similar to New Zealand in their reform profiles.

Cautious: Continental European Reformers and Canada

The next two groups in our typology represent the Continental European countries and Canada. In the first group, we have placed the Nordic countries and the Netherlands and the second group consists of Germanic and southern European countries plus Canada. These countries do not regard radical NPM reforms as desirable (Pollitt and Bouckaert, 2000). Neoliberal ideology faces strong political opposition limiting marketization of governmental services in these countries (Kickert, 1997). The concept of the primordial role of the public sector in the society creates inherent tension between public and private management techniques. The neoliberal idea of marketization of the public sector and transferring the provision of public services to private firms through contracting-out challenges the traditional core concept of a 'good public sector' in the Nordic countries and the Netherlands, the civil obedience to government in the Germanic countries, and the idea that the public sector should watch over the polity in the southern European countries and Canada (Torres, 2004).

Nordic

In these countries, questions of legitimacy surround contracting out of public services, a parallel movement complementing the evolution of relationships between government and citizens. To decrease the gaps between the state and its citizens, governments initiated reformation of public services to bring administration and delivery closer to citizens, thus enhancing transparency, openness, accountability and, most importantly, fairness (Alford, 2002). Nordic countries have stressed the de-concentration of the provision of public services through transformation of many of the traditional government ministries into semi-public agencies. Sweden and the Netherlands are the countries with greater market-type reforms albeit as a complementary element of the provision of public services (Premfors, 1998). However, the Netherlands climate of public opinion is increasingly negative about drastic privatization and contracting-out of several monopolistic services and is in favour of returning some services to the state (Manning and Parison, 2004).

Behind the differences in public administration reforms and implementation of contracting-out, there are reasons related to countries' administrative traditions. The Nordic countries (Sweden, Norway, Finland, Denmark) and the Netherlands are unitary states with public administration models emphasizing the meeting of citizens' needs and collective responses (Torres, 2004). They have a tradition of negotiation and consultation and emphasis on the satisfaction of citizens' wishes in the search for efficiency and effectiveness.

Minimalists

The countries of Continental Europe and Canada can be labelled the 'minimalist' reformers. In countries influenced by the Germanic tradition – Germany, Austria and Switzerland – the bureaucracy model remains basically Weberian in the framework of a complex federal system and a complex inter-relationship between federal government and the Lander (member of the Federation with sovereign state power). Especially in Germany a federal system makes the public administration varied and complex (Pollitt and Bouckaert, 2000) and the introduction of homogeneous reforms and contractual relationships becomes very difficult. The Länder retains sovereign state power of its own and defines its own public administrations reform programme, resulting in a vertical and horizontal variance and fragmentation (Wollmann, 2001).

Southern European countries (France, Italy, Portugal, Spain) and Canada have service delivery processes built around a strong concept of administrative law (Rouban, 1997). One basic concern is to provide equal levels of public services throughout the country through a centralized state apparatus.

Politicians and the general public believe that only government may guarantee that services arc distributed equally and efficiently. In these countries the central government sets common service futures for the whole country, collects most of the tax revenues and maintains offices in provinces (Torres, 2004).

In summary, Continental European countries modernize their public administration processes, but are cautious about contracting-out services to private providers.

Devolution: Asian Reformers

The 1990s economic crisis pushed the national governments of South Korea, Thailand, Malaysia and Singapore to initiate privatization policy with contracting-out as the most common form. Contracting-out was seen as one of the major tools for reforming government and making it more efficient and productive. The reform included the reduction of the size of bureaucracy, the introduction of commercial principles and competition in government, and making government accountable and customer-oriented (Park, 2004). All these were in line with the Anglo-American model of reform. Based on these ideas, national governments contracted-out operational services and, using financial mechanisms, pressed local authorities to contract out their services. For instance, the South Korean government used a mandatory established number (20 per cent) to cut down the size of local government and its manpower (Park, 2004). After implementing early retirement, local governments contracted-out many of its social welfare services in order to satisfy the mandated per cent of reduction.

Asian administrative culture with its strong command character makes implementation of contracting-out quite different from the Anglo-American model. On the national level, governments contract only operational tasks that are mostly blue-collar types of work or the running of public facilities. Governmental core activities and strategic functions are rarely contracted-out. Since the majority of services are provided by the local governments, the per cent of contracted-out services are greater at the local level than at the regional or national. Local governments contracted-out most of the social welfare services and recreational services. Waste-water treatment, garbage collection and garbage incineration are often contracted-out (Park, 2004; Manning and Parison, 2004). Although the ideas of competition and customer satisfaction were initially introduced, national governments are not very successful in creating competitive environments and mechanisms to motivate a better performance by contractors (Kim, 1998). Moreover, low public support makes it difficult for local governments to further implement contracting-out policies (Khan, 1998). Among the Asian countries, Singapore is more successful than the other Asian countries in implementing 'budgeting for results' and contracting-out policy based on some elements of the New Zealand model (Schick, 1998).

Central Resource Control and Decentralized Delivery

Latin America
During the 1990s many Latin American countries (Chile, Mexico, Brazil, Argentina) started public administration reforms according to the managerial model of Anglo-American countries. Governments privatized state-owned companies that produce goods widely available in private markets, created distinct policy-making ministries and autonomous agencies operating under a management contract, and permitted private organizations to provide public services that are 'non-exclusive' to the state. These reforms led to a system characterized by the combination of a centralized, rigid control of resources with decentralized implementation of service provision. Governments continuously emphasize pro-market economic policies, extending the role of the private sector in certain areas while keeping government responsible for ensuring that services are delivered. Chile introduced more advanced managerial reforms, contracting-out substantial activities to the private sector in education, public health, housing and social welfare (Manning and Parison, 2004).

Central and Eastern European Countries and Russia
Central and eastern European countries (Hungary, Poland, Romania, Czech Republic, Slovenia, Lithuania, Latvia, Estonia), and to some extent Russia, started complex political and socio-economic reformation in 1989. Local authorities acquired more responsibility for service delivery and the use of market solutions, but they are often subject to the centre's legal review. The restructuring of public administration through complex legislation was implemented in 1999 within the agenda of accession to the EU (Manning and Parison, 2004). Although governments introduced total privatization of industrial enterprises and natural monopolies, there has been limited privatization and contracting-out in the health sector, education, social welfare services and utilities. National governments continue to play a major role in the provision of public services.

Isomorphic Pressures and Infrastructure Needs: Selected Developing Countries

During the 1990s, governments of some African and Asian countries, for instance Zimbabwe, Ghana, Tanzania and Mongolia, introduced public administration reforms, privatization programmes and market mechanisms. Under the pressure of international organizations, WB, IMF, and the successful examples of New Zealand, Australia, UK and the USA, national governments sold natural monopolies, infrastructure and utilities (Cook and Uchida, 2003; Parker and Kirkpatrick, 2004; Farazmand, 2002). As research on the selling of state enterprises shows (World Bank, 2004), governments of developing countries failed to develop market mechanisms and regulation over the activities of privatized entities, although the necessity to improve regulatory regimes and effectively supervise the private sector is now being recognized (Schick, 1998). In recent years, several developing governments have engaged external parties (international experts) in the administration of regulatory tasks. A recent World Bank study (2004) estimates that governments dedicate a considerable share of their annual budgets (over 20 per cent) to hire external expertise.

Governments in developing countries contract out such regulatory functions as tariff reviews, monitoring compliance, data gathering, development of new rules and dispute settlement for a variety of reasons, including limited in-house capacity and lack of expertise and competence as well as a desire to improve the quality and credibility of regulation, to foster the independence of regulatory process from short-term political capture, and in order to attract investors, particularly in countries with weak institutional capacity. The World Bank study (2004) concludes that for contracting-out to be successful, governments should seek to foster competition in the provider's market, introduce mechanisms for ensuring transparency in the selection process to avoid corruption, and establish systems for strong performance monitoring.

IMPLICATIONS OF THE VARIETY OF REFORMS

Although many of the reform programmes were driven by the need of governments to solve similar problems (notably concern about inefficiency, poor service delivery, responsiveness and accountability, and fiscal pressures), it is noteworthy that a common reform paradigm has not emerged. As described above, some of the reform programmes illustrate a fuller acceptance of the ideas which are now called New Public Management while in other cases these reforms, including the use of contracting, have been shaped by the countries' degree of centralization, efforts at devolution and historical acceptance of a more collectivist ideology. It appears that most reform programmes have been driven primarily by political and civil service elites rather than pressure for change from the public (Pollitt and Bouckaert, 2000). Responding to public discontent and dissatisfaction clearly was important to these political elites, but there is a chicken-and-egg issue here. In many cases it appears public dissatisfaction was encouraged by the efforts to reform and served to justify and accelerate the reform programmes.

For some groups of countries, basic reforms are likely to include some minor changes of responsibility among levels of government and some equally minor reductions in service provision. Contracting-out will be restricted to the easily specified support tasks. Advanced reformers implemented major reallocation of responsibilities from central to sub-national government, radical service shedding of previously accepted government tasks, and the extensive use of contracts across the public sector, not just in easily specified areas of maintenance and cleaning. Devolution to the lowest possible appropriate level of government has been an important component of these reform programmes. This level of change also includes contracting-out core functions, well beyond the usual janitorial and clerical services to the policy and broader programmes undertaken by government. These more advanced areas for outsourcing include payroll, some aspects of policy formulation, human resource development and some areas of audit inspection.

In the countries that have accepted advanced reforms, such changes have led to the setting up of what may appear to be a bewildering array of new autonomous or semi-autonomous public bodies in place of relatively homogeneous and integrated ministries. Executive agencies have been established in Australia and the United Kingdom, special operating agencies in Canada and crown entities in New Zealand. Such reforms create a need for a greater degree of explicitness in performance management and accountability arrangements. Contractualism is certainly not the only way to go. Other advanced reformers have also increased the flexibility available to managers while increasing the focus on monitoring performance – balancing enhanced autonomy with a greater emphasis on results and measuring achievements (Manning and Parison, 2004).

To the extent that many governments were driven by very similar sets of concerns, the question arises, why did they pursue different reform activities (e.g. different level of contracting-out)? One set of answers must lie in country-specific political economy. The particular alignment of interests and the historical momentum that different factions have obtained must be a major factor (Flynn, 2000; Manning and Parison, 2004). The Manning and Parison (2004) comparative study looks at the institutional arrangements within government that have given traction to reformers. Much of the pattern of reform can be explained by the leverage that was available to reformers and the intrinsic malleability of state structures. There is a diverse range of levers available to some reformers. Public management reforms, including contracting, can be traced to the presence of one or a combination of a strong, central agency, single-party majority, integrated ministerial careers, degree of heterogeneity of the public sector and the sponsorship of innovation of reform ideas.

Many forces outside this set of internal and institutional arrangements could be considered as levers. A discontented public can be a radical force for reform. Another set of opportunities outside the public sector arises from the pressures that can be mounted and contributions that can be made by think tanks, management consultants and academics. The examples of the United Kingdom and New Zealand suggest that these radical reformers were helped considerably by the presence of intellectually, financially and politically powerful think tanks.

While reformers may have distinctively different leverage in the public sector, the basic institutions of the public sector also can be more or less malleable (Manning and Parison, 2004). A strong political lead in the United Kingdom was able to produce radical changes with remarkably few legislative obstacles. Centralization provides considerable malleability. Governments in states that have divided authority constitutionally between levels of governments are less able to drive through comprehensive and uniform reform programmes. Political neutrality at senior levels also fosters malleability, because when the majority of senior public official positions are politicized, with consequent high levels of turnover with a change of government, it is harder to sustain a reform effort. In opposition, the Germanic state traditions provide some legal rigidity. By contrast, the Anglo-American state tradition is peculiarly compatible with recent reform efforts. Also, extensive trade union membership in the public sector makes substantial resistance to reform more probable.

Other countries have had their own special set of pressures. Pressure was put on developing countries during the first stage (1970 in Latin America, 1980 in Africa and Asia, 1990s in post-communist countries) of so-called 'wild privatization', when international investors had made privatization a condition of loans or aid funds (Martin, 1999). Sponsored by developed countries, many international aid and development organizations, World Bank, International Monetary Fund, United Nations Development Programmes, also required some types of administrative reforms in their assistance programmes to less developed countries. For example, Meacham (1999) points out that many of the reforms in Latin America have followed external pressures, especially from international monetary organizations and have been influenced by the US because of its dominant role in the region. India's experience of reforms of public sector enterprises such as nationalization, divestment and contracting-out was influenced by international pressure as well (Sapat, 1999). The adoption however is not always well timed. As the Nixon and Walters (1999) study shows, Mongolia's adoption of the New Zealand contractual model reform has been driven by external pressure and ideology, rather than pragmatism, and the reform may well be inadequate in coping with the immediate economic problems.

Thus, contracting-out as a part of the global reform movement to transform governance has been implemented in different countries through a complex mixture of environmental pressures and historical and institutional contexts. International trends of contracting-out have characteristics of universality, but they have also been transformed in the diffusion process when they encounter national contexts. Contracting-out does not have one specific starting point nor a specific path or specific destination for one single neat package of reform elements.

SELECTED TRENDS IN CONTRACTING-OUT

The trends and predictions for contracting-out are multiple and sometimes contradictory. First, contracting-out will continue to be bundled with other initiatives that share the ideological perspectives of New Public Management. In the beginning of the twenty-first century, contracting-out became embedded in governmental practice and policy as a desired goal as part of New Public Management. Pollitt and Bouckaert (2000) specifically list key characteristics of the shifts that occurred: a focus on outputs, measurement, flat organizational forms, substitution of contract-like relationships, market mechanisms, emphasis on a consumer orientation, blurring of the public and market and voluntary sectors, and emphasis on efficiency and individualism. Most developing countries also plan to continue to contract in the future according to a 2004 World Bank survey. In fact, Kettl (2000), Pollit and Bouckaert (2000) and Rosenbloom and Kravchuk (2002) as well as others state that New Public Management has demonstrated staying power.

Second, contracting-out becomes part of other techniques and philosophies that increase the interdependence among organizations and organizational units. The movement became an inevitable part of the general reformation process where government is struggling to adjust existing structures to new processes and conditions of complete interdependence of all societal actors – public and private. At the turn of the twenty-first century, governmental service provision became 'increasingly dependent on complex networks of contractors, grantees, and other partners' (Kettl, 1996:9). Today, it is virtually impossible to identify any public programme that a single government agency can manage on its own without relying on some partnership with other public agencies of private or non-profit organizations.

A third trend is 'second-generation outsourcing' – so called because 'first generation' outsourced services are put up for bid again. While any first-generation outsourcing is complicated enough if it is done across the entirety of a complex technology-driven infrastructure, doing a second-generation outsourcing is even harder, as the services, data, key personnel and other basic elements are not in the contracting authority's possession. The Driver and Vehicle Licensing Agency (DVLA) in Great Britain went through such a process in 2002, the beginning of a wave of second-generation public sector outsourcings as the contracts that really took off in the mid-1990s now began to come to an end. Second-generation outsourcings will be a much bigger feature of the public sector outsourcing environment (Public Sector: Public Providers, 2004).

Fourth, a controversial trend is that of 'outsourcing' to other countries. A report of the Washington Alliance of Technology Workers warned that increasing numbers of offshore contractors are preparing themselves for contract work from the US state governments, particularly in information technology (IT) services. A recent news article in the United States notes that 18 offshore companies have already taken work in the IT sector worth at least $US75 million (Communication Workers of America, 2004).

Somewhat contradictory of the others, a final trend is the tendency on the part of scholars and government officials to insist on a better evaluation of the methods of New Public Management, including contracting-out. Australian scholars John Halligan and Jill Adams (2004:91–92) note, 'A new phase of public management is now well established. It is characterized by less emphasis on the competition and contractualism of the 1990s; government responses to reassessment of high devolution and its consequences; and new people in key leadership positions.' The infatuation with applying competition principles has abated somewhat. Compulsory IT outsourcing was terminated once a more mature contingent approach was accepted. The contracting of the public service has been most dramatically turned around. Developing countries are also demanding more evidence of the effectiveness of policy changes. A spreading conclusion is that privatization and contracting-out will not be effective without well-developed market mechanisms and regulatory functions of governments over the activities of privatized firms (World Bank, 2004; Kettl, 2000; Hodge, 2000; Farazmand, 2001).

EFFECTIVENESS OF THE IDEA

These reform activities show remarkable diversity, but the real test of a policy lies in its eventual impact on service delivery, accountability improvements and aggregate expenditure. Case by case, there are undoubtedly many examples of specific improvements in particular services or in the work of ministries or other organizations. There is, however, remarkably little evidence of the overall impact of reforms. Cost has been studied but part of the reluctance in the literature to make definitive statements is the difficulty of before and after comparisons in terms of actual costs of activities, matching true scope of tasks and calculating a fair rate for the administrative costs of contracts. However, most of the studies do conclude that contracting-out has saved money although how much is often debated (Savas, 2000; Hodge, 2000; Bourbeau, 2004). The conclusion, however, on whether contracting sacrifices some quality for costs in developed nations is much more mixed (Bourbeau, 2004).

Although surveys in the 1990s showed that privatization and contracting-out were not effective for developing countries, later studies (World Bank, 2004) indicate contracting-out regulatory functions along with services is effective. A World Bank study of 51 agencies revealed that 61 per cent rated results from contracting-out as good whereas 39 per cent said it was average; 41 per cent of responses indicate that contracting has helped reduce costs and improve quality (World Bank, 2004). According to the survey, contracting-out helps improve organizational competence (91 per cent), but also independence (62 per cent) and trust with key stakeholders (71 per cent). Yet the top challenges are budgetary constraints (70 per cent) and small supply market (under 50 per cent).

The advantages and disadvantages of contracting have been in continuous debate even as the practice and policy of contracting have become firmly established around the world. As far back as a mid-1970s study (Fisk, Keisling and Muller, 1978) of the US experience in contracting-out, researchers identified contracting advantages as the following: costs less or provides better performance; provides specialized skills; limits the growth of government; permits greater flexibility; produces better management. Its disadvantages were identified as the possibility of poor service for citizens; may increase corruption; may displace public employees; may entail problems in enforcing public policy; may fail to guarantee adequate competition. New points from critics were added in the 1990s. The increasing number of semi-autonomous service providers, run on more businesslike lines, that are found within the public sector may be individually more efficient but collectively more fragmented and hard to control. Efficiency, then, is bought at the price of coordination. Some commentators and some politicians have expressed concerns that contractualism leads to erosion of a public service ethos and a loss of continuity and institutional memory (Schick, 1998). Important future research directions will include trying to understand how costs, quality and effectiveness may vary by the type of tasks, discrete or relational contracts, and level of government.

CONCLUSION

A plethora of advice exists on how to engage in contracting-out (World Bank, 2004; Flynn, 2000; Kettl, 2000; Pollitt and Bouckaert, 2000; OECD, 1997). In developed countries, the capacity of public managers needs to be developed so that they can become smart buyers, buyers who can determine in advance what they want to buy, define specifications carefully and assess the quality of what has been bought (Kettl, 2000). Aggressive and thoughtful oversight is needed for contracting to succeed. An appreciation of the complexity of the interdependence of the networked world should be taught to and reinforced for public managers. As Kettl (2000:458–459) notes:

> When a substantial part of governmental activity lies outside the direct control of government managers, however, the job becomes much harder. Government managers lose control over the goals, indicators, and measurement processes. The more government builds nongovernmental partnerships to do its work, the harder the job becomes.

In transition countries, there is a lack of regulatory capacity and a lack of market mechanisms (Martin, 1999). Thus, for these countries, contracting-out and any public administration reform will be unsuccessful without development of effective market mechanisms, competition, business ethics and contract law. The recent World Bank study (2004) concludes that for contracting-out to be successful, governments should seek to foster competition in the provider's market, introduce mechanisms for ensuring transparency in the selection process to avoid corruption and establish systems for strong performance monitoring. Finally, and perhaps most important, we agree with Donald Kettl, 'And, in the end, it all must be focused squarely on achieving the public interest' (Kettl, 1997:459).

REFERENCES

Alford, J. (2002), 'Defining the client in the public sector: a social exchange perspective', *Public Administration Review,* **62**, 337–47.

Antal-Mokos, Z. (1998), *Privatization, Politics, and Economic Performance in Hungary,* Cambridge: Cambridge University Press.

Blejer, M.I. and M. Skreb (eds) (2001), *Transition. The First Decade,* Cambridge, MA and London: MIT Press.

Borzutzky, S. (2003), 'Social security privatization: the lessons from the Chilean experience for other Latin American countries and the USA', *International Journal of Social Welfare,* **12** (2), 86–95.

Bourbeau, J. (2004), 'Has Outsourcing/Contracting Out Saved Money and/or Improved Service Quality?', Blacksburg, VA: dissertation for the Virginia Polytechnic Institute and State University.

Boyne, G. (1998), 'Bureaucratic theory meets reality: public choice and service contracting in U.S. local government', *Public Administration Review,* **58** (6), 474–84.

Chai, J. (2003), 'Privatization in China', in David Parker and David Saal (eds), *International Handbook on Privatization,* Cheltenham, UK and Northampton, MA, USA: Edward Elgar, pp. 235–61.

Christensen, T. and P. Laegreid (2001), 'A transformative perspective on administrative reforms', in Tom Christensen and Per Laegreid (eds), *New Public Management: The Transformation of Ideas and Practice*, Aldershot, UK: Ashgate, pp. 13–39.

Colman, W. (1989), *State and Local Government and Public–Private Partnerships: A Policy Issues Handbook*, New York: Greenwood Press.

Communication Workers of America (2004), 'Offshore contractors target state government work', Reindeer's Rants, 22 July, accessed 29 July at http://reindeer.radioleft.com/blog/_archives/2004/7.

Cook, P. and Y. Uchida (2003), 'Privatization and economic growth in developing countries', *Journal of Development Studies*, **39** (6), 121–54.

Dittrich, E. (ed.) (2001), *Wandel, Wende, Wiederkehr. Transformation as Epochal Change in Central and Eastern Europe: Theoretical Concepts and Their Empirical Applicability*, Wurzburg, Germany: Syndikat.

Domberger, S. (1998), *The Contracting Organization: A Strategic Guide to Outsourcing*, Oxford: Oxford University Press.

Dudley, L.S. (1997), 'New insights in old theories: contracting relationships and the separation of powers', *Journal of Health and Human Services Administration*, **20** (2), 129–45.

Eagle, K.S. (2005), 'New Public Management in Charlotte, North Carolina: A Case Study of Managed Competition', Blacksburg, VA: dissertation for the Center for Public Administration and Policy, Virginia Polytechnic Institute and State University.

Elam, L. (1997), 'Reinventing government privatization-style – avoiding the legal pitfalls of replacing civil servants with contract providers', *Public Personnel Management*, **26** (1), 15–34.

Farazmand, A. (ed.) (2001), *Privatization or Public Enterprise Reform: International Case Studies with Implications for Public Management*, Westport, CT: Greenwood Press.

Farazmand, A. (2002), 'Reorganization, reform, and revolution in contemporary Iran', in Ali Farazmand (ed.), *Administrative Reform in Developing Nations*, Westport, CT: Praeger, pp. 143–56.

Ferris, J. and E. Graddy (1986), 'Contracting out: for what? With whom?', *Public Administration Review*, **46**, 332–44.

Fisk, D., H. Keisling and T. Muller (1978), *Private Provision of Public Services: An Overview*, Washington, DC: Urban Institute Press.

Fixler, P. and R. Poole (1987), 'Status of state and local privatization', in Steve H. Hanke (ed.), *Prospects For Privatization*, New York: Academy of Political Science, pp. 164–78.

Flynn, N. (1997), *Public Sector Management*, London: Prentice Hall/Harvester Wheatsheaf.

Flynn, N. (2000), 'Managerialism and public services: some international trends', in John Clarke, Sharon Gewirtz and Eugene McLaughlin et al. (eds), *New Managerialism, New Welfare*, London, UK and Thousand Oaks, CA: Open University/Sage, pp. 45–91.

Halligan, J. and J. Adams (2004), 'Security, capacity and post-market reforms: public management change in 2003', *Australian Journal of Public Administration*, **63** (1), 85–93.

Hatry, H.P. (1983), *A Review of Private Approaches for Delivery of Public Services*, Washington, DC: Urban Institute Press.

Hodge, G.A. (2000), *Privatization: An International Review of Performance*, Boulder, CO: Westview Press.

Hughes, O. (2003), *Public Management and Administration: An Introduction*, New York: Palgrave.

Kaboolian, L. (1998), 'The New Public Management: challenging the boundaries of the management vs. administration debate', *Public Administration Review*, **58** (3), 189–93.

Kettl, D. (2000), *The Global Public Management Revolution: A Report on the Transformation of Governance*, Washington, DC: Brookings Institution.

Kettl, D. (1997), 'The global revolution in public management: driving themes, missing links', *Journal of Policy Analysis and Management*, **16**, 446–62.

Kettl, D. (1996), 'Governing at the Millennium', in B. Guy Perry and Jon Pierre (eds), *Handbook of Public Administration*, San Francisco, CA: Jossey-Bass, pp. 5–18.

Kettl, D. (1993), *Sharing Power: Public Governance and Private Markets*, Washington, DC: Brookings Institution.

Khan, M. (1998), 'Patron–client networks and the economic effects of corruption in Asia', in Mark Robinson (ed.), *Corruption and Development: An Introduction*, London: Frank Cass, pp. 15–29.

Kim, S.Y. (1998), 'What are the factors for successful results from contracting out in social services?' *Korea Journal of Public Policy*, **7** (3), 87–120.

Kingdon, J.W. (1995), *Agendas, Alternatives, and Public Policies*, New York: HarperCollins.

Kickert, W. (ed.) (1997), *Public Management and Administrative Reform in Western Europe*, Cheltenham, UK and Lyme, US: Edward Elgar.

Klausen, K. (1992), 'NPM in the Nordic countries; a vitalization of or an end to the Scandinavian model, International Public Management Network, pp. 22–27, Postdam, Germany.

Klingner, D. (2000), 'South of the border: progress and problems in implementing New Public Management reforms in Mexico today', *American Review of Public Administration*, **30** (4), 365–73.

LaPanet, P. and M. Trebilcock (1998), 'Contracting out social services', *Canadian Public Administration*, **41** (1), 21–51.

The Lawyer (2004), 'Public sector: public providers', 31 May, 25 London.

Lynn, L. (1996), *Public Management as Art, Science, and Profession*, Chicago, IL: University of Chicago.

Manning, N. and N. Parison (2004), *International Public Administration Reform*, Washington, DC: World Bank.

Martin, Roderick (1999), *Transforming Management in Central and Eastern Europe*, New York: Oxford University Press.

McCourt, W. (2001), 'The NPM agenda for service delivery: a suitable model for developing countries?' in Willy McCourt and Martin Minogue (eds), *The Internationalization of Public Management*, Cheltenham, UK and Northampton, MA, US: Edward Elgar, pp. 107–28.

McIntosh, K., J. Shauness and R. Wettenhall (1997), *Contracting Out in Australia: An Indicative History*, Canberra: Centre for Research in Public Management, University of Canberra.

Meacham, C.E. (1999), 'Administrative reform and national economic development in Latin America and the Caribbean (post-dictatorship)', *Policy Studies Review*, **16** (2), 41–64.

Megginson, W. and J. Netter (2001), 'From state to market: a survey of empirical studies on privatization', *AEA and Journal of Economic Literature*, June, 321–89.

Ministry of Government Administration and Home Affairs [Korea] (MOGAHA) (2003), *Manual for Contracting Out*, May #005, accessed 1 July 2004 at: http://www.moleg.go.kr.

Nixon, F. and B. Walters (1999), 'Administrative reform and economic development in Mongolia, 1990–1997: a critical perspective', *Policy Studies Review*, **16** (2), 147–74.

Organisation for Economic Co-operation and Development (OECD) (1997), 'Public Management Contracting Out Government Services', occasional papers no. 20, Paris.

Oswald, S. (2000), 'Economic transition in the Czech Republic: attempts to privatize the health system', *Administration and Society*, **32** (2), 227–58.

Park, Se-Jeong (2004), 'Contracting out in Korean local governments: current situation and challenges ahead', *International Review of Administrative Science*, **70** (3), 497–509.

Parker, D. and C. Kirkpatrick (2004), 'Economic regulation in developing countries: a framework for critical analysis', in Paul Cook et al. (eds), *Leading Issues in Competition, Regulation and Development*, Cheltenham, UK and Northampton, MA, US: Edward Elgar, pp. 92–113.

Pollitt, C. and G. Bouckaert (2000), *Public Management Reform*, New York: Oxford University Press.

Premfors, R. (1998), 'Re-shaping the democratic state: Swedish experiences in a comparative perspective', *Public Administration*, **76**, 141–59.

President's Commission on Privatization (1988), *Privatization: Toward More Effective Government*, Washington, DC: General Accounting Office.

Reeves, E. and M. Barrow (2000), 'The impact of contracting out on the costs of refuse service collection: the case of Ireland', *Economic and Social Review*, **31**, 129–50.

Rehfuss, J. (1989), *Contracting Out in Government*, San Francisco: Jossey-Bass.

Rosenbloom, D. and R. Kravchuk (2002), *Public Administration: Understanding Management, Politics, and Law in the Public Sector*, Boston, MA: McGraw-Hill.

Rouban, L. (1997), 'The administrative modernization policy in France', in Walter Kickert (ed.), *Public Management and Administrative Reform in Western Europe*, Cheltenham, UK, and Lyme, US: Edward Elgar, pp. 143–58.

Sapat, A. (1999), 'Privatization strategies adopted for public sector reform in India: determinants and constraints', *Policy Studies Review*, **16** (2), 99–132.

Savas, Emanuel S. (1987), *Privatization: The Key to Better Government*, Chatham, NJ: Chatham House.

Savas, Emanuel S. (2000), *Privatization and Private–Public Partnership*, New York: Chatham House.

Schick, A. (1998), 'Why most developing countries should not try New Zealand reforms', *World Bank Research Observer*, **13** (1), 123–31.

Simon, D. and P. Jensen (1997), 'Contracting out by the public sector: theory, evidence, prospects', *Oxford Review of Economic Policy*, **13** (4), 67–79.

Smith, F. (1987), 'Privatization at the federal level', in Steve H. Hanke (ed.), *Prospects for Privatization*, New York: Academy of Political Science, pp. 179–89.

Thekildsen, O. (2000), 'Public sector reform in a poor aid-dependent country: Tanzania', *Public Administration and Development*, **20**, 60–70.

Torres, L. (2004), 'Trajectories in public administration reforms in European Continental countries', *Australian Journal of Public Administration*, **63** (3), 99–112.

Washington Alliance of Technology Workers (2004), 'Report', Asia Africa Intelligence Wire, 24 July. Accessed 30 August at: http://web3.infotrac.galegroup/itw/infomark/498/796/78063388w3/purl=rcl_ITOF_0_A119837580&dyn=8!xrn_8_0_A119837580?sw_aep+viva_vpi.

Wettenhall, R. (1998), 'Who owns what? Some implications of the Humphry Report on government business enterprises', *Australian Journal of Public Administration*, **57** (3), 110–16.

Wollmann, H. (2001), 'Germany's trajectory of public sector modernization: continuities and discontinuities', *Policy and Politics*, **29** (2), 151–70.

World Bank (2004), 'Contracting out utility regulatory functions', environmental resource management report, accessed 1 August, at http://rru.worldbank.org/Documents/PapersLinks/2550.pdf.

4. Public–private partnerships: a public policy perspective

Carsten Greve

INTRODUCTION

Public–Private Partnerships (PPPs) are the talk of the (global) town these days. PPPs have been called 'the latest chapter in the privatization book' (Hodge, 2002). As with all such concepts, a variety of meanings have been attached to it, with some noting the 'multiple grammar of meanings' (Linder, 1999). PPPs can loosely be defined as 'co-operation of some sort of durability between public and private actors in which they jointly develop products and services and share risks, cost and resources which are connected with these products' (Van Ham and Koppenjan, 2001:598). In this definition, cooperation has to take place over time, ruling out short-term contracts as partnerships. Both parties to the contract have to take responsibility and share responsibility. Furthermore, both parties run a risk of some kind, and so in some ways it is a journey into the unknown because the final product of the partnership is not always known beforehand.

There is little doubt that PPPs are now a global policy phenomenon, and that learning from international experience with PPPs is already under way (Hodge and Greve, 2005; Osborne, 2000). Experiments with partnerships are going on in North America, Australia, the Netherlands, Norway, Denmark, Germany, the United Kingdom and several other places. Partnering is a current topic in the European Union (Commission of the European Communities, 2004), the OECD and the World Bank (Estache and Serebrisky, 2004). Professional meetings and academic conferences are organized around the theme of PPPs globally.

The attractions of PPPs are not difficult to see: partnering is the promoted activity over adversarial behaviour, and rewards are promised for all participants, while the potential losers of partnerships have not received much attention yet. As several observers have mentioned, the discussion on how to combine private sector activity with public purposes is far from new, and history is full of examples of public–private cooperation (Wettenhall, 2003, 2005). What is new is the global attention paid to these views.

The purpose of this chapter is to examine PPPs from a public policy perspective, with particular focus on agenda setting. If PPPs fit into the 'privatization story', how exactly are they placed? The chapter concentrates on three questions: Why did PPPs get onto the public policy agenda? Who pushed for PPPs to come onto the agenda? What is the prospect of PPPs being an enduring concept that will survive the initial interest?

A key hypothesis for the chapter is that PPPs are best viewed as a global public policy idea that must support particular country studies if the full dynamic of the partnership concept is to be understood.

The chapter will employ a theoretical public policy perspective in discussing these questions. Recent developments in theories of the policy process (Sabatier, 1999) have inspired the use of the Multiple Streams Framework (MSF) (Kingdon, 1995; Zahariadis, 1999) and the Advocacy Coalition Framework (ACF) (Sabatier and Jenkins-Smith, 1999). The first perspective looks at how public policy agendas are formed, while the two other perspectives are useful in examining which actors are active in shaping the policy agenda.

The chapter is divided into three parts. The first part briefly discusses the theoretical framework of 'multiple streams' and actor strategies connected to it. The second part discusses why PPPs have come onto the global policy agenda and who pushed for it. The third part concludes the chapter by discussing whether PPPs will stay in our focus or retreat as the 'policy window' perhaps closes again.

THEORETICAL FRAMEWORK: PROBLEMS, POLICIES, POLITICS

How does the policy process unfold in complex societies? This question has triggered many explanations and theoretical frameworks. In recent times, a number of alternative approaches to the traditional 'stages model' of public policy making have also appeared, and many of them are presented in Sabatier's (1999) helpful overview. One of the approaches – the Multiple Streams Framework (MSF) – stresses ambiguity as a condition under which public policy making is taking place. As the reasons and the conceptualization of PPPs happen to be marked by a certain level of ambiguity, MSF seems a good point of departure for thinking theoretically about the policy process. The first question of how PPPs came onto the agenda can be addressed by using MSF. Developed by John Kingdon (1995) and later on supplemented by the work of Zahariadis (1999), this theoretical framework builds on the famous garbage can model developed by Cohen, March and Olsen (1972) that characterized organizations as 'organized anarchies'. The question is 'why some agenda items are prominent and others are neglected' (Zahariadis, 1999:76). In other words, why did PPPs appear on the horizon in the late 1990s as one of the 'big new ideas' in public policy making? MSF identifies three different streams to look out for. The first stream is about 'problems', and the question is why policy makers pay attention to particular problems. Problems can occur because findings of outputs and outcomes indicate that something needs to be altered; disasters or emergency situations can call attention to problems. The second stream is termed 'policies' (and was called 'solutions' in the organizational theory version). These are ideas for new initiatives developed by policy units, think tanks, etc. Policy proposals have to be reasonably sane to stand a chance of becoming adopted, but they are out there with many proposals competing for attention. The third stream is called 'politics', and in Kingdon's version this is about 'the national mood, pressure group campaigns, and administrative or legislative turnover' (Zahariadis, 1999:77). Like in the original garbage can model, these streams are considered independent analytically and they will be 'coupled together' either by chance or by design by policy 'entrepreneurs' in what is termed 'policy windows'. An important feature is that these policy windows are open only temporarily. If the open policy window is missed, the brilliant policy proposal may never be coupled with the relevant problem or the rising political opportunity. There are, of course, many questions to be asked about the MSF, and Zahariadis (1999:81–87) addresses some of them. The main difference between the original garbage can version and the policy windows approach is that the former was much more sceptical about design and management of the process, preferring instead to stress the 'fatalist' tendency of the framework (Hood, 1998).

Turning to our question of which actors supported the agenda, the MSF has some shortcomings. MSF examines only 'traditional actors' like legislators, the government and interest groups. A possibility is to add more elaborate theories of networks and policy communities. First, it is important to look at the role of technical knowledge and the groups that advance technical knowledge about a policy issue. The Advocacy Coaliton Framework (ACF) (Sabatier and Jenkins-Smith, 1999) can help focus on how knowledge is used and produced in public policy making and how key actors are organized in competing advocacy coalitions. ACF examines how policy subsystems evolve. An advocacy coalition consists of 'people from various governmental and private organizations that both (1) share a set of normative and causal beliefs and (2) engage in a non-trivial degree of coordinated activity over time' (Sabatier and Jenkins-Smith, 1999:120). Advocacy coalitions include policy advisers, journalists and researchers, who in other frameworks are 'neutral' in public policy making.

Actors have a hierarchical belief structure divided into 'deep core beliefs', 'policy core beliefs' and 'secondary aspects of a belief system' (ibid.:121–122). Deep core beliefs are similar to religious persuasions and cannot normally be changed while policy core beliefs may be changed although this is difficult. Secondary aspects will include more tactical goals and can therefore be sacrificed more easily by actors in advocacy coalitions.

The shared beliefs that a coalition can have can also be elaborated upon. The concept of 'epistemic communities' (Haas, 1992) might be helpful here. An epistemic community consists of 'professionals from a variety of disciplines and backgrounds that have a shared set of normative beliefs, shared causal beliefs, shared notions of validity and a common policy enterprise, i.e. a common cause they want to advance' (Haas, 1992:3). These people are normally professionals (economists, for example), but they can also include other groups. The important thing about an epistemic community is that it shares and advances knowledge on specific policy issues in a consistent and coherent way.

There is an overlap between the ACF and the notion of epistemic communities in that they both emphasize the shared belief system and the shared causal beliefs (which are based on accumulating technical knowledge about processes). Both frameworks also recognize that the number of potential members of the policy community can vary, but that it usually extends beyond the usual participants in Parliament and government administration, and that it includes networks of actors pursuing a common policy.

WHY DID PPPs APPEAR ON THE POLICY AGENDA?

PPPs arrived in full power in public policy making across the globe in the late 1990s. But the term itself was not new. In the 1980s, the term PPP was used mainly for urban redevelopment projects in the UK and the USA. In a book on contracting-out from 1993, the American scholar Donald F. Kettl (1993) noted how PPPs had been an integrated part of American public policy making since 1945. The term was used to cover all kinds of public–private cooperation as Wettenhall (2003) has clearly pointed out. If the MSF is employed, we might consider the recent entry of PPPs as a coupling of different kinds of streams: a problem stream, a policy stream and a politics stream.

The 'problem stream' consists of two main problems: finance and disappointment with the principal–agent model of contracting-out. The first and most visible 'problem' has been that of lack of finance for funding public services. PPP in one of its incarnations (the British Private Finance Initiative) was conceived by the former Conservative government in Britain as a way to fund public services and infrastructure in a period of financial pressure. Lack of resources meant that the government had to look to other ways to fulfil election promises. Attracting the private (financial) sector to do deals with the public sector seemed a bright idea at the time. When New Labour came to power in 1997, the PFI version of PPP survived. New Labour made promises to renew the welfare state, to provide better services and provide better infrastructure, but at the same time did not want to raise taxes. One of the options was to carry on with PFI. In the literature (on the PFI version), financial pressure has been mentioned as one of the key 'problems' that the PPP concept was going to solve. Since then, the official purpose of PPPs from the New Labour government has shifted (Flinders, 2005), and now it is not only about relief of financial pressure.

The second 'problem' was widespread disappointment with traditional contracting in principal–agent terms. The distance between the purchaser as principal and the provider as agent was conceived to block cooperative behaviour, foster low-trust relationships, fragment the public sector and hollow out the state (Milward and Provan, 2000). Purchasers and providers were getting too far apart. The disenchantment with traditional contracting-out meant that the opportunity for new concepts and new best practices were widely sought after in the late 1990s. In academia, the network and governance approaches began to overtake the New Public Management (NPM) approach that had been the dominant doctrine in public management reform.

The 'policy stream' consists of the PPP concept itself. It is an ambiguous term that both promises new organizational forms of managing relations between different actors, but it also has rhetorical power in underlining cooperation instead of competition, trust instead of mistrust and sharing of powers and risks instead of separating power and risks (Teisman and Klijn, 2002). In the PFI version of the PPP concept, there is a clear financial model that many governments found attractive. Both in normative and regulative aspects, the PPP model has something to offer. Evaluating PPP models is hard because the partnerships are supposed to work over long periods of time. The jury is still out on PPPs (Hodge, 2005), and there is no clear evidence yet of what constitutes failure and success.

The 'politics stream' consists of national moods, pressure group campaigns and administrative and legislative turnover. Internationally, the mood, or the fashion, seemed to swing in favour of PPPs rapidly within a few years. Private sector companies embraced the strategy. Danish-based company, International Service Systems (ISS), that has operations in countries worldwide, declared its opposition to 'raw contracting-out' and its support for partnerships as the organizational framework of the future. Books have come out on privatization and public–private partnerships. Opportunity arose for governments around the world to locate themselves in the partnership debate. In 2004, the Danish government, for example, issued an 'Action Plan for Public–Private Partnerships' (Regeringen, 2004). The international organizations EU, OECD and the World Bank began to publish documents and policy papers on PPPs.

Pressure group campaigns have been subtle. The role of financial experts and finance companies have been noted (Hodge, 2005). Financial experts and legal experts have clear interests in developing a PPP industry, especially as the PFI deals are extremely complex. A PFI deal cannot be handled by a Ministry of Finance alone, but will normally seek help from consultants. There is as yet little hard evidence of how much influence the financial and legal experts have had in making PFI deals. Another pressure group might be the construction companies that have gained new market shares in public sector infrastructure projects. Unions have been bewildered over what kind of actions they should take, although unions are aware that something new is going on and they need to be a part of it.

Finally, administrative and legislative turnover has played a part. The election of the Blair government in Britain has boosted the interest in PPPs. Although the PFI policy was originally created under John Major's Conservative government, the advocacy by the Blair New Labour government when it came to power has attracted interest in PPPs from around the world. As was the case with privatization in the 1980s under Mrs Thatcher's government, another British government seems to have pointed the way to the 'next big policy' by promoting the PPP agenda. In Britain alone, the advent of the Institute of Public Policy Research's Commission on Partnerships in 2001 attracted attention, and the papers remarked how a think tank report had never been more anticipated. The election of the Blair government certainly seemed to have renewed and then later sustained the interest in PPPs.

The argument is that there has been a 'policy window' open since the late 1990s for the PPP idea to come onto the agenda. PPPs are now being implemented in countries such as Norway, Denmark, Sweden, Germany and the Netherlands, although many of the projects are still in their early stages. The three streams of problems, policies and politics have been coupled together at this particular time in history. One explanation could be that the problems – financial pressure and disappointment with traditional contracting – were so great that something had to turn up. Had it not been PPPs, then another concept would have appeared. Another explanation might be that the policy – PPPs – was on the lookout for problems to become attached to it. PPPs are not about financial relief for present-day governments; a PPP represents an idea that was promoted by certain key actors such as consultants, in conjunction with governments wanting to distance themselves from the NPM agenda and appear more 'caring' and outreaching to stakeholders.

The ambiguity of the concept itself has played a part. PPPs are still seen both as PFI-like financial arrangements and a broader organizational mode of connecting people, resources and objectives from various actors. The lack of an authoritative definition leaves the concept open to interpretation.

We now turn to the actors, or the 'players of the game'. The coalitions in the previous privatization discussions have been visible. Hodge (2002) has talked about the 'privatization wars', noting how advocates of market-based solutions have battled advocates of public sector solutions. Recent research on advocacy coalitions in contracting-out have identified a pro-contracting-out coalition (consisting of Conservative and Liberal political parties, industry and private sector organizations), and an anti-contracting-out coalition (consisting of parts of the Labour Party, parts of the unions and less organized groups such as individual citizens and taxpayers). Research has also shown how little learning between coalitions has taken place (Greve and Ejersbo, 2005). Sabatier and Jenkins-Smith (1999) use the term 'policy brokers' to name those actors that have a role in bringing different coalitions together and exchange in deliberation on the basis of new 'technical' material and reports. The brokers in contracting-out have been government departments that organize meetings and knowledge networks, and consultants to a certain extent.

In partnerships one could in theory expect the situation to be the same: a pro-partnership advocacy coalition and an anti-partnership advocacy coalition. If we look at the policy discussions surrounding the PPP debate, we find few anti-partnership actors. What is amazing is that the pro-partnership coalition (and a very broad one at that) seems to be dominating, judging from the international debate. Advocates are found among government departments, private sector companies, pressure groups and consultants and experts who all get a piece of the action. The potential losers, such as current and future taxpayers, are not very well organized around this issue as the complex partnership/PFI deals seems to be too difficult to grasp.

However, the situation in 2006 is different because most of the actors appear to group together in an 'pro-partnership advocacy coalition'. This is probably due to the ambiguity that surrounds the concept still, which allows almost everybody to maintain their own understanding and experience of what a PPP is or should be. We examine this coalition here as an epistemic community.

People and organizations have stopped talking about the shortcomings of contracting-out and have begun debating the opportunities that PPPs provide. In Germany and Scandinavia, for instance, the debate on partnerships has gradually taken over the debate on traditional contracting-out even though these countries have little actual experience with implementation of PPP projects (Greve, 2003; Oppen, Sack and Wegener, 2005; Almquist and Högberg, 2005).

The 'PPP epistemic community' seems to be a powerful community. Private sector construction companies have teamed up with politicians from nearly all political parties, government departments, legal experts and financial experts, international organizations and even some researchers in promoting the partnership idea. With alliances like that, who can be against partnerships? The 'brokers' (in ACF terms) are not even neutral, as most broker organizations have been more in favour of continuing with the PPP policy than abandoning it. A good example of this was the Institute of Public Policy Research report in Britain (IPPR, 2001). On the surface it appeared as a balanced report delivered by a commission, but it also made recommendations of more use of PPPs in the future that New Labour could use immediately. Examining the conditions of a community more closely, a characteristic of the PPP epistemic community seems to fulfil most of the criteria pointed out by Haas (1992). First, a number of professionals – bankers, accountants, economists, private sector chief executive officers – share the notion that PPPs are a commendable feature that will help the modern-day public sector in surviving by collaborating with private sector companies on a variety of issues. Second, there is a shared set of causal analyses. The economic logic of a cheaper and more efficient governance system is being anticipated when private sector organizations, for example, build, own, operate and transfer public assets. There is an equation of using PPP/PFI = saving money and improving governance and management routines. The economic rationale has been argued for in various reports (the Arthur Andersen/LSE report is one memorable document, indicating the 17 per cent savings promise). More recently, British economist Michael Pollitt (2005) has shown that the PFI models do, in fact, deliver results in terms of saved money and adherence to timetables. Others, however, remain more sceptical, and the IPPR report warned that PPPs might seem 'the only show in town' for a period, when, in fact, there were more shows than one in town, and that governments do not have to go down the PPP road if they do not want to. Third, there is a growing shared notion of validity concerning PPPs. PPPs as PFI-type arrangements or economic partnerships are clearly being validated on behalf of the economic success of the deals. However, as Hodge and others have shown, there are other criteria as well, and 'governance risks' are probably as serious as any economic or financial risks that governments and private sector companies run. A fourth criterion is the 'common policy enterprise', and there seems to be an understanding that PPP/PFI can actually help the public sector in being more efficient and adopting new organizational models. Especially among the core group of bankers, accountants and international bodies like the OECD and the World Bank, this is a shared notion. Yet, there are researchers in the academic community for whom the PPP idea still seems too good to be true to work in practice and who remain sceptical concerning the long-term success of economic partnerships. Some are openly critical, such as Shaoul (2005) and Wettenhall (2005) who do not see the evidence for both the argument that PPPs are new and the argument that it will save money and help build new infrastructure facilities. If PPPs will do society any good remains a contested question among most academic researchers in public policy.

IS THE POLICY WINDOW FOR PPPs ABOUT TO CLOSE?

According to Kingdon (1995), policy windows do not stay open forever, but are likely to close after a certain period of time. There are five reasons for closure of policy windows (Zahariadis, 1999:82): the issue has become addressed sufficiently; there is no action; there is now an available alternative; the people that argued for the policy have gone to do other things; and the 'crisis' or the 'focusing event' has disappeared from the scene again. The question is then whether any of these criteria are met by PPPs. This section will discuss if the conditions behind the policy window suggest that it is about to close, or whether enough policy implementation is in motion to allow PPPs to become institutionalized.

The arguments supporting the prospect of immediate closure of the policy window for PPPs include the following: not enough action is generated; the action that has been generated has been flawed and spawns new problems for governments and taxpayers; the financial crisis or focusing event has diminished; several countries lack central PPP policy units or sincere governmental backing; the regulatory state may squeeze the flexibility originally hoped for in PPPs; advocacy coalitions only agree on changing secondary aspects of policy beliefs while showing no sign of changing their policy core beliefs or their deep core beliefs when the surface of the commitment is scratched.

The arguments opposing the closing of the policy window include the following: the international professional dialogue is still revolving around PPPs and shows few signs of exhaustion; results from implementation are beginning to be visible and there are some economic and political gains to be harvested; PPPs are taking hold in particular sectors making the policy subsystems more likely to continue to develop the PPP policy; genuine policy learning is taking place among key actors, who, having shed the 'privatization' and 'contracting-out' language, now appear to be engaging in a more frank policy dialogue involving change in policy core beliefs without sacrificing deep core beliefs about markets and politics.

First, let us examine the arguments on the closure of the policy window. A primary reason for thinking that PPPs' time may soon be up is that PPPs have not been as big a part of the public and the private sectors' activity as maybe first expected. The IPPR (2001) report made the point that it is only a small part of public sector infrastructure investment that comes from PPP projects. Overwhelmingly, investment is traditional public sector investment drawing on government's own funds or on capital raised on behalf of the government at the government's credit rating. PPPs have not become the only show in town, far from it. In Denmark, for example, the government is only beginning to make suggestions for a handful of PPP projects (notably a new National Archive building, a new prison and a primary school). In the UK and Australia the situation is different, as here dozens of projects are in their implementation phase or have been completed (Hodge, 2005). A second argument is that one of the key problems PPPs were about – lack of capital for funding new projects – was probably only a big problem in the UK in a particular historical setting. Evidence from Ireland and Denmark for example, suggests that governments do have access to (relatively) cheap available capital. The Ministry of Finance in Denmark has noted how, in reality, the rationing of capital is not the main problem. Local governments in Denmark have not used all of their possibilities for borrowing from central available funds. In short, the chief reason for PPP in the UK's PFI version is not a real and ongoing reason in all countries. Perhaps it is not so surprising then, that in terms of rationale, the British government has changed its focus at least three times during the lifetime of PPP policy (Flinders, 2005).

The less prominent place of the financial reason throws the future of the PPP in the PFI version in some doubt, and it remains unclear at this point if governments can keep generating the enthusiasm for PPPs. A regularly heard argument, also from private sector companies, is that PPPs are more about new cooperative organizational forms than about cheap capital and financial resources per se. But the proof of the pudding is in the eating, so it will be interesting to watch if that argument will continue to gain currency among central decision makers in both public sector and private sector organizations.

A third argument is that some of the people and organizations that have promoted PPPs shift their attention to other policies. In some countries there has been a central PPP unit (like in the UK and in the Netherlands), but in other countries where the institutionalization is less built into the governmental system, the people interested in PPPs have a hard time holding central policy makers to their promises. In Denmark, the government was behind a central policy proposal in the beginning of 2004, but the responsibility for the various projects is dispersed among various ministries, making a coordinated effort more difficult.

A fourth argument is that PPPs will simply be killed by 'the regulatory state' in the long run. The term 'the regulatory state' has gained wide influence among social science researchers (see Jordana and Levi-Faur, 2004). The problem for PPPs is that there is no tailor-made regulatory structure that fits all partnerships (James, 2003). Consequently, partnerships have to be in compliance with European Union procurement rules to a certain extent. One of the key problems is that most PPPs are about long-term contracts while the EU procurement rules have encouraged competition and frequent bidding. Public sector policy units are struggling with this at the moment, and private sector companies are likely to become frustrated that all the big ideas about partnering and trust-based relationships will be regulated to death. The private sector companies that eye opportunities for long-term contracts will naturally support the partnership idea. But smaller companies that rely on frequent bidding may be less pleased about the trend towards long-term partnerships. Anecdotal evidence suggests that some private companies may not be patient forever as the market share for PPPs is not overwhelming anyway.

These are some of the main arguments suggesting that the place of PPPs in the sunlight is not going to last that long, and that the current enthusiasm for PPPs will diminish at some point.

We now turn to arguments about the sustainability of PPPs. A primary argument is that the policy ball is simply on a roll now, and cannot be stopped easily. PPPs are interwoven in much of the current discourse and policy proposals that come out of organizations like the OECD, the World Bank and the EU. As with privatization in the 1980s, the policy is set to gain momentum, and what might have appeared as a British or Australasian 'new idea' is going to become a full-blown policy feature in most modern governments globally. According to this argument, we have seen only the beginning of what is to come. Depending of course on how broadly PPPs are defined, the need for public–private cooperation in today's interconnected world is too strong to resist. If this is true, then we will see further exposure of the PPP idea in many parts of society, and the focus on infrastructure projects will soon have (has already?) shifted towards the social sector, including childcare, elderly care and welfare state services. Much will depend on the political gains that governments stand to make on PPPs, but also the involvement of policy subsystems plays a role.

A second argument, related to the first one, is that policy learning is actually taking place. Private sector companies and public sector executives sit down and talk to each other, they make deals and they are interested to learn more about each other's strengths and weaknesses in a way that the previous privatization and contracting-out discussion never allowed them to do.

A third, but certainly contested, argument is that PPPs are showing results. Pollitt (2005) argues for at least some economic improvement for PFI deals. Hodge (2005) examines the CityLink road project in Melbourne that was completed as a PPP, but emphasizes how 'the jury is still out' on the performance of PPPs generally. There are critics who openly dispute the performance of PPPs (Shaoul, 2005). The British IPPR report was not all critical about PPPs, but stated that PPPs may be of use in certain policy areas rather than others. The main problem with evaluating infrastructure PPP projects is that the contracts run 30 years or more, so logically it is hard to evaluate the problem completely. We also don't know what is going to happen to the projects after the contract expires. Will they be turned over to the government again as promised, or will the quality of the buildings leave room for argument among (former) partners?

One of the most challenging aspects of PPPs is about the actors behind it.

Inspired by the ACF we can point to a new pro-PPP advocacy coalition which can be seen as an epistemic community on PPPs. The extraordinary fact is that many of the stern pro-privatization supporters have managed to convert themselves into a more 'softer' side supporting PPPs. It is almost as if PPPs are 'the human side of privatization' (or 'pink privatization' as David Levi-Faur has called it). On the other side, people and organizations that were against privatization also find themselves supporting the PPP idea because they see it as a way for government still to play a role even though it is as a 'partner'. In the terminology of the ACF we can say that what we are witnessing is a change in the secondary aspects of policy beliefs where organizations alter their views for mostly tactical reasons. In an epistemic community view, groups are beginning to share a set of causal beliefs on what PPPs might bring in economic and financial gains. But there is also movement in the policy core beliefs, the beliefs that actors normally hold dear. That is because actors can be for PPPs and still maintain their identity as public sector organizations and private sector organizations. Most organizations are probably not going to give up their deep core beliefs, so private sector companies entering a partnership with a public sector organization will still believe in market forces and competition in their hearts. Public sector organizations will continue to believe in the primacy of politics and the rule of law. This could be the work of the 'policy brokers' that Sabatier and Jenkins-Smith describe, whose role it is to create professional forums where different organizations can meet and exchange views on technical information over periods of time. Brokering is going on with PPPs in a grand way at present with lots of conferences, professional meetings and government seminars being arranged on the topic of PPPs.

CONCLUDING REMARKS

Why have PPPs been dominating the public policy agenda in recent years? This chapter has used a Multiple Streams Framework to show how three 'streams' intersected to enable PPPs to come onto the international policy agenda: (a) A problem stream focusing on a lack of funding and disappointment with traditional contracting-out; (b) A policy stream presenting an open-ended PPP concept that is subject to interpretation from a variety of actors; (c) A politics stream concerning election of a New Labour government in Britain in favour of PPPs. The British government's promotion of PPPs inspired governments around the world to seek knowledge on PPPs. The politics stream is also about an international mood towards PPPs among leading international organizations such as the EU, OECD and the World Bank, which have been coupled at a particular time in history to open a 'policy window' that promotes the PPP idea.

Why PPPs have come onto the policy agenda is partly to do with the strong push from key actors or policy entrepreneurs. The thesis in this chapter is that these entrepreneurs are assembled in a pro-PPP advocacy coalition, and that this coalition is fast turning into an epistemic community that consists of both public sector organizations, private sector companies and international organizations and perhaps also selected journalists and researchers. The epistemic community behind PPPs is believed to be relatively strong and has not met much opposition, except from some academic research scholars. Some members of this epistemic community, notably private sector organizations, have managed to transform themselves from being former privatization and contracting-out advocates. It does seem as if the PPP concept is sufficiently open to interpretation that it can bridge different groups along the public–private interface.

The future of PPPs is about whether the 'policy window for PPPs' will stay open long enough for the PPP policy to become institutionalized. The chapter has examined the arguments for and against. Arguments for closure of the policy window included: Not enough action is generated. The action that has been generated has been flawed and spawns new problems for governments and taxpayers. The financial crisis or focusing event has diminished. Several countries lack central PPP policy units or sincere governmental backing. The regulatory state will squeeze the flexibility originally hoped for in PPPs. Arguments opposing closure of the policy window included: The international professional dialogue is still revolving around PPPs. Results from implementation are beginning to be visible. PPPs are taking hold in particular sectors making the policy subsystems more likely to continue to develop PPP policy. Genuine policy learning may be taking place among key actors.

A huge challenge facing the public policy aspect of PPPs is how the dynamics of internationalization will affect the fate of PPPs. An international policy dialogue is taking place in an epistemic community on PPPs. PPPs can hardly be discussed only within national borders of each country. The dynamics of PPP policy making resembles the earlier privatization debate in many ways. Future research will be concentrating on how will the destiny of the PPP differ from the destiny of the privatization policy debate, and what kind of results are PPPs going to be judged on in the long run?

REFERENCES

Almquist, R. and O. Högberg (2005), 'Public–private partnerships in social services – the example of the City of Stockholm', in G. Hodge and C. Greve (eds), *The Challenge of Public–Private Partnerships: Learning from International Experience*, Cheltenham, UK and Northampton, MA, USA: Edward Elgar, pp. 231–56.

Arthur Andersen and LSE Enterprise (2000), 'Value for money drivers in the Private Finance Initiative', report commissioned by the UK Treasury Task Force on public–private partnerships, London: The Stationery Office.

Cohen, M., J. March and J. Olsen (1972), 'A garbage can model of organizational choice', *Administrative Science Quarterly* **17** (1), 1–25.

Commission of the European Communities (2004), *Green Paper on Public–Private Partnerships and Community Law on Public Contracts and Concessions*, Brussels: Commission of the European Communities.

Estache, A. and T. Serebrisky (2004), 'Where do we stand on transport infrastructure deregulation and public–private partnership?', World Bank policy research working paper.

Flinders, M. (2005), 'The politics of public–private partnerships', *British Journal of Politics and International Relations*, **6** (4), 215–39.

Greve, C. (2003), 'Public–private partnerships in Scandinavia', *International Public Management Review*, **4** (2), 59–68, accessed at: www.ipmr.net.

Greve, C. and N. Ejersbo (2005), *Contracts as Reinvented Institutions in the Public Sector: A Cross-Cultural Comparison*. Westport, CT: Praeger.

Haas, P.M. (1992), 'Introduction: epistemic communities and international policy co-ordination', *International Organization*, **46** (1), 1–35.

Hodge, G. (2005), 'Public–private partnerships in Australasia', in G. Hodge and C. Greve (eds), *The Challenge of Public–Private Partnerships. Learning from International Experience*, Cheltenham, UK and Northampton, MA, USA: Edward Elgar, pp. 305–11.

Hodge, G. (2002), 'Who steers the state when the government signs public–private partnerships?', *Journal of Contemporary Issues in Business and Government*, **8** (1), 5–18.

Hodge, G. and C. Greve (eds) (2005), *The Challenge of Public–Private Partnerships: Learning from International Experience*, Cheltenham, UK and Northampton, MA, USA: Edward Elgar.

Hood, C. (1998), *The Art of the State*, Oxford: Clarendon Press.

Institute of Public Policy Research (IPPR) (2001), *Building Better Partnerships*. London: IPPR.

James, O. (2003), *The Executive Agencies Revolution in Whitehall*, London: Palgrave.

Jordana, J. and D. Levi-Faur (eds) (2004), *The Politics of Regulation: Institutions and Regulatory Reforms for the Age of Governance*, Cheltenham, UK and Northampton, MA, USA: Edward Elgar.

Kettl, D. (1993), *Sharing Power: Public Governance of Private Markets*, Washington, DC: Brookings.

Kingdon, J. (1995), *Agendas, Alternatives and Public Policy,* 2nd edn, New York: Longman.

Linder, S. (1999), 'Coming to terms with the public–private partnership: a grammar of multiple meanings', *American Behavioral Scientist*, **43** (1), 35–51.

Milward, H.B. and K. Provan (2000), 'Governing the hollow state', *Journal of Public Administration Research and Theory*, **10** (2), 359–79.

Oppen, M., D. Sack and A. Wegener (2005), 'German public–private partnerships in social services: new directions in a corporatist environment?', in G. Hodge and C. Greve (eds), *The Challenge of Public–Private Partnerships: Learning from International Experience*, Cheltenham, UK and Northampton, MA, USA: Edward Elgar, pp. 269–89.

Osborne, S. (ed.) (2000), *Public–Private Partnerships*, London: Routledge.

Pollitt, M. (2005), 'Learning from UK private finance initiative', in G. Hodge and C. Greve (eds), *The Challenge of Public–Private Partnerships: Learning from International Experience*, Cheltenham, UK and Northampton, MA, USA: Edward Elgar, pp. 207–30.

Regeringen (Danish Government) (2004), *Handlingsplan for offentlig-private partner-skaber* [*Action Plan for Public–Private Partnerships*], Copenhagen: Ministry of Economics and Industry.

Sabatier, P. (ed.) (1999), *Theories of the Policy Process*, Boulder, CO: Westview Press.

Sabatier, P. and H. Jenkins-Smith (1999), 'The advocacy coalition framework: an assessment', in P. Sabatier (ed.), *Theories of the Policy Process*. Boulder, CO: Westview Press, pp. 117–66.

Shaoul, J. (2005), 'The private finance initiative or the public funding of private profit?', in G. Hodge and C. Greve (eds), *The Challenge of Public–Private Partnerships: Learning from International Experience*, Cheltenham, UK and Northampton, MA, USA: Edward Elgar, pp. 190–206.

Teisman, G.R. and E.H. Klijn (2002), 'Partnership arrangements: governmental rhetoric or governance scheme?', *Public Administration Review*, **62** (2), 197–205.

Van Ham, H. and J. Koppenjan (2001), 'Building public–private partnerships. assessing and managing risk in port development', *Public Management Review*, **3** (4), 593–616.

Wettenhall, R. (2005), 'The public–private interface: surveying the history', in G. Hodge and C. Greve (eds), *The Challenge of Public–Private Partnerships: Learning from International Experience*, Cheltenham, UK and Northampton, MA, USA: Edward Elgar.

Wettenhall, R. (2003), 'The rhetoric and reality of public–private partnerships', *Public Organization Review – A Global Journal*, **3**, 77–107

Zahariadis, N. (1999), 'Ambiguity, time, and multiple streams' in P. Sabatier (ed.), *Theories of the Policy Process*, Boulder, CO: Westview Press, pp. 73–93.

5. Private sector development strategy in developing countries

Paul Cook

INTRODUCTION

There is little doubt that privatization and economic liberalization introduced in the 1980s placed the private sector in the centre of the stage for development policy. The origin of the ideas behind the change in development policy emerged in the 1970s as a challenge to Keynesianism, and was led on many fronts by the influential works of Harry Johnson, Ian Little and Bela Balassa. Collectively their works reflected the belief that the problems of economic development could be solved only by an economic system with freely operating markets and minimal intervention by government (Toye, 1993). The World Bank (1985:1) led the change in development policy stating that 'The new vision of growth is that markets and incentives can work in developing countries. But they are filtered through government policies and agencies, which, if inappropriate, can reduce or even negate the possible benefits.'

In terms of the thrust towards the private sector by the World Bank, whether through privatization or support for the general conditions for the growth of private enterprises, change was relatively slow. The pace of privatization in the early 1980s was at a trickle and concentrated in only a few developing countries (Cook and Kirkpatrick, 1995). Support continued for the development of the small enterprise sector in developing countries, and for the restructuring of ailing state-owned enterprises. In the latter case to reform them to insulate them from excessive political interference and to provide them with incentive structures that resembled their counterparts in the private sector.

The disjuncture between changes in development thinking, as outwardly expressed in multilateral development agency policy statements, and practice, reflected to a large extent the structural rigidities in the ways in which funds were disbursed and technical assistance was delivered. The international development agencies provided their support for both state activities and the private sector in developing countries predominantly through government-controlled agencies. The gap between policy and practice was, however, to change in the 1980s with growing conviction within the World

Bank directorate that more effort ought to be placed on privatization and private sector development and less on public enterprise reform. The acceleration of policy reform in this direction was facilitated by the collapse of foreign private capital to developing countries, following Mexico's suspension of debt service in 1982. This considerably enhanced the ability of the World Bank and the International Monetary Fund to impose policy conditions with their lending activities. Following from this, privatization and the focus on private sector development gained ascendancy within the community of international development agencies. By 1988 the World Bank had established a task force to assess the role of the private sector in development and to provide guidance on how the Bank could assist member countries to strengthen their private sectors' contribution to development (World Bank, 1989). In 1991 the World Development Report stated that non-market approaches to development had proved less effective than had been expected, and that as a consequence a consensus has been formed in favour of a 'market-friendly' approach to development. This consensus came from an increasing number of countries that recognized that competitive market signals and entrepreneurial actions lead to more efficient resource allocation.

However, the support for privatization and private sector development within the international development agency community took a jolt in the mid-1990s with the findings of the World Bank's report, *Bureaucrats in Business* (World Bank, 1995). One of the main findings of this influential report was that the amount of privatization in developing countries was considerably below expectations and the public sector was still as large in many countries, particularly in the lower-income countries, as it was when market-oriented reforms were initially introduced in the early 1980s (Cook, 1998). The World Bank considered this as a relative failure of their privatization efforts (Shirley, 1998). Although the analysis in the report indicated what might constitute a more successful programme for privatization, the emphasis in this area declined in relative importance. In the four years following the *Bureaucrats in Business* report policy conditionality towards privatization and public enterprise reform in structural adjustment lending declined substantially, while support for the development of the business environment in general and for private participation in infrastructure, including privatization, became predominant (World Bank, 2002). This trend has been reinforced in recent years by the spate of strategies towards private sector development (PSD) that have emerged from all the major international development agencies, including the World Bank, the Asian Development Bank, the Inter-American Development Bank and the African Development Bank, as well as the majority of bilateral aid donors.

The purpose of this chapter is first, to examine policy and practice towards private sector development by the major multilateral and bilateral development agencies. Following this the chapter discusses the issues that have emerged as policy towards the private sector has evolved, and reviews some of the outcomes. Finally, the chapter concludes by assessing what lessons have been learnt.

DEVELOPMENT OF PSDs

The clear shift in policy away from interventionist planning towards a neo-classical, market-oriented view of the development process and policy witnessed a stronger commitment on the part of the major international development banks to increase their support for private sector development. Initially, this meant reducing the bias in lending towards public sector investment, although this was to prove to be less than straightforward.

The shared vision of the international agencies that emerged in the early 1980s was twofold. First, all agencies emphasized the need to establish the appropriate national macroeconomic framework within which private enter-prises could operate. This was clearly evident in the types of policy conditions that were instrumental in both sector and structural adjustment lending to developing countries. Second, there was a view that the choice between private and public enterprises was itself dependent on whether the right oper-ating environment in recipient countries was established. Once a competitive environment was established, the choice of enterprises would be determined by efficiency rather than by the type of ownership. In this respect, the multi-lateral development banks differed from the more ideologically focused stance of some bilateral agencies, for example USAID. This then implied that it was developing country governments who could decide on which type of owner-ship to support. Their preferences were reflected in lending practice, since most of the earlier World Bank structural adjustment loans (73 per cent) speci-fied some form of public enterprise reform rather than privatization.

In the 1980s there were three main ways in which the international lending institutions assisted private sector development in developing countries (Cook, 1988). The first was through the process of policy dialogue and particu-larly through policy-based lending. Of the 40 World Bank structural adjust-ment loans to 21 countries between 1980 and 1985, 62 per cent called for the deregulation of pricing and licensing legislation, which would permit the private sector to compete more effectively in sectors in which public enter-prises predominated (Mosley, 1988). The second was by lending to the private sector. Table 5.1 shows the main ways the major international lending agen-cies channelled funds to the private sector. Lending to the private sector was either direct, in the form of loans or equity, or through government and finan-cial institutions which on-lent to the private sector. At this time the major

Table 5.1 Comparison of main channels for lending to the private sector in developing countries

| Recipients | Lending Institutions | | | | | |
| | World Bank Group | | IFC | Inter-American Development Bank | | Asian Development Bank |
	IBRD	IDA		(IDB)	(IIC)	(ADB)
DFIs or governments and re-lent to private sector	Assists private sector through SALs to govt Extends credit lines to DFIs	Charter flexible regarding guarantee Extended credit to involved sector only via govt on concessional terms	Lending to DFI Lending to enterprises with govt capital	Credit lines to DFIs Some loans for working capital		Bulk of lending through credit line to DFIs Govt guarantee
Extends credit lines	Through commercial banks Apex credit lines to several DFIs					
Private enterprises	Lending to private sector with govt guarantees		Lending to private sector without guarantees	Charter allowed lending to private sector with govt guarantees	Could lend to private sector without govt guarantee	Charter permitted direct lending without govt guarantee
Co-financing	Co-financing and B-loan programme with commercial banks*		Co-financing with commercial banks and other agencies			Co-financing with commercial banks and other agencies
Equity			Participated in equity and quasi-equity schemes	Did not generally engage in equity investment		Growing but limited equity participation

Note: *World Bank guarantees the later maturity of commercial bank loans

Source: Compiled from various reports of the respective institutions

banks were lending to the private sector without government guarantees through their affiliated institutions. Lending in this way was led by the International Finance Corporation (IFC) and was later followed by the Inter-American Investment Corporation (IIC). The Asian Development Bank began to lend directly to the private sector without government guarantees through its private sector division.

In the 1980s, however, the largest proportion of loans to the private sector was channelled through the development finance institutions (DFIs) in developing countries, and direct lending to individual enterprises accounted for a relatively small share of total private disbursements. A characteristic of lending to the private sector in the 1980s was the large share provided to the lower-middle- and upper-middle-income countries, and within these groups, the highly concentrated pattern of lending to a few countries such as South Korea and Pakistan.

Third, the international agencies also acted as a catalyst for private sector investment. This was particularly important when foreign commercial lending was severely constricted in the early 1980s. This left the international agencies in an extremely strong position in being able to instigate policy conditions attached to lending that was in relatively short supply. Indeed, the existence of policy-based lending in a developing country acted, in many instances, as a pre-condition for the resumption of foreign commercial bank capital inflows towards the end of the 1980s. Private banks were not in a position to impose restructuring conditions on developing country governments, but could effectively piggyback on the conditions imposed by the international agencies. This was likely to increase repayment and reduce the risk of major default.

The gradual movement into lending directly to the private sector in the 1980s posed a number of problems for the international development banks and may have constrained the volume of lending to this sector. First, loans to the private sector would not be guaranteed by the government since they were not going to the private sector through government agencies or DFIs. Previously, loans to the private sector by the international development banks were guaranteed and channelled through government-controlled DFIs, but there were concerns over how effectively these institutions were managed and over the criteria used for on-lending. In some instances the international development banks imposed conditions on the DFIs which included interference, and in some cases, virtual takeover of their management practices. Lending directly to the private sector, however, raised the risk to the international development banks and placed an even greater emphasis on the need to secure the most appropriate investment. A high proportion of non-guaranteed lending in their portfolios had the potential to adversely affect their banks' ratings in international capital markets, and hence their ability to borrow. It also had implications for their ability to act as a catalyst for private foreign investment.

Second, the shift towards lending directly to the private sector created the conditions for a potential conflict of interest between the development side of the international development banks and their role as a lender and shareholder. There was a danger that the increasing use of policy conditionality could be influenced by the need to preserve the integrity of the banking side which would lead to compromises being made in relation to the broader developmental objectives established for these agencies.

The response of the international development banks to these issues was initially to modify their internal structures, for example, by strengthening their affiliate bodies that specialize in lending to private enterprises. It was felt such moves would reduce the potential conflict between their roles in poverty alleviation and economic growth.

However, it was soon apparent that a separation of the approach adopted for private sector development into developmental and commercial divisions was not tenable for a development agency. As a consequence an alternative approach was being called for that would bring the aims of growth and development under one strategy. This was delivered by the task force set up by the World Bank to assess the role of the private sector's contribution to development, and identify how best the World Bank could help strengthen the private sector in developing countries. A new private sector strategy was unveiled in 1989. The strategy was based on five main considerations (World Bank, 1991):

1. Private sector development should go hand in hand with measures to assume sustainability and equity, such as human resource development, poverty reduction and environmental protection.
2. Possibilities exist to pursue private sector development in virtually every sector.
3. Research and policy analysis should be undertaken to improve the understanding of relatively unexplored areas and develop new tools.
4. Private sector development requires both expanded competition and improved government capacity to correct abuses and regulate wisely.
5. There are differences among member countries in economic, political and social objectives, as well as in the stage of development of their private sectors, that must be weighed.

After two years of operation and a stocktaking exercise, the World Bank (1991:v) concluded that there 'was a need for a more integrated approach to address systematically the constraints inhibiting private investment in different countries'. This would entail a focus on broad economic policy reform with increased attention to specific constraints to private sector activity. Within this, constraints were divided into several categories relating to distortive incentive policies; excessive government production, consumption and regulation; weak support systems for private enterprises; and constraints associated with economic uncertainties that affect business decisions, including political and macroeconomic instability.

The specific actions undertaken as part of the private sector development strategy were operationalized as components of various types of lending instruments, such as adjustment loans, investment through financial intermediaries and direct investment. Out of all World Bank operations in 1990, totalling 228, 150 included private sector development components, and direct investment featured strongly (World Bank, 1991).

CURRENT WAVE OF PSDSs

In recent years there has been a proliferation of new private sector development strategies adopted by multilateral, as well as bilateral, development agencies. Recent examples are the Asian Development Bank's Private Sector Development Strategy (ADB, 2000), the World Bank's Private Sector Development Strategy – Directions for the World Bank Group (World Bank, 2002) and the Inter-American Development Bank's Private Sector Development Strategy (IDB, 2004). The main components of these strategies are summarized in Tables 5.2, 5.3 and 5.4.

Table 5.2 provides a summary of the three strategic elements to the ADB's approach to private sector development. It highlights the role of government in creating the enabling conditions for private sector development which includes financial and capital market reforms. Privatization remains on the agenda as an element in creating business opportunities, although in its newer form of supporting infrastructure development. The third element includes the priority for channelling investment in specific sectors such as infrastructure, financial institutions and small enterprises.

Competition policy appears in the ADB's strategy, as well as in others, but was noticeably absent in earlier structural adjustment programmes. Its inclusion in the current wave of PSDSs in part reflects the past failure of economic reforms in the 1980s that overly relied on trade liberalization to promote domestic market competition. World Bank structural adjustment conditionality did not stipulate conditions for domestic competition policy (Gray and Davis, 1993). The lack of success in linking trade liberalization to the stimulation of competition raised questions concerning the direction of causality between trade and competition, and to the view that success in trade was itself dependent on establishing a competitive domestic environment. The emphasis on developing competition law is reiterated in the World Bank's private sector strategy in Table 5.3 and contributes to the aim of improving the investment climate for private enterprise development.

Table 5.2   Private sector development strategy (ADB). Three strategic thrusts: targeted outcomes and instruments

Strategic thrusts	Public sector operations		Private sector operations
	Creating enabling conditions	Generating business opportunities	Catalysing private investments
Targeted outcomes	• Sound macroeconomic policy • Appropriate competition policy • Investment and trade liberalization • Legal and judicial reform • Public administration reform • State enterprise reform • Tax reform • Product markets reform • Financial sector reform • Capital market reform • Pension and insurance reform • Labour and land markets reform • Sound environmental and social standards • Reform of infrastructure and other sectors • Good physical, social and technological infrastructure	• Private sector participation in Asian Development Bank (ADB)-financed public sector projects through contracts for – supply – construction – management – concession – leasing • ADB-designed model build-operate-transfer and other types of projects with poverty-reduction impacts • ADB-supported privatization programmes	• Private sector projects with development impacts and/or demonstration effects • Priority to be given to – infrastructure facilities – financial institutions – investment funds – specialized financial institutions for small and medium-sized enterprises and microenterprises – pilot health and education projects
Instruments to use	• Policy dialogue • Economic and sector work • Programme loans • Sector development loans • Project loans • Technical assistance • Co-financing • Partial credit guarantees	• Technical assistance • Programme loans • Sector development loans • Project loans • Co-financing • Partial credit guarantees	• Loans without government guarantees • Equity investments • Hybrid instruments • Co-financing • Partial risk guarantees • Partial credit guarantee

Source: ABD (2000)

Table 5.3 *World Bank private sector development strategy, 2002*

Strategic thrust	Extending the reach of markets	Access to basic services
Targeted measures	**Investment climate** • Continued policy-based lending, consultation and reforms to build competition law, simplify business procedures • Reduce unjustified obstacles to private business investments • Legal and judicial reforms • Establish secure property rights regimes for poor people • Conduct systematic investment climate surveys and assessments to identify pro-poor investment climate features, track changes and compare countries • Institutional capacity building and improve corporate governance **Direct public support to firms** • Continued support to entrepreneurs including rural credit and micro-finance • Improve performance of public financial and advisory support • Limit domestic taxpayers of poor countries by providing credit through IFC, not subsidies through WB • Target subsidies to capacity building/institution building activities and make transparent • Require minimum rate of return of lending and ensure subsidies are transparent	**Infrastructure supply** • Support private participation in infrastructure • Improve regulatory regimes and build institutions to supervise the private sector • Develop principles for regulatory regimes reflecting emerging best practices of policy makers and regulators **Social sectors** • Continue investments in private health and education projects • Assess options for privatization based on infrastructure experience • Pilot 'Output-Based Aid' projects that disburse public funds backed by donors for basic public services • Evaluate the effectiveness of pilots in the medium term and assess contracting and regulatory risks • Capacity building of public and private institutions

Source: Developed from World Bank (2002a: pp. i–vi, and annex 1) in Hodge (2004)

Table 5.4   Inter-American Development Bank PSD strategy

---

1. Developing an enabling environment for business

    •   Identification and elimination of barriers to the private sector

2. Financial support for specific private sector projects

    •   Infrastructure projects
    •   Finance to small-scale enterprises

3. Leveraging developmental impact in underserved markets

    •   Attention to smaller-scale enterprises and the problems of informality

4. Engaging the private sector in dialogue and action

    •   Building consensus on the goals of private sector development with business, government and civil society and international institutions

---

Source: IDB (2004)

Table 5.4 outlines the approach adopted by the Inter-American Development Bank which again emphasises the support required for an enabling environment including finance for infrastructure and small enterprises and the removal of obstacles to private enterprise development.

The bilateral donors have also adopted new programmes or developed earlier ones aimed at strengthening the private sector. A compendium of approaches among bilateral donors is provided in Table 5.5, constructed by Schulpen and Gibbon (2002). The consensus of bilateral donors at the end of the 1990s was similar to that derived by the multilateral agencies. Economic growth was central to development, and economic growth was best achieved through the private sector, with government acting as a facilitator to the private sector and ensuring that the growth contributes to poverty reduction. To the major donors, the publication of Dollar and Kraay's (2000) study *Growth is Good for the Poor* provided the empirical evidence to reinforce the consensus. They used data from 137 countries over a 40-year time period, and reported that the incomes of the poor rose proportionately with average income growth.

There have been few published evaluations of the recent donor programmes for PSD. The World Bank produced its first report on the 2002 strategy in 2003 (World Bank, 2003). It is, however, instructive to identify the similarities and differences between the multilateral and bilateral PSDSs, and to ask in what ways these newly developed strategies are different from earlier approaches. First, as noted by Schulpen and Gibbon (2002) bilateral and multilateral donors have given attention to the 'enabling environment' for private sector

Table 5.5   Donor's PSD programmes – a compendium

Instrument	Short description
Instruments of non-financial aid/technical assistance/business developmental services	
Technical aid	Technical assistance at macro level (legislation, privatization, good governance, etc)
Technical aid	Technical assistance at meso and micro level
Vocational and technical aid	Either in developing country or in the donor country by training consultants from the donor country
Export training	Training about production, quality control and regulations for export, e.g. about markets, regulations, etc., marketing studies, quality control
Information provision	
Management provision	Help in finding and recruiting capable management, including expert programmes and training programmes
Investment advice	Investment related advisory services
Consultant Trust Funds	Providing own consultants for multilateral donor programmes supporting private sector
Study grants	Feasibility studies, normally in the start-up phase of a joint venture, followed by training, advice and study visits
Instruments of financial aid	
Grants or loans	Financial support at macro level (infrastructure, health, education) for local enterprises (often through
Loans and equity financing	intermediaries) and/or for own private enterprises (e.g. FDI, joint ventures)
Risk capital	Providing capital directly to commercial projects
Guarantees	A sort of insurance in case of trade or investment
Mix of loans, grants and financing	Combination of different instruments in one programme – the financial packages
Mixed credits/ concessionary credits	Export credits, tied to imports of goods and services from the donor country
Lines of credit	Credit to local financing institution for on-lending to small and medium-size enterprises
Microloan programmes	Financial systems serving the microenterprises

Sources: DAC (1995:31–110); van den Bosch (1998); DGIS (2000); NORAD (1999); NZODA (1991); CIDA (1999); DAC (1997b,c); AusAID (2000); Danida (1999); Pietila (2000); and Schulpen (2000).

development, and this falls within the mainstream of contemporary development thinking. But few bilateral donors have concerned themselves with the detail that is required to satisfy the macro-level conditions for private sector development.

Second, there also appears to be a broad convergence between bilateral and multilateral agencies with respect to the selection of programmes to be included in a private sector development strategy. Although, the multilateral agencies appear to be better informed than the bilateral agencies about recent trends and the basis for the intellectual justification required to identify and support specific courses of action.

Third, the bilateral programmes place a large emphasis on the transfer of technology and expertise between enterprises in recipient and donor countries, and the transfer of expertise through short-term consultancy activities. Again, Schulpen and Gibbon (2002) have indicated, this approach may be outdated as the more recent literature emphasizes that more effective transfers develop from long-term, path-dependent relationships between specific enterprises and a few key suppliers and customers (Uchida and Cook, 2005). Indeed, all strategies appear to ignore the importance of developing national systems of innovation, a complex of nationally grounded and interlinked research institutions and business networks (Lundvall, 1992).

Fourth, although most strategies refer to the importance of new relationships between public and private sectors, competition and the regulatory environment, the models adopted continue to be those principally developed and rooted in the institutional sophistication of the developed economies (Cook et al., 2004). Associated with the question of the origin of policies and the appropriateness of what is transferred, is whether this amounts to a 'one size fits all' approach – a claim which most donors have continued to reject in their latest strategy documents. For example, the Inter-American Bank claim, 'there is no single reproducible process to achieve private sector development that can be applied in all cases, all regions, all countries, all industries or all enterprises. Each solution must be tailor-made to the institutions, actors and markets that define the initial conditions' (IDB, 2004:24).

Consultants and consultancy organizations have played a role in developing the emphasis on private sector development. This can most vividly be seen in the earlier attempts to introduce privatization in developing countries. There are numerous examples of consultancy companies and merchant banks pushing the privatization agenda (mainly those involved in UK privatization) in terms of assisting developing country governments to establish priority sectors for divestiture, restructuring and liquidation. Interestingly, the intensity of this activity appears to pre-date the World Bank's own push towards privatization in developing countries and was most virulent when empirical evidence on the merits of privatization was weak (Cook and Kirkpatrick, 1988).

Consultancy companies continue to be actively engaged in private sector development but with less bravado than in the days when privatization was centre stage. Consulting firms tend to have a wider perspective nowadays, working through consortiums to form strategic partnerships with local entrepreneurial initiatives, and sometimes extending the agenda to incorporate such elements as social corporate responsibility (Utting, 2002).

CONCLUSION

The pertinent questions to address in assessing the current wave of PSDSs relate to the extent to which they differ from past approaches, and whether lessons have been absorbed and acted upon in these newer strategies. A number of points can be made in this respect. First, it has been claimed that the current group of actions more closely reflects a public policy framework rather than the notion of a strategy as a designed set of actions that sets corporate direction (Hodge, 2004). In some respects, however, the agencies have been consistent in this approach. Earlier frameworks for private sector development have not necessarily been portrayed through strategies but as policy frameworks, and current PSD strategies are accompanied by the proliferation of a whole range of new strategies, along public policy lines, such as poverty reduction and financial development, into which they must draw linkages.

This leads to the second point which concerns the absence of the specific links and channels to poverty and poverty reduction. Of course, this is subsumed in the underlying aggregate framework linking growth and development, but the specifics are as absent in the new strategies as they were in the old. Of course the intention, largely unstated, may be to achieve greater integration across all strategies. In practice, this could prove difficult without a clearer understanding of the ways in which private sector development and the policies supporting private enterprise affect the poor.

Third, in principle the movement away from lending to the private sector through government-controlled development finance institutions, with entrenched views on the role of public enterprises, removes some of the resistance to private sector development, but does not remove the potential conflict between commercial interest and the developmental role of the international agencies.

Fourth, new strategies, particularly among the multilateral agencies, appear to build on earlier experiences through their emphasis on the need for a more systematic approach to the understanding of the constraints facing private sector development. In this respect the development of country surveys as a basis for improved technical assistance and lending activities evident in the World Bank's strategy, not only builds on the weakness of earlier programmes but provides a platform for further lending. In particular, the World Bank 2003 evaluation report points to the need for more detailed surveys, in line with the recently produced Doing Business Indicators (World Bank, 2004), and is rather critical of some of the more highly aggregated indices of competitiveness and business climate that have emerged in recent years.

Fifth, it is interesting to see the re-emergence of subsidies in the policy framework for private sector development. This appears to be a more innovative approach to project finance that accompanies traditional ways of financing. Under output-based aid, introduced in the World Bank strategy, service delivery (e.g. water) is delegated to third parties under contracts that tie payment to the outputs or results actively achieved. The intention is to shift performance risk to the private sector, which will assist the targeting of developmental outcomes, while providing a sufficient level of incentive to deliver. In effect, public subsidies supported by donor funding are intended to satisfy developmental objectives and not increase the profitability of the private sector. So far pilot schemes have been applied in a number of areas including rural water and sanitation, access to energy and rural telephone connections. In Paraguay connection subsidies for water are used through a negative concessions approach in a selected number of towns. Here service providers bid for the concession on the basis of the subsidies they require, rather than the fees they would pay, to obtain the concession.

Finally, over time, the trend in investment lending for the World Bank has been to withdraw direct support to state-owned enterprises and individual investments that the private sector might be in a better position to undertake. The IFC has become the main instrument for direct assistance to private enterprises, supported by guarantee activities through the Multilateral Investment Guarantee Agency (MIGA). The share of lending and guarantee products by the IFC and MIGA in total World Bank financial products has increased from 3.3 per cent in 1980 to 25 per cent in 2000. The World Bank currently adopts a hierarchical approach to investment guarantees adhering to the principle of the market first, then MIGA/IFC instruments, followed by World Bank guarantees. The last are deployed according to when particular risk conditions apply. Although, over time the IFC's investments have become increasingly concentrated in relatively low-risk rather than high-risk countries, and include significant investments in the financial and infrastructure sectors.

REFERENCES

Asian Development Bank (ADB) (2000), *Private Sector Development Strategy*, Manila: ADB.
AusAID (2000), *Private Sector Development through Australia's Aid Program*, Canberra: AusAID.

Bosch, F. van den (1998), *De ontwikkeling van de particuliere sector – beleid, organisatie en programma's in de DAC donorlanden*, The Hague: DGIS.

CIDA (1999), *CIDA's Draft Policy for Private Sector Development in Developing Countries*, Quebec: CIDA.

Cook, P. (1988), 'Recent trends in multilateral development bank lending to the private sector in developing countries: policy and practice', *Development Policy Review*, **6** (1), 165–82.

Cook, P. (1998), 'Privatization, public enterprise reform and the World Bank: has "Bureaucrats in Business" got it right?', *Journal of International Development*, **9** (6), 887–97.

Cook, P. and C. Kirkpatrick (1988), *Privatization in Less Developed Countries*, Brighton: Wheatsheaf.

Cook, P. and C. Kirkpatrick (1995), *Privatization Policy and Performance: International Experience*, Hemel Hempstead: Prentice Hall.

Cook, P., C. Kirkpatrick, M. Minogue and D. Parker (eds) (2004), *Leading Issues in Competition, Regulation and Development*, Cheltenham, UK and Northampton, MA, USA: Edward Elgar.

DAC (1995), *Private Sector Development – A Guide to Donor Support*, Paris: OECD/DAC.

DAC (1997), *Survey of DAC Members' Cooperation for Capacity Development in Trade*, Paris: OECD/DAC.

Danida (1999), *Review Report – Danida's Private Sector Development Program*, Copenhagen: Danida.

DGIS (2000), *Ondernemen tegen armoede – notitie over economie en ontwikkeling*, The Hague: DGIS.

Dollar, D. and A. Kraay (2000), *Growth is Good for the Poor*, Washington, DC: World Bank.

Gibbon, P. and L. Schulpen (2002), 'Comparative appraisal of multilateral and bilateral approaches to financing private sector development in developing countries', United Nations University discussion paper no. 2002/112, Tokyo.

Gray, C. and A. Davis (1993), 'Competition policy in developing countries pursuing structural adjustment', *Antitrust Bulletin*, Summer, 425–67.

Hodge, G. (2004), 'Private sector development strategy: some critical issues', in P. Cook, C. Kirkpatrick, M. Minogue and D. Parker (eds), *Leading Issues in Competition, Regulation and Development*, Cheltenham, UK and Northampton, MA, USA: Edward Elgar, pp. 129–45.

Inter-American Development Bank (IDB) (2004), *Private Sector Development Strategy*, Washington, DC: IDB.

Lundvall, B. (ed.) (1992), *National Innovation Systems: Towards a Theory of Innovation and Interactive Learning*, London: Pinter.

Metcalfe, J.S., R. Ramlogan and E. Uyarra (2002), 'Economic development and the competitive process', Centre on Regulation and Competition working paper no. 36, Manchester.

Mosley, P. (1988), 'Privatisation, policy-based lending and world bank behaviour', in P. Cook and C. Kirkpatrick (eds), *Privatisation in Less Developed Countries*, Brighton: Wheatsheaf, pp. 125–40.

NORAD (1999), *Strategy for Norwegian Support of Private Sector Development in Developing Countries*, Oslo: NORAD.

NZODA (1991), *A Strategy for Implementing NZODA to the Private Sector in Developing Countries in the South Pacific*, Wellington: NZODA.

Pietila, T. (ed.) (2000), *Promoting Private Sector Development – Issues and Guidelines for Aid Agencies*, policy papers I/2000, Helsinki: Institute of Development Studies.

Schulpen, L. (2000), 'Private sector development and poverty reduction: an inbuilt incoherence?', in T. Pietilä (ed.), *Promoting Private Sector Development – Issues and Guidelines for Aid Agencies*, policy papers I/2000, Helsinki: Institute of Development Studies.

Schulpen, L. and P. Gibbon (2002), 'Private sector development: policies, practices and problems', *World Development*, **30** (1), 1–15.

Shirley, M. (1998), 'The economics and politics of government ownership', *Journal of International Development*, **9** (6), 849–64.

Toye, J. (1993), *Dilemma of Development*, Oxford: Blackwell.

Uchida, Y. and P. Cook (2005), 'The transformation of competitive advantage in East Asia: an analysis of technological and trade specialisation', *World Development*, **33** (5), 701–28.

Utting, P. (2002), *Regulating Business via Multi-Stakeholder Initiatives: A Preliminary Assessment in Voluntary Approaches to Corporate Responsibility: Readings and Resource Guide*, NGLS/UNRISD: Geneva.

World Bank (1985), *Research News*, **6** (1).

World Bank (1989), *Developing the Private Sector: A Challenge for the World Bank Group*, Washington, DC: World Bank.

World Bank (1991), *Developing the Private Sector: The World Bank's Experience and Approach*, Washington, DC: World Bank.

World Bank (1995), *Bureaucrats in Business: The Economics and Politics of Government Ownership*, Oxford: Oxford University Press.

World Bank (2002), *Private Sector Development Strategy – Directions for the World Bank Group*, Washington, DC: World Bank.

World Bank (2003), *World Bank Group Private Sector Development Strategy Implementation Progress Report*, Washington, DC: World Bank.

World Bank (2004), *Doing Business in 2004*, Washington, DC: World Bank/Oxford University Press.

PART II

Market development

6. The 'consultocracy': the business of reforming government

Graeme Hodge and Diana Bowman

INTRODUCTION

Governments have always had a strong relationship with the business sector. Traditionally, the use of consultants by the public sector has been somewhat subdued. In bygone decades, the differences between cultures in the two sectors was of such magnitude as to minimize the use of consultants, so that the infrequent use of external resources would be perhaps on the basis of either occasional expertise or on the basis of short-term project resource needs. Governments behaved, as did most business entities, as self-reliant organizations staffed primarily by full-time and loyal employees. All this has changed over the last few decades. The business sector is now a trusted adviser, an essential human resource and even a strong reform ally in governing today. And in the growing arena of public sector reforms in developing countries, the consulting sector is today recognized as a major commercial player in the provision of aid.

This chapter outlines how the gradual commercialization of government along with the increasing trend of governments to draw on the advice of the business sector have led to the creation of what has been termed 'the consultocracy'. But how is this consultocracy defined, and how should its influence be understood by those interested in the movement around the world of privatization ideas? This chapter firstly observes the reasons for which governments are increasingly relying on the consulting sector, and the consequential growth in international consulting business is then briefly outlined. A series of concerns regarding the increasing use of the business consulting sector in government are then presented and several charges against the role now being played by businesses in government are acknowledged and examined. Overall, the argument pursued through this chapter is built around the idea that there is, today, a global business in reforming government. The desire to gain a regular slice of the resulting commercial 'reform transactions' is hardly new, but is rarely acknowledged by reforming governments or international development banks. Whilst consultants will and indeed should, remain free to advise governments and provide professional services as the political need arises, the consultocracy as a phenomenon does need to be recognized by government as a new and powerful interest group. As a consequence, governments now need to consider new and innovative ways in which it makes explicit, or removes, the many conflicts of interest that are created through its contracts with the consultocracy.

THE GROWTH OF THE CONSULTANT ROLE

The increased role of consultants in today's government has several sources. First, we should observe that the growing role of the management consultant in private market sector businesses has been instrumental over the past two decades. The increasing need for stronger professionalism in businesses along with a relentless search for productivity gains on behalf of shareholders have produced an insatiable desire for new ideas and new techniques for improving business performance. For senior executives, the trend has been to adopt business reforms when in doubt rather than be accused of remaining stagnant. This market sector trend has effortlessly translated to the public sector as government, itself, has become steadily more commercial and efficient. Under the influence of New Public Management ideas (Hood 1991, Pollitt 1993, Consodine and Painter 1997, Alford 1993), greater use of contracts and contractors, performance reward schemes and business logistics models have all seen operating differences between the two sectors narrow. Now, similarities appear to outweigh the differences and a growing managerialist culture within the public sector increasingly relies without question on reforms straight out of the business sector. The currency most advertised in these reforms has been knowledge, and consulting companies have been quick not only to see such knowledge as a resource, but also as a form of authority (Stone, 2003).

As well as general efficiency reforms, governments have also relied increasingly on consultants for high-level expertise across a range of professional managerial and policy arenas. These range from information management to competition policy, and from business process outsourcing to defence and security policy advice. Increasingly professionalized incoming political leaders have also expected access to a broader range of ideas and options from professional colleagues and groups not aligned with previous governments. We might also question the extent to which the ethos of government as a purchaser of services (whether this is simply collecting the garbage or buying a public–private partnership deal for a multi-billion-dollar piece of infrastructure) has also translated to an expectation of governments to 'purchase solutions' for complex policy problems as if 'off-the-shelf'. In any event, there has certainly been an increasingly strong role played by consultant groups in providing the intellectual backbone of government reform packages, so that consulting groups acting as policy entrepreneurs (Kingdon 1984) have been paid as allies, or even foot-soldiers, in the midst of policy reform battles.

THE CONSULTOCRACY

First described by Hood and Jackson (1991), the 'Consultocracy' alludes to the increasing influence of private sector management consultants on the reform and agenda processes of the public sector. The concern voiced through this label is that the interests of profit-maximizing management consultants from the business sector may become key determinants of managerialist policies (Saint-Martin 2000:193). Whilst the historical foundations of today's global consulting companies can be traced back to the nineteenth century, significant market development did not occur until the late twentieth century. The more recent evolution of this field of commerce is perhaps best illustrated by the growth in estimated global consulting revenues, as shown by Figure 6.1.

As illustrated by Figure 6.1, the development of the management consulting market has accelerated since the 1990s despite global economic downturns. Indeed, revenues in 2003 were estimated at almost 20 times the level that one might have expected simply on the basis of growth in line with the consumer price index. In this continuing period of global recovery, Kennedy Information (2004) estimated that the size of the global management consulting industry in 2004 will have seen continued growth yielding an annual

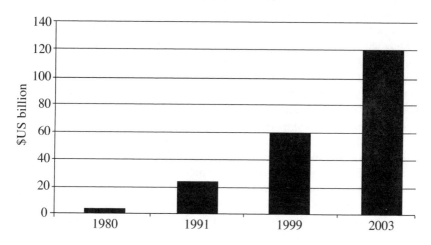

Source: UN (1993); Christensen (2003)

Figure 6.1 Estimated global consulting revenue (1980–2003)

market value of an estimated $US125 billion. It does not appear that growth of 'the consultocracy' is about to stall, with Kennedy Information (2004:1) anticipating that the 'profession will register a compound annual growth rate of nearly 5% through 2006', with solid financial growth anticipated within North America and the Asia Pacific region.

The increasing fiscal importance of the management consulting industry from the 1980s onwards parallels the rise of 'the new managerialism' or 'New Public Management' (Hood, 1991). Whilst this does not itself indicate a growth in the utilization of management consultants by the public sector, studies have indicated a growing trend in public sector expenditure on private sector management consulting services (HMSO Efficiency Unit, 1994; Northern Ireland Audit Office, 2004). The establishment of government consulting divisions within many of the larger consulting firms during the 1980s (Saint-Martin, 2000) appears to demonstrate the forecasted long-term expansion and potential for profit within this sector. Kennedy Information (2004) further suggest that today, the provision of consulting services to the public sector is the largest industry segment for consulting revenue, thereby displacing the financial sector.

But does increased spending on management consultants necessarily create a 'consultocracy'? Arguably yes and no. Pollitt (1996:84) on the one hand suggests that the increasing importance of management consultants is illustrated by the degree to which we witness consulting firms 'contributing important ideas about how to manage large and complex organisations'. Saint-Martin (1998:320), however, takes a more measured view, arguing that 'there is no direct and simple causal link between increased spending and increased influence'. There is little doubt that there has been a growth in public sector spending on management consultants, but it is also important to acknowledge that the increasing utilization of consultants is not solely about the 'packaging, selling and implementing' of policy (Greer, 1994:29) or solely about issues of management reform. In reality, consulting revenues are more likely to be earned from the provision of a wide range of service areas associated with IT services, customer services and security (Kennedy Information, 2004) than solely matters of policy reform.

When considering the rise of 'the consultocracy', it is also important to reflect on the nature and size of individual firms within the global network. However, given the generally unregulated nature of the market (United Nations, 1993) and taxonomy problems associated with defining industry boundaries (Kuber, 1986), literature examining the impact of management consultants on the public sector has generally focused on the role of the large transnational firms. This is not to say that the impact of small to medium-size management consulting firms has not been significant; but rather, as illustrated by Figure 6.2, with four firms in 2003 accounting for 45 per cent of the global market, their impact and role in 'the consultocracy' has been easier to examine.

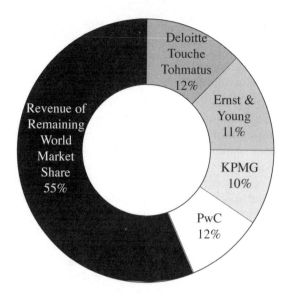

Source: Derived from Consulting Times (2004)

Figure 6.2   Global market share of aggregate consulting revenue (2003)

Colloquially referred to as the 'Big Four', Deloitte Touche Tohmatsu (Deloitte), Ernst & Young (EY), KPMG and PricewaterhouseCoopers (PwC), are the surviving firms of an industry that has been dominated by consolidation, mega-mergers and development. Once the 'Big Eight' and then the 'Big Six', today's 'Big Four' are an oligopoly of accounting firms which in the words of Saint-Martin (1998) 'dominate the world's management consulting market'. Despite the principal founding members of these four firms predominantly deriving from English accountancy firms (with the exception of Ernst & Young[1]), three of the Big Four are today US-owned[2] (Saint-Martin, 1998). As Table 6.1 below indicates, the Big Four have developed into extensive international firms in terms of human resource levels and international coverage. Indeed, the $US 71.1 billion total revenues in 2005 from these companies, and the employment of 462 500 people overall, are both a testament to the potential power of this industry sector.

Motivated by self interest and the creation of new markets for their services (Christensen, 2003), we have also witnessed a diffusion of the consultocracy from the developed countries to the developing nations. Today, every one of the Big Four firms has offices in 140 or more countries throughout the world. The extent to which this geographic spread has occurred is evidenced in the following examples of international offices:

Table 6.1 Key statistics on the 'Big Four' global consulting companies

Key statistics for 2005	Deloitte	Ernst & Young	KPMG	PwC
Aggregate revenue (2004/05 financial year in $US billion)	$18.2	$16.9	$15.7	$20.3
People	121 300	107 000	104 000	130 200
Partners	n.a.	n.a.	6 600	8 019
Countries	148	140	144	148
Number of offices/ member firms	670	700	715	771
Primary business/ services	Audit	Assurance & advisory	Audit	Audit and assurance
	Tax	Emerging & growth markets	Tax	Crisis management
	Consulting	Human capital	Advisory	Human resources
	Enterprise risk services	Law in Continental Europe		Performance improvement
	Financial advisory services	Tax		Tax
		Transactions		Transactions

Industries

9	7	8	23
Aviation & transport services;	Financial services;	Financial services information;	Aerospace & defence;
Financial services;	Technology, communications & entertainment;	Communications & entertainment;	Automotive;
Public sector;	Energy, chemicals & utilities;	Industrial markets;	Banking & capital markets;
Consumer business;	Health sciences;	Consumer markets infrastructure;	Chemicals;
Life sciences & health care;	Industrial products;	Government & health-care;	Education & non-profit;
Real estate;	Real estate, hospitality & construction;	Special focus groups;	Energy, utilities & mining;
Energy & resources;	Retail & consumer products	Private equity;	Engineering & construction;
Manufacturing;		Japanese practice	Entertainment & media;
Technology, media & Telecommunications			Financial services;
			Forest, paper & packaging;
			Government/public services;
			Health-care;
			Hospitality & leisure;
			Industrial manufacturing;
			Insurance;
			Investment management;
			Metals;
			Pharmaceuticals;
			Real estate;
			Retail & consumer;
			Technology;
			Telecommunications;
			Transportation & logistics

Source: Deloitte (2005); EY (2005); KPMG (2004, 2005a, 2005b), PwC (2005)

- Albania, Estonia, Indonesia, Nigeria and Yemen (Deloitte, 2005)
- Cameroon, Congo, Gabon, Rwanda and Vietnam (EY, 2005)
- Angola, Cambodia, Ghana, Laos, Papua New Guinea and Sri Lanka (KPMG, 2005a)
- Algeria, Botswana, Bulgaria and Senegal (PwC, 2005).

In which arenas do these international giants generate this revenue? It is here, on such matters of service revenues, the spread of revenues across different countries and on national employment numbers, the picture begins to get rather cloudy. It is nonetheless possible to glean some insights from Figure 6.3, which shows aggregate revenues across the primary firm business areas for each of the Big Four in 2005.

Although the nomenclature used by each firm to describe its services varies

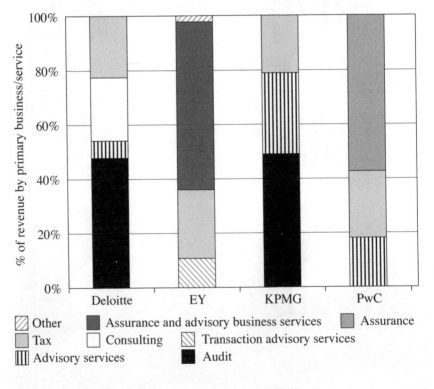

Source: Deloitte (2005); EY (2005); KPMG (2005a); PwC (2005)

Figure 6.3   2005 firm revenue (by per cent of total firm revenue) by primary business/service area

somewhat, it appears that auditing, tax and assurance services remain the core business of each of the Big Four. Interestingly, Deloitte is the only firm to have continued adopting the label 'consulting' as a specific service area, with $US4.3 billion (or 21.7 per cent) of total revenue attributed to this activity.

A similarly imprecise picture arises when examining the geographical spread of revenues, as shown in Figure 6.4. What is clear is that, at least for the period up to this 2005 data, the single global region dominating consulting revenues for most companies was the Americas. Furthermore, if we read between the lines in this figure, it appears that the combination of the Americas together with Europe seems to cover the majority of revenues.

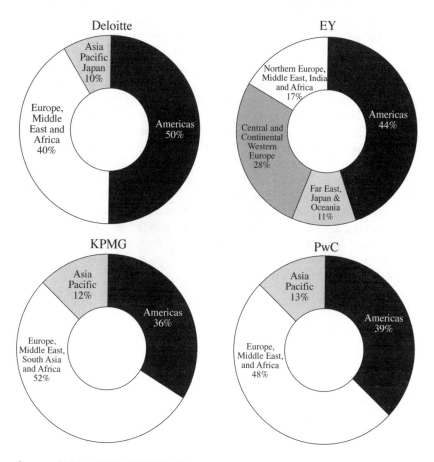

Source: Deloitte (2005); EY (2005); KPMG (2005a, 2005b); PwC (2005)

Figure 6.4   2005 revenue by geographical region

Thus, for example, of the $US18.2 billion in aggregate revenue recorded by Deloitte during 2005, the Americas contributed 50 per cent ($US9.1 billion), with 40 per cent ($US7.3 billion) of revenue from Europe/Middle East/Africa (EMEA) region (Deloitte, 2005). Similarly, 44.3 per cent (or $US7.5 billion) of EY's total 2005 revenue of $US16.9 billion originated from the Americas, in contrast to 10.6 per cent from the Far East, Japan and Oceania, and 27.8 per cent from Central and Continental Europe (EY, 2005). The concentration of revenues on the developed regions is expected to continue, notwithstanding the fast-growing markets of China, India, Latin America and eastern Europe (Kennedy Information, 2005:3).

And what of the distribution of employees around the world? Of course this distribution ought, in concept, be similar to revenue sources. But there is one significant difference. Compared with revenue proportions, the Americas were a slightly smaller base for employment than other regions. For instance, EY saw some 44 per cent of its aggregate revenue in 2005 coming from the Americas, while only 35 per cent of all EY employees were located within this region. In contrast, EY's Far East, Japan and Oceania regional firms generated 11 per cent of its global revenue, but were supported by 20 per cent of all EY employees (EY, 2005). This trend, which can be broadly observed in all firms in this group, suggests higher per capita revenue within the Americas, which is likely to reflect higher fee structures.

Overall, it appears that the emergence of the Big Four within the developing world indicates a paradigm shift from the exclusive demand for management expertise within OECD countries (Pollitt, 1990), arguably to include institutional-building and major reform processes within the developing world.

There is thus no doubt as to the spreading influence of major consulting firms throughout the world. This spread, however, has not been without its critics. It is to this matter that we now turn.

THE CHARGES

The rising role of consultants in Australia, in common with other neoliberal economies such as Canada, occurred during the mid-1980s. In the words of Considine (1999, as cited in Correy, 1999:11),

> governments, including Labor governments in Canberra and State governments in Australia, developed a consensus that private sector type management inside the public sector was going to get them some of the things they were looking for.

A feature of both the Hawke and Keating Labor governments, the increasing use of private sector consultants was not the subject of any serious criticism.

One exception to this, however, was the airing of an ABC Radio National programme by journalist Stan Correy looking at the increasing role of management consultants in government and titled 'The Consultocracy' (Correy, 1999). Correy's central concern stemmed from his observation that the use of consultants in the public sector clouded the function of government, so that in the end, citizens were uncertain 'just where the Consultocracy ends, and where the elected government begins' (Correy, 1999:2). His programme enunciated 'nine charges' against the growing influence of consultants within administrative reform processes and associated with the evolution of government policy. Correy's nine charges are summarized in Table 6.2 below. Each of these deserves some attention.

Correy's first claim questioned the blurring of traditional conceptual boundaries between the public and private sectors. His concern was that as countries continue down the privatization and outsourcing pathways, traditional accountability mechanisms can be lost, and questions regarding 'who is influencing what? . . . and how?' become far more prominent. His second charge, that judgements about the success or failure of consulting work were essentially left to the market place (Correy, 1999:2), was more an observation that consulting work was neither a matter for citizens to make judgements on, nor a matter for open political processes. Whilst consultants worked inside

Table 6.2   'The Charges' as identified by Correy (1999)

The Charges

1. Blurring of the public–private interface (1999:2)
2. Judgement about their success or failure is left to the market place (1999:2)
3. The attitude and values of the private sector don't seem to include openness (1999:3)
4. Consultocracy is selling the reform agenda (1999:4)
5. The old policy processes have been replaced with new policy development processes (1999:4)
6. The consultocracy is intended for the presidential style of American politics and not for Australia's Westminster system (1999:6)
7. Consultants are too powerful today (1999:12)
8. There is a new language created by the private sector, focused on outputs and outcomes, that is being imposed on the public sector (1999:12)
9. Governments are in danger of becoming too reliant on the private sector for advice (1999:14)

governments, they somehow remained outside government accountability structures. The third charge was critical of the 'culture, attitude and values of the private sector' (Correy, 1999:3) which was increasingly spreading through government. The culture of secrecy through the use of 'commercial-in-confidence' agreements between the two sectors was central here, in that citizens no longer appeared to have the right to know 'what governments [were] doing' (Correy, 1999:3).

Arguably even more important was the fourth charge – that 'the consultocracy' was in the business of selling reform agendas to government. For Correy (1999:4) the crux of this charge was the observation that,

> Government is elected to carry out those policies it makes for the running of the country. The questions are, what is it that the non-elected consultants are selling to government? And does this relationship make the consultants key political players in our parliamentary democracy?

Critical to this charge was the question of just how influential the consultants appear to have become. Correy's fifth charge rested on the claim that traditional policy processes have been superseded, or even corrupted, and 'replaced . . . by the practices of private consultancies, with confidential briefings, and less and less by open processes of consultations' (Correy, 1999:4). Likewise, with three of the Big Four now exclusively owned by US parent companies, considerable scepticism of the appropriateness of such consulting firm structures and style for Australia was the foundation of the sixth charge. Saint-Martin (1999, cited in Correy, 1999:6) had previously questioned the suitability of these management systems and experience outside of the US, but Correy (1999) went further, noting Al Gore's gushing praise of David Osborne as 'the man who literally wrote the book on reinventing government'.[3] To Correy, 'its most basic thrust [was] to clear the way for Wall Street capitalism, for free market entrepreneurs . . . [who] see State rules and regulations, and state control of assets and information, as obstacles to the freedom to do business'.

The seventh charge, that consultants are too powerful today, was one of considerable gravity. While Correy (1999:12) acknowledges that consultants are not yet equal to the 'old style power elite: business, media barons, powerful politicians and Party power brokers' he (1999:13) argues that,

> the consultants are enormously adaptable and persuasive. They make government and management seem much easier. They give advice, they tender for outsourced services, and for the software to run it.
>
> Their networks of influence are now deeply entrenched . . . And if they're not always working all that well, it's too late to change now. They handle staffing and 'strategies' and any 'reform agendas' that are still [to] be implemented. Their political clout is different from that of a Rupert Murdoch or the head of Western Mining, but it is undeniable.

Importantly, this charge concerning growing influence appears to be central to Hood and Jackson's (1991) coining of the term 'consultocracy'. Guthrie (1999, as cited in Correy, 1999:12) articulates the eighth charge as one involving management consultants fashioning 'a new language that's being imposed on the public sector'. Thus, a new business reform language has now become commonplace with words such as contracting, results and performance incentives, and the use of models through which departments are seen as service producers of outputs and outcomes. Correy's final charge asserted that governments were in danger of becoming too reliant on the private sector for advice. This idea is not new, and has been a feature of many of the critiques within privatization and outsourcing debates.[4]

Investigating the Charges

It is now several years since Correy (1999) enunciated his nine charges against the consultocracy in the context of Australia's public sector reforms. Since then, several others have echoed his concerns, particularly at the international level, where the spread of policy reform ideas around developing countries has been characterized in terms of the spread of 'neo-liberal capitalist order . . . primarily focused on economic liberalization and market globalization' (Stone, 2003). It is therefore an ideal time to reflect and investigate the degree to which these claims might be substantiated, both within the broader context of developed countries as well as developing nations. Importantly, this provides the opportunity to inquire more broadly about the relevance of these claims in the twenty-first century to the spread of the privatization family of policy ideas and the potential policy implications of this maturing relationship.

A critical investigation of these charges reveals a large degree of commonality and overlap amongst them. Indeed, we might posit two larger primary concerns:

- First, the concern is that old-style policy processes are now obsolete and that policy reform solutions are now sold by consultants rather than offered up front by elected representatives. The result is that consultants have become a powerful interest group with undue influence underneath a less democratic policy development process.
- Second is the concern that government accountability to citizens has been reduced through secrecy in contract arrangements, and through the invisibility and lack of acknowledgement of the consultant role in democratic policy making and in the polity.

Thus, whilst consultants do play an important role in government today, they have also become a powerful interest group, although it is yet to be clearly acknowledged. As well, concerns around the consultant's role in secret or confidential policy or contractual matters can represent a shift of power from citizens to the government–business partnership. But to what extent do such concerns have any foundation? All of these concerns were central to the tone of the consultocracy as coined by Hood and Jackson (1991). However, in determining whether these charges carry substantive weight, it is important to avoid demonizing the role of consultants and painting a picture based on either a romanticized public sector equivalent, or as Christensen (2003) says, attitudes 'contaminated by nostalgia'. The following section investigates these concerns more carefully in an effort to more clearly determine the extent to which the 'consultocracy' might have influenced privatization policy within countries as well as assisting in its spread across the globe.

EXAMINING THE CONSULTOCRACY

New, Less Democratic Policy Processes?

The primary concern with policy processes in today's privatized state has been that as the strength of 'the consultocracy' has grown, non-elected consultants have increasingly had the opportunity 'to make their voices heard in the inner circles of decision-making' (Saint-Martin, 1998:319). This charge would appear to be supported by the likes of Bakvis (1997) and Peet (1998) who note the importance of private sector consulting firms in the development and implementation of the New Public Management reform agenda in the 1980s. The rise in 'the consultocracy' is therefore seen to parallel a decline in democracy for the citizenry. There are several relevant points to make here.

There is no doubt that there has been, over the past several decades, a blurring of the public–private interface. But it is also true that this trend is the latest in a long-running story of public service provision that goes back centuries. The need to have a professional, trustworthy, competent, merit-based and full-time public service bureaucracy was recognized over a century ago and was a major advance on the previous system based on patronage and corrupt practices. Weber's neutral, consistent and rule-driven public service systems, however, also brought with them a tendency for slow decision making and a resistance to change. By the 1960s the Fulton Committee in the United Kingdom, and Glassco Committee in Canada judged public service operations to be still following nineteenth-century philosophies with out of date management systems (Saint-Martin, 1998:335). As much of the work of the public sector was progressively seen logically to have many similarities to other service organizations, the work of management consultants was given more credence. And as Saint-Martin (1998:323) noted, the state was more likely to use consulting knowledge to develop NPM policies after consultants first acquired a certain reputation as experts in business management. Furthermore, rather than leading reform, it is likely that consultants followed behind politically charged reformers. Supporting this point, Saint-Martin (2000:468) again notes that 'while the state certainly contributed to the growth of consulting, historically, it is the production needs of the economy that first instigated the creation of and development of management consulting knowledge'.

Of course, there is also no doubt that consultants lobby for change. Self-interest drives this, and whether they were able to get a slice of the $US100 billion per year enterprise sales market revenues worldwide throughout the 1990s, a slice of the accompanying outsourcing trend,[5] or else a slice of the more recent public–private partnerships market,[6] the motivating principle of self interest still holds. However, as willing foot-soldiers of political change rather than its masters. Claims that the consultocracy sells the reform agenda to a simple-minded government are too simplistic in most jurisdictions.[7] But the related charge that the consulting business needs to be seen as a new advocacy group in its own right is legitimate. Moreover, it also has the consequence that as the government's relationship with this interest group grows stronger, there is a real risk that the government may become monopolized by advisers' arguments and their private interests rather than keeping its eye on the public interest.

At the international level, the policy influence of consultants is undoubted. At an academic level, there is also a wide array of possibilities here, rather than some sort of simple conspiracy. Stone (2001:4) presented a wide array of labels for this policy influence, as follows: 'lesson-drawing' (Rose 1993), 'policy band-wagoning' (Ikenberry, 1990), 'policy borrowing' (Cox, 1999), 'policy shopping' (Freeman, 1999), 'systematically pinching ideas' (Schneider and Ingram, 1988), 'external inducement' (Ikenberry, 1990), 'direct coercive transfer' (Dolowitz and Marsh, 1996), 'exporting ideas' and 'policy pushing' (Nedley, 1999). To these, we could also add the notions of Bennett (1991) who talked of policy emulation, harmonization, elite networking and penetration. It is also crucial to recall that in addition to this array of policy influence mechanisms, there are many different non-state actors who are actively engaged in the transfer of policy ideas: think tanks (or research institutes), foundations and academia as well as consultants (Stone, 2001:22). There are evidently many possibilities for policy influence. But there is also a less flattering and darker side to this, with critics such as Wedel (2005:37) referring to highly visible, jet-setting economists as 'econolobbyists', who appear 'to be more concerned about public relations and their own publicity than they are about dispensing serious policy advice'. Moreover, she argues that these triumphal 'fly-in, fly-out' consultants are part of a new mobile global power elite, who are accused by local citizens as inadvertently making their biggest contribution to the local economy through the provision of hard currency to hotels, restaurants, taxis and translators rather than policy advice of any veracity.[8]

So, have old policy processes been replaced with new consultant-driven policy development discussions? Not really. Whilst it is true that the era of the conservative government in places such as the UK has indeed seen the age of the management consultocracy (Beale 1994), it is misleading to believe that the growing influence that consultants now have in the policy process has been caused only by Thatcherism or by the rise of the New Public Management (NPM) (Saint-Martin, 1998). This rise had in fact, on Saint-Martin's reading, been steadily occurring throughout the preceding 1960s and 1970s as well, at least in the UK. And in any case, as we noted above, governments have for some considerable time been using consultants for their own purposes as well as the other way around. There is symmetry to the confluence of interests here.

Over time, there has, as Edeldman (1977) and Parsons (1995) both pointed out, certainly been a corruption of the policy discourse so that in the new postmodern age of policy spin, almost anything appears possible. But the largest issue here is that useful performance framework ideas had been around for some decades prior to the rise of the consultant – they did not monopolize, but perhaps helped to spread the performance measurement and improvement gospel. The systems engineering language of inputs, process, outcomes and evaluation against programme objectives goes back to the age of management by objectives and earlier programme budgeting ideas of the 1960s. Whilst this language was reinforced through subsequent waves of reform (including zero-based budgeting, programme budgeting, programme priority and planning, performance indicators and performance budgeting to name just a few), it was not sourced simply from the private sector nor was it forced onto public servants solely by consultants. Today's performance measurement culture has had a long lineage, and the language of outputs and outcomes has simply become more widely used and fashionable over the past two decades. Thus, the change in language occurred as well within the broader managerial revolution. So again, consultants became the 'foot-soldiers' in the war, but did not start it.

Reduced Government Accountability to Citizens

The advent of the phrase commercial-in-confidence has indeed sent shivers up the spines of numerous citizen groups and auditors general as moves to contractualize and outsource have gathered pace (Barrett, 2003). It has suited many incoming governments in their reform wars to rely on the prevailing attitude and values of the private sector – which do not automatically include openness to citizens. The unavailability of administrative law remedies for the case of private contracts, and uncertainty around freedom of information legislation have both also probably contributed to a weakening in public accountability. Some jurisdictions have overcome these concerns by ensuring that private contracts with government must as a general rule supply information to citizens, with any exceptions to this being explicitly vetted by Parliament, rather than the other way around.

Weakened accountability to citizens is partly also related to the lack of explicit acknowledgement of the increasing role of consultants in government, and to a healthy scepticism of the notion that because many New Public Management reforms have been fundamentally concerned with management they are therefore somehow apolitical. On the first point, there is an understandable reluctance for modern governments in power to highlight the degree to which they have effectively outsourced the day to day business of governing and passed over the public administration role to the business sector. On the second point, we might observe that whilst most management reforms have inevitably been sold as neutral and outside the political domain, this is clearly not the case. Work undertaken for any government department is, by its very definition, political to some degree. Whilst the strength of this varies from agency to agency, the principle that government work is not apolitical, does not. Having said this, it is also reasonable to argue that whilst citizens often do not directly judge the quality of management consulting projects, market reputations and competitive pressures are most likely to be the major determinants of their ultimate success or failure. As with any advice tendered to the business sector, the quality of advice tendered to government will usually stand on its own terms, and on the competitive nature of alternative options inevitably canvassed.

The combination of concerns around secrecy and concerns around weak accountability to citizens does leave one with a certain negative image of the consultocracy. In the words of Considine (cited in Correy 1999:14),

> This has, in a way, become the single most disturbing feature of the Australian case, and the one that overseas countries look at with both fascination and alarm, that in the absence of strong central programs and controls, and with an increasing resort to the delivery of programs through third parties, private contractors . . . in effect, we know less and less about what's actually happening, and we know less and less about how taxpayer's money is spent, we know less and less about what's happening to people who are accessing those government services. And the 'we' in this case is not just we citizens, but it's also central authority holders like Auditors General, like Senate and House Committees, even in many cases, Ministers.

There is also no doubt that the ability of the US consultant to sell reform ideas is second to none. And whilst this may well have initially been intended for the presidential style of American politics rather than others, the use of consultants in other political jurisdictions is not necessarily problematic.

Consultancies are dynamic organizations and adapt quickly to the needs of different clients. And in any case, democratically elected governments no doubt adopt a wide range of different methods to institute reforms and will continue to do so.

Central to all these matters is the argument that consultants are too often silent on the strong conflicts-of-interest that they experience. Being essentially 'transaction merchants', their success in terms of revenues earned does not equate to privatization reform success for citizens in terms of better services, greater choice and lower prices. As Hodge (2000) pointed out, the question of success in any part of the privatization arena needs to be qualified – 'success for whom?' is the more accurate issue.

So, how might these findings on the role of the consultocracy be interpreted within the context of the global movement of privatization family mechanisms? And what are the lessons here?

THE CONSULTOCRACY AND THE PRIVATIZATION REFORM FAMILY

Clearly, the consultocracy at the level of national reforms is more a lubricant in public sector reform than the policy reform machine itself. It has enabled government policy changes to be implemented with considerably greater speed and ruthless completion than might have otherwise been the case traditionally. And the strength of the consultocracy varies. Saint-Martin (1998; 2000), found from his analysis of historical institutional interrelations between management consultants and the state in the United Kingdom (UK), Canada and France, that it was strong in the UK, of medium strength in Canada and weak in France. His finding was that in the former two countries, the management consultancy profession emerged earlier, and more strongly than in the latter. The observation was made that because British and Canadian consultants had been involved in building the management capacity of the state for the past three decades, they acquired experience and built networks with the state. This resulted in their voices being progressively heard closer and closer to inner circles of policy making (Saint-Martin, 1998). This trend for strong links in some areas and weak links elsewhere is very likely to be the case at the international level as well.

What is also clear is that whether we view consultants as a 'shadow government' in the words of Guttman and Willner (1976) or as Hood and Jackson's (1991) 'consultocracy', the power of reforms under way will inevitably rely on the legitimacy or otherwise of policy reform directions and the degree of democratic support that reform policies attract. In terms of the spread of privatization ideas, the literature reminds us that:

> In Eastern and Central Europe, consultancy firms have been prominent in providing advice throughout the transition processes becoming central actors in privatisation, legal reforms and financial liberalisation in the post-communist states. (Wedel, 1998, cited in Stone 2001:25)

Well-implemented enterprise sales have no doubt produced benefits for governments and citizens, but implementation through either undue haste or insufficient attention to post-regulatory requirements as occurred in the former USSR, for instance, have been disastrous (Stiglitz, 2002; 2003). Stiglitz argues that the International Monetary Fund's (IMF) ideological pursuit of quick privatizations resulted in too little attention being given to corruption minimization, and privatization being known comically as 'briberisation' (Stiglitz, 2002:58). Divestitures in the former USSR were pursued at all costs, with the result that rather than creating wealth, assets were stripped at every level. Russian industrial production fell by 60 per cent – worse than the GDP loss suffered in the Second World War; poverty increased tenfold (from 2 per cent in 1989 to 23.9 per cent by 1998); and Russia today has 'a level of inequality comparable with the worst in the world' (Stiglitz, 2002:153–154).

The Harvard Institute for International Development's (HIID) management of distributing $US350 million of US economic aid money to Russia and its $US40 million bill for doing this work is one case in point. This body, working exclusively with a group centred around Anatoly Chubais, an indispensable aid to Boris Yeltsin through much of the 1990s (Wedel, 2000) was responsible for privatizing the Russian economy. But, as Williamson (1999) testified to the US House of Representatives, this privatization saw 'the new elite learn everything about the confiscation of wealth, and nothing about its creation'. As Wedel (2005:44) noted, rather than the fruits of the free market, 'instead, largely in the hands of the Harvard–Chubais transactors, it helped to create a system of tycoon capitalism run for the benefit of a half a dozen corrupt oligarchs . . . [thereby nurturing] the "crony capitalism" for which we now criticise Russia'. Of course the real question here is the role played by international consultants such as those from Harvard University as well as the policy reform effectiveness itself. But what is clear from this example is the absence of any early acknowledgement as to the clear conflicts of interest of consultants whose revenues depended not on success from the perspective of citizens, but on the completion of ideologically driven reform project transactions under contract.

Interestingly, even the World Bank, dubbed as 'the apostle of privatization', has recently been reported as having a 'crisis of faith' (Phillips, 2003). Kessides (2004) from the World Bank has also noted that 'privatisation has been oversold and misunderstood', with huge public dissatisfaction with the reform. He quotes recent disapproval ratings of some 90 per cent in Argentina and 80 per cent in Chile. Nonetheless, he also reports privatization in telecommunications as contributing to faster growth in phone line availability (from around 7 per cent to over 20 per cent per annum) and sharply increased labour productivity in railways. Belatedly, he nominates the two most common traps for enterprise sales as privatization without competitive restructuring, and weak regulatory capacity. As a consequence, he calls for more attention to proper scope, pace and sequencing of future reforms (Kessides, 2004:263).

For the case of enterprise divestitures, more case study analyses are required in order for the role of international consultants to be better articulated. What is clear thus far, is that consultants have inevitably been the foot-soldiers for the political and public policy directions taken by international reform agencies such as the World Bank and the IMF, as well as being front-line players within national public sector reform efforts. In both cases, it is also clear, as has been acknowledged elsewhere, that consultants have been one of the biggest winners from enterprise divestiture reforms to date (Hodge, 2000).

For the case of other members of the privatization reform family such as contracting-out services, partnerships and private sector development strategy, the international role of consultants also needs more consideration. But a few things are crystal clear.

First, the effectiveness of many privatization family reforms such as contracting-out has enjoyed mixed success in developed economies, let alone their application to developing economies. For instance, Hodge and Rouse (2004) detail the example of Australia's Whole of Government IT Infrastructure Outsourcing Initiative ('WOGITIOI'), in which cost savings of 20 per cent were promised by the federal government amounting to over $A1 billion. The reality of this reform, though, was that these savings were not delivered – despite being a textbook case of outsourcing using best practice. Importantly, the Auditor General (Australian National Audit Office (ANAO), 2000) found that costs had blown out. As Rouse and Corbitt (2003a:82) put it,

> Most of these cost blow outs were related to the costs of specialist international consultants, including . . . accounting firms, outsourcing advisors, and the outsourcing legal specialists, Shaw Pitman . . .

The Auditor General (ANAO, 2000) also found that, contrary to government claims, only one of the first four contracts, the contract for Cluster 3, was likely to deliver any savings,[9] and that 'actual savings after twelve months [in this case] were less than half of those projected at the time the contract was signed'. Overall, the total cost savings[10] for the group probably amounted to something closer to a few per cent, an order of magnitude smaller than the initial policy promise. Despite such mixed performances from developed jurisdictions, unquestioned recommendations to adopt these types of privatization family reforms throughout developing economies continues.

Second, when public administration work is itself outsourced, there are fundamental governance risks at stake.[11] Returning to the Russian privatization management debacle mentioned earlier, there is a salutary lesson here. Wedel (2005:44) explained the case as follows:

> In 2000, the US government sued Harvard University, the Harvard project's two principals – Andrei Shleifer, . . . and Jonathon Hay, and their wives . . . The suit alleged that the principals misused 'their positions, inside information and influence, as well as USAID-funded resources . . . to advance their own personal business interests and investments'. The investments, which the defendants did not deny, included securities, equities, oil and aluminum companies, real estate, and mutual funds – many of the same areas in which they were being paid to provide 'impartial' advice to help develop the Russian economy. In June 2004, a federal court in Boston ruled that Shleifer and Hay conspired during the 1990s to defraud the US government while supposedly representing US interests.

In this case, as Wedel (2005:45) says, Harvard project staff took advantage of 'government by third party'. They bypassed legitimate traditional institutions, they operated organizations such as the Russian Privatization Center, which was 'sometimes private, sometimes state, sometimes bureaucratic, sometimes market focused, sometimes Russian, sometimes American', and they operated as individuals who changed their roles to suit personal and group agendas so that the same person could represent the US in one meeting and Russia in another.[12]

The conflicts of interest in international policy as well as narrower commercial and personal interests were all palpable here. And there is also a remarkable parallel between the above Australian IT outsourcing case, and this case in the huge differences between the rhetorical policy promises advertised by the consultant reformers and the realities on-the-ground; the public policy promises morphed into far longer-term aspirations, whilst the short-term fees remained the real pay-off.

Third, in the arena of Public–Private Partnerships (PPPs), there has been some success, although again the evidence is not consistent, in both developed and developing economies. For example, PPPs as applied to infrastructure provision in developing countries have seen successes (see Kessides, 2004), as well as failures. The difficulty of evaluating these reforms against the next best alternative is legendary, but we might tentatively observe that there appear to be only a minority of cases where development agencies claim success. This may be due as much to the complexity of reform requirements as it is due to any potential success of privatization reforms per se or the successful role of an international consultant.

In developed economies, there is also no doubt that there is a diversity of experience with the PPP phenomena (Hodge and Greve, 2005). Moreover, it is instructive to note that we are increasingly turning our research attention now to questions of how to resolve conflicts of interest in the completion of PPPs.

Both governments and private sector companies have such conflicts in the world of partnership deals. In the former case, Hodge (2004) points out that,

> as the values of the state's public servants have been progressively managerialised, many of the traditional guardians of the public interest, both public servants generally and central institutions such as treasury departments, have shifted ground. There has been a subtle shift away from the dominant traditional, conservative, neutral stewardship and administration role towards a more dominant policy advocacy and implementation function. Executive employment contracts tied to implementation performance measures, for instance, have no doubt produced greater compliance and a more effective managerial machine for the implementation of political ideals. But advocacy compromises stewardship . . . Put bluntly, government Treasury departments . . . now sell PPP policies. But in doing so, they take on multiple and conflicting roles. These include the roles of policy advocate, project promoter, in-house manager, city planner, contract developer, financial steward and project assessor, legislator, contract regulator for subsequent decades, and trusted parliamentary adviser.

In the case of private companies, conflicts of interest may be both parallel or serial. For the case of a parallel conflict of interest, one party is not in a balanced position in which to make a decision on the proposal because it is in that party's own interests for the deal to proceed. The classic parallel conflict of interest is the recommendations of share traders who more often than not recommend investors buy 'hot stocks' without disclosing that they themselves profit from each trade irrespective of whether share prices subsequently rise or fall. This anecdote is mirrored today when, just like the staff of the Harvard Institute for International Development in Russia, private consulting companies advocate for governments to go ahead and finance public infrastructure through schemes from which they themselves would profit. But conflicts of interest may also be of a 'serial' type. Here, an individual uses knowledge and contacts (derived, say, from their position in government), to gain an unfair advantage in business (or vice versa). Numerous examples of both conflict types are present in the literature. A few are sufficient here to exemplify the issue.

Parallel Conflicts of Interest

- The UK Labour Party was accepting free accounting services from KPMG, which was also involved in more than £12bn of government contracts (Maguire, 2003). The party's finance director, Stephen Uttley, was reported as being on a secondment from the management consultancy, which continued to pay his wages. This news came shortly after the Labour leadership refused to review PFI contracts despite an overwhelming vote at the party's conference for an investigation into deals which critics argued gave taxpayers poor value for money but made vast sums for private firms.[13]

- Vasagar and Evans (2002) reported that KPMG had 'alarming' conflicts of interest. It noted the practice of supplying both audit services and advisory services to companies with Private Finance Initiative (PFI) works granted by the British government. It also observed that KPMG had offices in 24 of the 32 tax havens the OECD is currently trying to tighten up on, and questioned the completion of an assessment made by the consultant on the debt-ridden Caribbean country, Belize. This country was apparently failing to collect enough tax revenue because it had extravagant tax exemptions. Furthermore, it noted the seconding of KPMG staff to the government Inland Revenue Office, and KPMG's subsequent boasting 'to its commercial customers that it can help tax avoiders run rings around Whitehall, thanks to inside knowledge'.[14]

Serial Conflicts of Interest

- In Australia, Mr Peter Reith (former Federal Minister for Defence) took up a paid consulting position with Tenix Group, the country's largest defence contractor (Tenix, 2005) 'reportedly . . . the day after ceasing to be a minister in November 2001' (Australianpolitics.com, 2002).[15]
- Mr Alan Stockdale (former Victoria Treasurer) 'moved from his Treasury Place office – fresh from privatising major infrastructure – into Macquarie Bank's infrastructure investment arm' (Schuber and Koutsoukis, 2004). Likewise, Mr Bob Carr (former NSW Premier) joined Macquarie Bank in a part-time position three months after retiring from politics, with this role expected to pay around $500 000 per year (Frew, 2005).
- In the USA, Mr Dick Cheney left his position as CEO of Halliburton in 2000 (1995–2000) to run for Vice President of the USA, at which time he reportedly received Halliburton stock options of approximately $US33 million (Minority Staff, US House of Representatives, 2003). Halliburton received a $US7 billion contract for reconstruction work in Iraq that was secretly awarded. Mr Cheney continued to derive, while the Vice President, an annual income from Halliburton through deferred compensation payment of approximately $US160 000 (Minority Staff, US House of Representatives, 2003).
- Perhaps the ultimate accusation of such conflicts of interest was the case of a John Battersby in the UK, who, after drafting the inheritance tax laws in 1986, then went on and worked for KPMG Private in Switzerland advising 50 high net worth individuals, for a price, as to how to circumvent this legislation.

These, of course, are not isolated cases, and in the US, the matter of professional lobbying has institutionalized such conflicts of interest. Indeed, the Center for Public Integrity (2005) found that 'the revolving door is turning dizzyingly fast. Nearly 250 former members of Congress and agency heads are active lobbyists, and more than 2 000 lobbyists used to work in senior government positions. There is a large financial incentive for the move.'

We might also note in passing that 'Canada and the US have a two-year moratorium on senior figures – including top public servants in the US – working in an industry for which they once had "direct responsibility". In Britain, departing ministers must seek permission from an independent advisory committee, which can enforce a two-year delay' (Schuber and Koutsoukis, 2004:5). No such constraint exists in Australia, nor most developing countries, where newspapers are awash with accusations of conflict.[16]

There is a clear need to better acknowledge, and then openly manage such conflicts to avoid the assessment that privatization components such as PPPs, for instance, can become a legalized form of corruption. In any event, our existing empirical knowledge from other privatizations has shown the importance of strong and independent regulatory arrangements underpinned by legislation and practices that maximize transparency to citizens. This is also likely to be needed to maximize citizen benefits in the arena of PPPs as well as simply greater transparency.[17] In all cases, conflicts need firstly to be acknowledged, and then separated out to ensure roles are undertaken explicitly and transparently.

The area of Private Sector Development Strategy (PSDS) has also seen international consultants playing a major role in development and implementation. Whilst numerous evaluations of reform efforts have been undertaken, and a wide range of often positive benefits have been found (World Bank Operations Evaluation Department 2005; Nellis 2005), the observations made earlier in terms of enterprise divestitures, contracting-out services and partnerships are also likely to hold for this broader arena. PSDS involves numerous techniques, including many associated with governance and rule of law reforms as well as improved financial management. If we learn one thing from the above case studies and from the analysis of commentators such as Christensen (2003), it is that consultants will do very well from reforms such as the distribution of international aid or the introduction of accrual accounting in the public sector, irrespective of any questions concerning policy effectiveness.

To sum up then, the consultocracy is certainly an effective lubricant of the public sector reform machine, albeit not per se a reform machine itself, both at the international level and at the domestic level. This does not mean, however, that no action is necessary to improve governance. In the arena of conflicts of interest, there is now a strong onus on both government accountability bodies and public policy commentators to keep a watchful regulatory eye over behaviour. We also need to investigate further cases of implementation success and failure from consultant experiences, so that we may better understand their role in privatization reforms

CONCLUSION

The growth of the consulting business over the past two decades has been spectacular. The biggest four players in the sector now employ almost half a million people across more than 140 countries and earn revenues of more than $US71 billion. Whilst some critics have dubbed consulting companies a 'consultocracy', this chapter has examined this claim and found it largely unsubstantiated. Many of the criticisms launched against consulting companies have had their roots in far earlier times than the more recent advent of managerialism and the use of techniques such as outsourcing of government services. Nonetheless, the business of reforming government itself needs to be recognized by governments worldwide as having produced a new, powerful professional interest group.

Whilst the notion of a consultocracy leading and implementing public policy reforms ahead of government policy directions is probably too strong, government nevertheless does now need to consider ways in which it makes explicit, or removes, the many conflicts of interest that are created through its contracts with consulting firms. The place of international consulting firms in the spread of the privatization family of ideas around the globe is assured as a lubricant for political and policy reforms, but it is also destined to remain controversial.

NOTES

1. For a history of the Big Four firms, refer to Deloitte Touche Tohmatsu (2005), Ernst and Young (2005), KPMG (2005a) and PricewaterhouseCoopers (2005).
2. With the exception of KPMG, which is a Swiss cooperative.
3. See Osborne, D. and T. Gaebler (1992), *Reinventing Government: How the Entrepreneurial Spirit is Transforming the Public Sector*, Reading, MA: Addison-Wesley.
4. For instance, in terms of the 'hollowing-out' of the state, it is exemplified through examples of outsourcing failures including outsourcing the task of internal auditing, a part of which required the consultant to check on the engagement of consultants (Correy, 1999:9). A further example was that of a consultant requested by a central government agency facing an assessment by the state's auditor general who insisted that the task of documenting the government's original policy objectives for outsourcing in the first place had to be undertaken by a consultant 'as that function had been outsourced' (Hodge, 2000).
5. For the sole case of Australia, the 1990s saw some $A11 billion outsourced to private companies according to Russell, Waterman and Seddon (2000).

6. HM Treasury (2003:13) reports that PFI commitments had risen from £667 million in 1995 to £7.6 billion in 2003–04 with some 457 completed projects. The proportion of investment made up by PFI was between 10 and 15 per cent. In Australia, this preference for the private finance of public infrastructure has also been pursued.

7. Of course it has always been possible for those elected in authority to listen more to the ravings and scribbling of madmen than to develop public policy on the basis of a more rational and evidence based philosophy (Parsons, 1995).

8. Wedel (2005:38) quoted one Slovak aid official as saying wryly that 'The Western consultants collect information, get the picture, then go home . . . We are solving the West's unemployment in this way.'

9. Rouse and Corbitt (2003a:83) further noted that despite relying on world-class consulting advice, the cost and savings projections were flawed, because decision makers had failed to take into account additional cash streams associated with equipment that would have been available at the end of the contract if the services were not outsourced. They had also underestimated the costs of leasing risks absorbed by the agencies. As a consequence of this, the auditor general 'determined that only Cluster 3 was likely to make any substantial savings from the outsourcing arrangements'.

10. We might also note that these cost savings calculations did not include the significant outlays spent on the Office of the Asset Sales and IT Outsourcing organization. These costs were viewed not as an additional cost to these four contracts, but as a separate sunk overhead.

11. We might reflect on the paradox that although debates around whether or not government functions might be outsourced are largely conducted in commercial terms, the experience of cases such as this suggests that it is higher-level governance risks that can in reality dominate the legitimacy of arrangements.

12. Wedel (2005:42) notes the example here of Harvard's on-site director in Moscow appearing to be acting interchangeably as a representative of the United States (with formal management authority through Harvard over other US contractors), Russia (being 'authorised to sign off on some high-level privatisation decisions on behalf of the Russian state'), as well as his girlfriend's companies.

13. What was most surprising in this episode was the government's response. Surprisingly, the government defended the relationship, saying his predecessor as finance director, Rees Aronson, had also been provided by KPMG! Adding petrol onto these flames, KPMG also stated that 'its employee had been seconded to Labour and said the Liberal Democrats were using the services of another member of its staff, with a third about to be placed with the Tories'! Crucially, a KPMG spokeswoman noted that this public arrangement had been declared to the electoral commission which monitors political donations. This did nothing to allay the fears of public sector unions who not surprisingly labelled this situation as an 'incestuous relationship'.

14. KPMG's involvement in taxation matters again hit the media more recently with the news that it 'was the latest of the big four international firms to clash with American regulators. In August [2005] it accepted a $US456 million fine and a period of supervision by a former head of the US Securities and Exchange Commission after admitting that it had helped wealthy American clients to evade tax' (Searjeant, 2005).

15. Another case here was that of Dr Michael Wooldridge (Federal Minister for Health) who 'promised $A5 million in taxpayers funds to the Royal Australian College of General Practitioners to set up an office in Canberra only months before he quit politics and joined the organisation as a consultant' (Australianpolitics.com, 2002).

16. Kirby (2004) reported on the closeness of Macquarie Bank to the state government of New South Wales in the following terms:

> Macquarie will need all the marketing research it can get, because there are perceptions that the bank is making big profits from exploiting the inadequacies of today's infrastructure market and the less sophisticated local, state and federal authorities it deals with. Deflecting the claims of government or bureaucratic connections will be even harder. Although other investment banks have former politicians from both sides of politics working for them, Macquarie has more than most.

Alan Stockdale, a former Liberal Victorian treasurer; Warwick Smith, a former Liberal opposition spokesman on communications; Max Moore-Wilton, a former secretary to the Prime Minister's Department; and Lucy Brogden, the wife of New South Wales Opposition Leader John Brogden, are all employed by the bank or entities closely associated with it. The bank's executive chairman, David Clarke, is a former federal treasurer of the Liberal Party. Even Crosby Textor, the consultancy behind the bank's attitudes survey, is run by Liberal Party stalwarts: Lynton Crosby is a former federal director of the Liberal Party, and Mark Textor was the pollster for the Liberal Party in the 2001 election.

17. The potential use of any mega-credit card arrangement by government should send waves of concern to citizens worried about the misalignment of political incentives in the short term compared with long-term implications and financial outcomes.

REFERENCES

Alford, J. (1993) 'Towards a new management model: beyond "managerialism" and its critics', *Australian Journal of Public Administration*, **53** (2), 135–48.

Australian National Audit Office (ANAO) (2000), *Implementation of Whole-of-Government Information Technology and Infrastructure Consolidation and Outsourcing Initiative*, audit report no. 9, Canberra: ANAO.

Australianpolitics.com (2002), 'Ex-ministers: jobs after government', 20 February, accessed 30 January, 2006 at www.australianpolitics.com/new/2002/02-02-20a.html.

Bakvis, H. (1997), 'Political-bureaucratic relations and the role of management consulting firm', paper presented at the Conference on Political Control of the Bureaucracy in Democratic-Systems, Ben Gurion University of the Negev, Beersheva, Israel.

Barrett, P. (2003), 'Public private partnerships – are there any gaps in public sector accountability?', speech given to Australian Council of Public Accounts Committees 7th Biennial Conference, Melbourne, 3 February.

Beale, D. (1994), *Driven by Nissan? A Critical Guide to the New Management Techniques*, London: Lawrence & Wishart.

Bennett, C.J. (1991), 'Review article: what is policy convergence and what causes it?', *British Journal of Political Science*, **21**, 215–33.

Center for Public Integrity (2005), 'Summary: lobbyists double spending in six years – Center for Public Integrity reveals extent of lobbying influence', accessed at: www.publicintegrity.org/lobby/default.aspx?act=summary.

Christensen, M. (2003), 'The "Big Six" consulting firms: creating a new market or meeting a public policy need?', *Australian Journal of Business and Social Inquiry*, **1** (1), accessed at www.scu.edu.au/ajbsi/papers/vol1/christensen.html.

Considine, M. (1999), as cited in Correy, S. (1999), 'The consultocracy', *ABC Radio National – Background Briefing*, 27 July, accessed at www.abc.net.au/rn/talks/bbing/stoies/s31095.htm.

Considine, M. and M. Painter (1997), 'Introduction', in M. Considine and M. Painter (eds), *Managerialism: The Great Debate*, Melbourne: Melbourne University Press, pp. 1–11.

Consulting Times (2004), accessed at www.consultingtimes.com.

Correy, S. (1999), 'The consultocracy', *ABC Radio National – Background Briefing*, 27 July, accessed at www.abc.net.au/rn/talks/bbing/stoies/s31095.htm.

Cox, R. (1999), 'Ideas, policy borrowing and welfare reform', paper presented to the Conference on Global Trajectories: Ideas, International Policy Transfer and Models of Welfare Reform, at the European University Institute, Florence, 25–26 March.

Deloitte Touche Tohmatsu (2005), 'Sustaining growth – Deloitte Touche Tohmatsu worldwide member firms 2005 review', Deloitte: New York, accessed at www.deloitte.com.

Dolowitz, D. and D. Marsh (1996), 'Who learns from whom: a review of the policy transfer literature', *Political Studies*, **44** (2), 343–57.

Edelman, M. (1977), *Political Language: Words that Succeed and Policies that Fail*, New York: Institute for the Study of Poverty.

Ernst & Young (2005), 'Global Review 2005', accessed at www.ey.com.

Freeman, R. (1999), 'Policy Transfer in the Health Sector', accessed at www.pol.ed.ac.uk/research/working_paper1.html.

Frew, W. (2005), 'Green Carr denies climate of conflict in new role', *Sydney Morning Herald*, 28 October, p. 2.

Greer, P. (1994), *Transforming Central Government: The Next Step Initiative*, Buckingham: Open University Press.

Guthrie, J. (1999) as cited in Correy, S. (1999), 'The consultocracy', *ABC Radio National – Background Briefing*, 27 July, accessed at www.abc.net.au/rn/talks/bbing/stoies/s31095.htm.

Guttman, D. and B. Willner (1976), *The Shadow Government: The Government's Multi-Dollar Give-away of its Decision-making Powers to Private Management Consultants, Experts and Think Tanks*, New York: Pantheon.

HM Treasury (2003), *PFI: Meeting the Investment Challenge*, London: HMSO.

HMSO Efficiency Unit (1994), *The Government's Use of External Consultants*, London: HMSO.

Hodge, G.A. (2000), *Privatisation: An International Review of Performance*, Theoretical Lenses on Public Policy Series, Boulder, CO: Westview Press.

Hodge, G.A. (2004) 'Governing with accountability: has parliament abdicated in the age of public–private partnerships?', paper presented to the National Conference of Parliamentary Environment and Public Works Committees, Melbourne, 11–14 July.

Hodge, G.A. and C. Greve (eds) (2005), *The Challenge of Public–Private Partnerships: Learning from International Experience*, Cheltenham, UK and Northampton, MA, USA: Edward Elgar.

Hodge, G.A. and A. Rouse (2004), 'Outsourcing government information technology services: an Australian case study', paper presented at the Determinants of Performance in Public Organisations Seminar, Cardiff University, 6–8 May.

Hood, C. (1991), 'A public management for all seasons?', *Public Administration*, **69**, 3–19.

Hood, C. and M. Jackson (1991), *Administrative Argument*, Aldershot: Dartmouth.

Ikenberry, G.J. (1990), 'The international spread of privatisation policies: inducements, learning and "policy band wagoning"', in E. Suleiman and J. Waterbury (eds), *The Political Economy of Public Sector Reform and Privatisation*, Boulder, CO: Westview Press, pp. 88–110.

Kennedy Information (2004), *Executive Summary: The Global Consulting Marketplace 2004–2006: Key Data, Trends and Forecasts*, Peterborough, NH: Kennedy Information.

Kennedy Information (2005), *Report Summary: The Global Consulting Marketplace 2005–2007: Key Data, Trends and Forecasts*, Peterborough, NH: Kennedy Information.

Kessides, I. (2004), 'Reforming infrastructure: privatization, regulation and competition', World Bank policy research paper, Washington, DC.

Kingdon, J. (1984), *Agendas, Alternatives and Public Policy*, Boston, MA: Little, Brown.

Kirby, J. (2004), 'Macquarie's enemies', *Business Review Weekly*, 26 (9) (11 March), 12.

KPMG (2004), 'KPMG International Annual Review 2004', accessed at: www.kpmg.com.

KPMG (2005a), 'KPMG International Annual Review 2005', accessed at: www.kpmg.com.

KPMG (2005b), 'KPMG Member Firms' Financial Performance', accessed at: www.kpmg.com.

Kuber, M. (1986), *Management Consulting: A Guide to the Profession*, Geneva: ILO.

Maguire, K. (2003), 'Labour "in conflict of interest"', *The Guardian*, 16 May, accessed 7 February, 2006 at www.guardian.co.uk/guardianpolitics/story/ 0,,957118,00.html.

Minority Staff, US House of Representatives (2003), 'Fact sheet – the Bush Administration's contracts with Halliburton', Minority Staff Committee on Government Reform, US House of Representatives, May, acessed at www.why-war.com/files/pdf_admin_contracts_halliburton_factsheet.pdf.

Nedley, A. (1999), 'Policy transfer and the developing-country experience gap: taking a southern perspective', accessed at www.york.ac.uk/depts/poli/esrc/papers/ nedley.htm.

Nellis, J. (2005), *Privatisation in Developing Countries: A Summary Assessment*, Cairo: Egyptian Center for Economic Studies.

Northern Ireland Audit Office (NIAO) (2004), *Use of Consultants: Report by the Comptroller and Auditor General*, Belfast: NIAO.

Osborne, D. and T. Gaebler (1992), *Reinventing Government: How the Entrepreneurial Spirit is Transforming the Public Sector*, New York: Addison-Wesley.

Parsons, W. (1995), *Public Policy: An Introduction to the Theory and Practice of Policy Analysis*, Aldershot, UK and Brookfield, US: Edward Elgar.

Peet, J. (1998), 'The new witch-doctors: a survey of management consultancy', *The Economist*, 13 February, 2–18.

Phillips, M.M. (2003), 'The World Bank wonders about utility privatization', *Wall Street Journal*, 21 July.

Pollitt, C. (1990), *Managerialism in the Public Services: The Anglo-American Experience*, Oxford: Basil Blackwell.

Pollitt, C. (1993), *Managerialism and the Public Services: Cuts or Cultural Change in the 1990s?*, second edition, Oxford: Blackwell Publishers.

Pollitt, C. (1996), 'Anti-statist reforms and new administrative directions: public administration in the UK', *Public Administration Review*, **56**, 81–7.

PricewaterhouseCoopers (2004), '2004 global annual review – perspectives and values,' accessed at www.pwc.com.

PricewaterhouseCoopers (2005), '2005 global annual review – perspectives and values,' accessed at www.pwc.com.

Rose, R. (1993), *Lesson Drawing in Public Policy: A Guide to Learning Across Time and Space*, Chatham, NJ, Chatham House.

Rouse, A.C. and B. Corbitt (2003a), 'The Australian Government's abandoned infrastructure outsourcing program: what can be learned?', *Australian Journal of Information Systems*, **10** (2), 81–90.

Rouse, A.C. and B. Corbitt (2003b), 'Revisiting IT outsourcing risks: analysis of a survey of Australia's top 1000 organizations', proceedings of the 14th Australasian Conference on Information Systems, Perth, 26–28 November.

Russell, E.W., E. Waterman and N. Seddon (2000), *Audit Review of Government Contracts: Contracting, Privatisation, Probity and Disclosure in Victoria 1992–1999, An Independent Report to Government*, vol 3, Melbourne: State Government of Victoria.

Saint-Martin, D. (2000), *Building the New Managerialist State: Consultants and the Politics of Public Sector Reform in Comparative Perspective*, Oxford: Oxford University Press.

Saint-Martin, D. (1998), 'The new managerialism and policy influence of consultants in government: an historical-institutional analysis of Britain, Canada and France', *Governance*, **11** (3), 319–56.

Schneider, A. and H. Ingram (1988), 'Systematically pinching ideas: a comparative approach to policy design', *Journal of Public Policy*, **8** (1), 61–80.

Schuber, M. and J. Koutsoukis (2004), 'All aboard the gravy train', *The Age*, 14 August, p. 5.

Searjeant, G. (2005), 'Global expansion pushes KPMG turnover up by 16%', *The Times*, 24 October.

Stiglitz, J. (2002), *Globalization and its Discontents*, London: Penguin Books.

Stiglitz, J. (2003), *The Roaring Nineties: A New History of the World's Most Prosperous Decade*, New York: W.W. Norton & Company

Stone, D. (2001), 'Learning lessons, policy transfer and the international diffusion of policy ideas', Centre for the Study of Globalisation and Regionalisation working paper no. 69/01, University of Warwick.

Stone, D. (2003), 'The "Knowledge Bank" and the global development network', *Global Governance*, **9** (1), 43–61.

Tenix (2005), 'The Tenix Group', accessed 12 December at www.tenix.com.au.

United Nations (1993), *Management Consulting: A Survey of the Industry and Its Largest Firms*, New York: UN.

Vasagar, J. and R. Evans (2002), 'KPMG: the government's friend', *The Guardian*, 1 July, accessed 7 February, 2006, at http://business.guardian.co.uk/story/0,3604,747089,00.html.

Wedel, J. (1998), *Collision and Collusion: The Strange Case of Western Aid to Eastern Europe*, New York: St Martin's Press.

Wedel, J. (2000), 'Harvard, the Chubais clan and Russia's ruin', *National Interest*, **59** (Spring), 23–34.

Wedel, J. (2005), 'U.S. foreign aid and foreign policy: building stronger relationships by doing it right!', *International Studies Perspective*, **6**, 35–50.

Williamson, A. (1999), testimony before the Committee on Banking and Financial Services of the United States House of Representatives, 21 September, Washington, DC.

World Bank Operations Evaluation Department (2005), '2004 annual review of development effectiveness: the World Bank's contributions to poverty reduction', accessed at www.worldbank.org/oed.

7. Regulation in the age of globalization: the diffusion of regulatory agencies across Europe and Latin America

Fabrizio Gilardi, Jacint Jordana and David Levi-Faur[1]

The era of privatization is also the era of regulation. This seems paradoxical since privatization and the family of policies that were associated with it was supposed to lead to deregulation and the promotion of freer markets. Yet, with the advance of privatization, it became clear that freer markets often imply more rules, regulatory agencies and regulators (Vogel, 1996; Levi-Faur, Jordana and Gilardi, 2005). A quarter of a century after the launch of the Thatcherite revolution, it is possible to conclude that the new economic order involves everything but deregulation. On the contrary, it may be better captured by the notion of 'regulatory capitalism'. The modern capitalist state, rather than hollowing out, is restructuring itself in a way that allows it to exert administrative controls over the economy. The major evidence of such a capacity is the mushrooming since the mid-1980s of new regulatory institutions worldwide. Surveying 36 countries in Europe and Latin America and 7 economic and social sectors, we were able to document the establishment of 174 agencies in the period up to 2002. Most of these agencies (107) were established in the 1990s. While specialized regulatory agencies were always important institutions in some sectors (largely finance) and countries (notably the United States), since the late 1980s they have become common across a broad range of sectors worldwide. Early work on regulatory capitalism concentrated either on broad changes that forced state structures to adapt (for example, Müller and Wright, 1994; Majone, 1997a) or on national and sectoral institutions and path dependencies that mediated reforms (for example, Eberlein, 1999). This chapter offers a new perspective by examining interdependencies in the diffusion of regulatory reforms among countries and sectors (Levi-Faur, 2002; Jordana and Levi-Faur, 2005, 2006; Gilardi, 2005a).

We have two aims. The first is to shed some light on the puzzle of a regulatory explosion amid privatization and other neoliberal reforms. The second is to examine three broad theories on the diffusion of regulatory agencies. In both cases we are taking the first steps in a discussion of these issues rather than providing conclusive answers. Instead of treating the process of the establishment of regulatory authorities across countries and sectors as an aggregation of discrete events, we examine the cases of the establishment of such authorities as interdependent events. We suggest that these regulatory reforms across countries and sectors are unlikely to be independent events. Thus, we aim to bridge the gap between 'structural' approaches to regulatory reforms and a diffusion perspective,[2] and to demonstrate that our perspective sheds some new light on the nature of the reforms and the meaning of the new order.

Our analysis draws on three broad theories. The first focuses on the dynamics of regulatory competition between countries and suggests that the major force behind the reforms is the state's dependency on capital and its consequent need to appease capital by committing itself to providing an attractive market environment and a stable regime for investment. The more privatized the economy is, the greater its dependency on private capital (Lindblom, 1977; Poulantzas, 1969) and consequently the greater the need to create a stable institutional design that is technocratic rather than political in its orientation. By way of exploring these relations, we examine the process of regulatory reforms both in economic sectors that are most likely to reflect the dependency on capital and in social sectors that are most likely to reflect social demands. The second theory focuses on regional integration processes and suggests that regulatory agencies and regulations in general are part of a new political, social and economic order that is characterized by processes of integration. The extensive processes of regionalization in Europe make it an interesting case whereby to examine these theories, while the weaker case of regionalization in Latin America extends the variations in our cases and thus provides some inferential leverage. The third theory highlights the role of policy learning and 'knowledge' actors in the diffusion of policy reforms. It suggests that the major agents of reforms are professionals who both enjoy the authority of expertise and participate in transnational networks and communities. Variations in the diffusion of the reforms across these spheres and regions reflect less the effects of regulatory competition and regionalism than the gaps in the power of the professional groups that dominate these spheres. Strong professional groups, mainly economists, promote the creation of autonomous regulatory agencies as an institutional resource that consolidates their position in the policy process. In this process they consolidate the power of a new group of professionals, the regulocrats (Levi-Faur, Jordana and Gilardi, 2005).

Our discussion proceeds as follows. We start with the explanandum and present a comprehensive picture of the diffusion of the reforms, presenting some indications of the strong association between privatization and the emergence of regulatory agencies. Each of the following three sections examines the process of regulatory change in light of our broad theories about the driving forces of regulatory diffusion – regulatory competition, regional integration and knowledge actors. We conclude by assessing the explanatory power of the three approaches and we offer some suggestions as to the direction of future research.

THE EXPLANANDUM: REGIONS AND SPHERES OF REGULATION

The empirical basis for our observations is expressed in a database that includes information on the creation of regulatory institutions in 36 countries across seven economic and social sectors. The data cover four economic sectors (telecoms, electricity, competition and securities and exchange) and three social sectors[3] (food safety, pharmaceuticals and environment). What we have identified, counted and classified are administrative agencies that have been separated from ministerial hierarchies. The agencies' degrees of separation vary widely across sectors and countries (Gilardi, 2002; 2005b), but their status as distinct entities and the central focus on regulation in their mission statement serve as criteria for inclusion in the database.[4] Looking at both social and economic sectors provides a more general view of the relations between regulation and privatization and allows us to test the three theories of regulatory diffusion across a broad set of sectors. For the same reason we also focus on Europe and Latin America, two large regions that were engaged during the 1990s in a frantic process of regulatory reform. We cover developments in 19 Latin American countries and 17 European countries (EU 15 before the latest enlargement plus Norway and Switzerland).

Figure 7.1 presents the growth of regulatory institutions across our data-set since 1960. It suggests immediately that, while not new, the phenomenon of the 'agencification' of regulatory agencies gained momentum in the 1970s and boomed in the 1990s. Figure 7.2 presents the growth of regulatory agencies since 1980 in each of the two regions. As can be seen, most of the new agencies (98 in total) are found in Europe, where the penetration rate is 82 per cent compared with 57 per cent for Latin America and 69 per cent for the data-set as a whole. Patterns of growth are similar between the regions but Europe seems to move forward much faster. Figure 7.3 adds information as it presents the growth of regulatory agencies across Europe and Latin America in the social and economic areas. Two points should be noted. First, the tendency to establish regulatory agencies is stronger in economic sectors than in social sectors. The 174 agencies identified in 2002 include 35 in telecommunications, 34 in securities and exchange, 32 in electricity and 25 in competition. The rest, with a significantly lower penetration rate, are in social regulation, including 18 in pharmaceuticals, 16 in environmental and 14 in food safety.

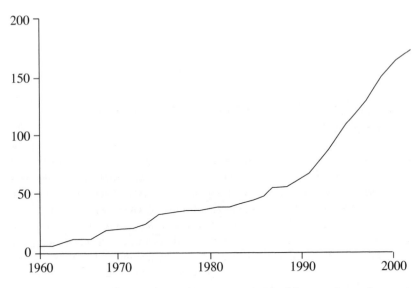

Figure 7.1 The diffusion of regulatory agencies in 36 countries and 7 sectors

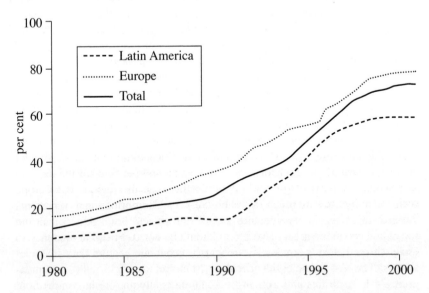

Figure 7.2 The diffusion of regulatory agencies: the general trend in Latin America and Europe

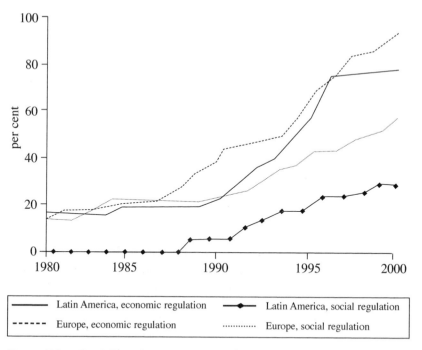

*Figure 7.3   The diffusion of regulatory agencies: Latin America vs Europe,
economic vs social regulation*

Second, most of the variation between the rates of penetration of regulatory
agencies in Europe and Latin America seems to be due to a significantly lower
rate of penetration in the social sectors (26 per cent for Latin America
compared with 64 per cent in Europe). While regulatory agencies are also
more popular in Europe than in Latin America in the economic arenas (with a
penetration rate of 98 per cent in Europe compared with 80 per cent in Latin
America), the difference is much smaller and is mainly due to the weaker
tendency to establish regulatory authorities in the area of competition in Latin
America (there is almost parity in the two utilities sectors and finance).

In an effort to capture comprehensively the similarities and variations,
Table 7.1 presents four different aspects of the process of change, comparing
the growth of social and economic regulation in the two regions. First, our data
unambiguously show a clear tendency to create more regulatory agencies
across both regions and both spheres of regulation (cell I). Second, and at the
same time, the diffusion of this institutional innovation is stronger in the field
of economic regulation than social regulation (cell II). Most countries have
established autonomous authorities in economic regulatory domains such as

*Table 7.1   The spread of regulatory agencies in Europe and Latin America:
variations and similarities across regions and spheres of
regulation*

	Similarities across social and economic regulation	Variations across social and economic regulation
Similarities across Europe and Latin America	**I** **Observation**: new regulatory agencies are established across both areas and across both regions (i.e., they spread in all cases)	**II** **Observation:** the spread of economic regulatory agencies is faster than that of social regulation
Variations across Europe and Latin America	**III** **Observation:** The spread of both social and economic regulatory agencies is greater in Europe than in Latin America across all spheres of regulation (largely due to competition agencies)	**IV** **Observation:** While there are variations between the spread of economic regulation agencies and that of social agencies in both regions, the gaps are larger in Latin America

utilities, whereas autonomous regulators are less common in social regulatory domains such as food safety and pharmaceuticals. Third, the spread of regulatory agencies in Europe is greater than in Latin America (cell III). This is true for both economic and social regulations. As mentioned above, in economic regulation the variations are mainly due to the gap in the number of competition agencies, and the gap is narrower in economic than in social regulations. Finally, while there are variations between the spread of economic regulation agencies and that of social regulation agencies in both regions, the gaps are larger in Latin America (cell IV). These variations in the spread of the regulatory agencies are useful sources of evidence about the factors that made these widespread changes possible (Levi-Faur, 2004).

DOES REGULATORY COMPETITION MATTER?

Can the theory of regulatory competition deal adequately with the patterns of variations and similarities that we found in the diffusion of regulatory agencies? The theory of regulatory competition suggests that the major force behind the reforms is the state's dependency on capital and its consequent need to appease capital through a commitment to an attractive market environment and a stable regime for investment (Tiebout, 1956; Geradin and McCahery, 2004; Radaelli, 2004). Good institutions are said to be causally linked to better economic performances (North, 1990; Williamson, 2000). In our context, institutions that reinforce delegation are expected to enhance the credibility of elected politicians and to improve the likelihood of private investment (Henisz, 2000, 2002; Carruth, Dickerson and Henley, 2000).

The establishment of autonomous regulatory authorities is interpreted as a signal to investors. This signal conveys the following message: we are serious about private investment and we assure you that we are committed to a stable institutional design that separates technocratic decision making from political decision making, and puts constraints on any reversal of policies. Delegating regulatory competencies to an agency that is independent from political pressure is a possible solution in that it is meant to enhance the credibility of commitment after market decisions are made (Spiller, 1993; Levy and Spiller, 1994; Majone, 1996, 1997b, 2001). The dynamics of institutional design in the context of regulatory competition is therefore a sequential game between investors and governments. Both sides are interested in investment at time t, but then, after more or less irreversible investment decisions have been taken, investors incur the risk that the government will renege on its commitment at time $t + 1$. If investors anticipate this, they may decide not to invest, so as to avoid expropriation. This outcome is suboptimal for both governments and investors. Governments may thus try to make their regulatory commitments more credible, and one of the major instruments in this credibility game is the autonomous regulatory agency. Very important from a diffusion perspective is not only the game between government and investors but also the game between governments who compete for investment. As soon as a government gains credibility by adopting a certain institutional design, other governments might want to narrow the credibility gap by adopting the same institutional design. This does not imply that the institutional design itself is efficient or otherwise; it may or may not have significant regulatory effects.[5] All that matters is that other governments have adopted it and that it has come to be perceived as a mechanism to enhance credibility. Thus, to explain the rapid diffusion of the institution itself we need to consider only the signal that it conveys to potential investors.

The theory of regulatory competition makes a lot of sense when examined against some of our observations. First, the theory expects a strong correlation in certain sectors between privatization and the likelihood of the establishment of regulatory authorities. This expectation is clearly documented in a study of the diffusion of privatization and regulatory agencies in telecoms and

electricity worldwide (Levi-Faur, 2005) as well as on the diffusion of regulatory institutions in Europe (Gilardi, 2005a). Second, the notion of regulatory
competition speaks directly to the interdependency of decisions taken in
different countries as they compete for capital, either with all other governments or perhaps especially with their peers (Elkins and Simmons, 2005).
Third, the notion of regulatory competition seems to be compatible with the
variations in the diffusion of regulatory institutions across economic and
social arenas. Since regulatory competition is tailored to private investment,
we can expect regulatory agencies to be more likely to appear in economic
than in social domains (Gilardi, 2002, 2005b). In this respect the theory of
regulatory competition seems to fit quite nicely with observation II (see
Table 7.1).

Yet the theory of regulatory competition makes less sense when examined
against some other aspects of our data. Take privatization, for example. We
have referred to the strong correlation between privatization and the establishment of regulatory agencies. Yet, when this relationship is examined across
two sectors where data are available worldwide (Levi-Faur, 2003), we find
that the likelihood of the establishment of regulatory agencies is stronger for
telecoms than for electricity. This is a counter-intuitive finding, as the problem
of policy credibility and policy reversal is more acute in electricity than in telecoms. In telecoms, a rapid technological cycle makes the financial returns on
telecoms investment relatively short (in some cases around five years), and
thus the risks for investors are less acute. By contrast, electricity investment
locks the investor into a commitment of a decade or more. If countries are
establishing regulatory agencies in order to attract investors, they should have
done so more in electricity than in telecoms. Moreover, the supply of money
for telecoms investment in the 1990s seemed to transform relations between
investors and governments: it was telecoms investors that were competing for
permission to invest, rather than governments competing for investors. The
theory of regulatory competition, while elegant and while certainly supplying
a good explanation for certain aspects of the establishment of regulatory agencies, seems to fall short of accounting for some of the puzzles of the new order.

The shortcomings of the theory of regulatory competition are evident also
with regard to three of the patterns of diffusion that we have observed. We
observe that new regulatory agencies are established around both areas and
across both regions (cell I, Table 7.1). Yet regulatory competition cannot deal
with the diffusion of regulatory agencies in social arenas, where regulatory
competition is only indirect. True, the establishment of regulatory agencies in
social arenas is a weaker trend than in the economic arena, but it is still a
meaningful one, and why should investors be more attentive to the effects of
economic regulation when social regulation is increasingly costly? In addition,
the theory of regulatory competition is not compatible with our expectation

about the establishment of regulatory agencies in the two regions when one considers the credibility gap between them. Since long-term investment in Latin America is more risky than in Europe, one might reasonably expect that the signals that Latin American governments would convey would be stronger than those conveyed by European governments. Yet the propensity of governments in the two regions to establish regulatory agencies in economic arenas was found to be similar (cells II and IV).

It could be suggested at this stage that the theory of regulatory competition does well when applied to the diffusion of regulatory agencies in economic sectors, but fails to account for patterns of variations when social sectors and regional variations are taken into account. On balance, it explains some of the most important observations well but falls short of explaining others. Overall assessment should, however, await comparison with other theories.

DOES REGIONALIZATION (EUROPEANIZATION) MATTER?

A second theoretical perspective focuses on theories of regionalization in general and of Europeanization in particular. The link between regulation and regional integration has been made most explicitly by Giandomenico Majone, who argues forcefully that the European Union is a 'Regulatory State' mainly because the EU has limited fiscal powers and human resources and thus finds it necessary to rely on regulation as a major tool of governance (Majone, 1994). Much of its budget is committed to specific policy goals (such as subsidies to farmers), and the 'Brussels bureaucracy' is, despite its image, very small in comparison with national bureaucracies. Under these constraints it makes sense to put special emphasis on the regulatory dimensions of policy making. Causality, according to Majone, runs from the EU to the member states: 'in order to take an active part in the formulation of all these new rules in Brussels, and then to implement them at national level, member states have been forced to develop regulatory capacities on an unprecedented scale' (Majone, 1997a:146). A broader application of Majone's thesis links regional organization in general to the development of regulatory institutions at the national level, and variations in the diffusion of regulatory reforms to the degree of depth of regionalization across Europe and Latin America and the scope of their interest (social versus economic). By Majone's own account, legal prohibitions (the Meroni Doctrine and Article 7 of the EC Treaty) constrain the ability of the EU to create fully independent regulatory institutions at the European level (Majone, 2002b); but the author portrays this situation as anachronistic, and forecasts that functional pressures will lead to the creation of an elaborate structure of regulatory institutions at the European level in the not too distant future (Majone, 2002c:303)

Certain aspects of the advance of regional integration are of particular interest for our discussion. The first is that the process of integration is stronger in Europe than in Latin America. This gap is evident at both the political and economic levels. The European Union is moving towards the creation of political structures that are in some respects federalist or at least aim to become so. Mercosur, the closest equivalent in Latin America, is much more limited in its scope (four core countries), newer (1991) and devoted mainly to trade issues.[6] While different in terms of institutionalization, in both regions economic reasoning is a major tool of legitimization. Regional integration is often directed towards the coordination of production (such as the coal and steel community), industrial policy (large projects such as the Airbus) and trade liberalization (the major issue since the 1980s). Social issues are secondary on the agenda of both the European Union (on the European social deficit, see Leibfried and Pierson, 1995) and Mercosur. Finally, it is important to note that regional regulatory powers are mainly entrenched in laws while administrative powers (and much room of manoeuvre) are left to the national level. More specifically, the administrative muscle of the European Regulatory State (and this is all the more true for Latin America) resides at the level of the member states and not at the regional level. To the extent that regulatory agencies were established at the EU level they were mainly established with limited competencies and (with the notable exception of the European Central Bank) in the social sectors.

Several dimensions of regional integration are intensively discussed in Europe. One dimension of the discussion deals with the continuum of coercion versus voluntarism: to what extent is the establishment of regulatory authorities at the national level a result of the coercive power of the EU? Another partly complementary view examines the effects of Europeanization in terms of a continuum of learning versus imitation: to what extent was the establishment of regulatory authorities at the national level the result of a process of policy learning within the EU as opposed to mimetic behaviour propelled by group pressures? Of these two conceptual dimensions, the latter seems the more useful as the 'coercive' powers of the European Union are limited in several respects. First, the EU is an agent rather than a principal, and hence its powers are largely derived from the delegation of authority from the member states to EU institutions. Second, the dominant decision making procedures are consensual and, while a dissenting country may have to acquiesce in certain policies even under consensual procedures, it is unlikely that many would find themselves in this position on any given issue. Third, the EU's powers do not touch on issues of ownership (so public versus private ownership is a matter for national discretion). Fourth, in all the relevant directives that deal with regulatory issues, member states are not required to establish regulatory authorities. While there is a requirement to separate ownership from regulatory functions in order to ensure that the regulator will treat all market actors fairly, the particular institutional design that is chosen need not include delegation, and is essentially a matter of national choice. This notwithstanding, the Commission has closely scrutinized the regulatory structures in place, and has repeatedly stressed that lack of independence is a strong market disincentive. Even though the Commission has been careful to note that the organization of a regulatory authority is a matter of national choice, its preference for independent regulatory agencies is quite clear (see, for telecoms, for example, European Commission, 1999:9–10, 2000:12–14, 2002:18). In some cases, such as Belgium, the Commission has explicitly pressed for greater independence for the regulatory authority (European Commission, 1999:10; 2000:12).

The limits of hierarchical models of EU policy making and politics are evident when the regulatory structures at the EU level are examined. Efforts to create European regulatory agencies either ended in failure (for telecoms, see Levi-Faur, 1999; Michalis, 2003) or did not eventuate at all (for electricity, see Jakobsen, 2004). The only case of a powerful regulatory agency at the European level, though hardly a marginal exception, is the European Central Bank (Jabko, 2004; McNamara, 2001). As an alternative to influential regulatory agencies at the regional level, which have proved so difficult to establish, the European Commission is promoting networks of national regulators and a coherent European identity in each sector through the exchange of information (Dehousse, 1997). A group of European telecommunications regulators was established in Paris in 1997 to coordinate on issues of market liberalization, as well as acting as an advisory body to the European Commission. For electricity, the Florence Forum of European regulators was established in 1998 and its existence formalized in 2003.[7] In the regulation of securities and exchange, a Federation of European Securities Commissions (FESCO) was set up in 1997 (Muegge, 2004). The common denominator of all these arrangements is their low level of institutionalization.

Developments in social regulation are somewhat more institutionalized, but are still soft in their nature. The European Environmental Agency was established in 1990, the European Agency for the Evaluation of Medicinal Products in 1995 and the European Food Safety Agency in 2002. However, the creation of European agencies could have stimulated the creation of national agencies in these sectors. It would be a mistake to examine the work of these agencies with the hierarchical models of domestic politics. They have no compulsory regulatory powers. The function of the environmental agency is to provide 'timely, targeted, relevant and reliable information to policy making agents and the public'. The mission of the pharmaceutical agency is to provide high-quality evaluation of medicinal products, to advise on research and development programmes and to provide useful and clear information to users and health professionals. Finally, the food agency focuses on the provision of 'independent scientific advice and clear communication on existing and emerging risks'. The emphasis of all three is on voluntarism in implementation and influence through the provision of information and the creation of networks of regulators across the member states (Dehousse, 1997).[8] The importance of these networks stems from the fact that regulators interacting in networks care about their professional reputation and thus attempt to preserve their autonomy (Majone, 2002a:387). In addition, a common professional identity can develop, thus favouring similar changes across countries. Thus, European agencies have contributed as coordinators of European networks to the creation of transnational professional and epistemic communities. As we will see in the following section, these have been important drivers of the diffusion of regulatory agencies.

Are these theories of regional integration consistent with the empirical evidence on the relations between privatization and regulatory reform? And how fit are they to deal with the various patterns of the diffusion of regulatory reforms? Our analysis indicates that they do so poorly. This is not to suggest that Europeanization and, by proxy, regionalization do not matter, but they matter perhaps to different issues and through different channels.

Let us first test what we know about regional integration processes in our two regions against our observations. Regional integration explanations are unconvincing when one examines the general patterns of the diffusion of regulatory agencies. They do somewhat better, however, in relation to variations in the diffusion of regulatory agencies in social arenas. First, they fare better in respect of the deficit in regulatory agencies in social arenas when compared with economic arenas, since the regional integration schemes of the 1980s and 1990s were oriented to economic issues. If regional integration is a relevant factor in the creation of regulatory agencies, it might well be that the social regulatory deficit at the national level is really a reflection of the same deficit at the regional level. Second, regional integration might account for the deficit in social regulation in Latin America when compared with Europe. The political ambitions of proponents of integrated Europe rest to a large extent on the democratic legitimacy of the European project. Responsiveness to social demands is one tool that may serve to enhance that legitimacy, a product of the political dimension of the EU that is missing in Latin America. Thus, European policies for social regulation may be considered a consequence of the much greater integration of Europe than of Latin America. The weakness of political ambitions of this sort in Latin America makes such considerations redundant and in consequence, so this line of reasoning suggests, there are fewer social regulatory agencies in that region.

DO TRANSNATIONAL NETWORKS OF PROFESSIONALS MATTER?

A third perspective on the diffusion of regulatory agencies suggests that regulatory change, captured here through the diffusion of new regulatory institutions, is too widespread and too intimately driven by knowledge actors to be explained exclusively by power and institutional configurations. Instead, it suggests that 'transnational networks of professionals' are major agents of change in general and regulatory change in particular. The argument fits well with the world-society literature that suggests that convergence on new institutions and policy is driven by 'Western rationality' (Meyer and Rowan, 1977; Meyer et al., 1997). The professionals and, more narrowly, the scientists are the transnational agents who spread this rationality through interaction in professional networks (Keck and Sikkink, 1998; Stone, 2003, 2004).

Five major suggestions of the world-society approach (WSA) are of special importance here. First, the WSA suggests that there are startling degrees of global cultural, social and organizational convergence across the world. Second, diffusion of cultural, social and organizational forms of governance from the centre to the periphery is increasing. Third, these processes of social, organizational and cultural convergence are driven by 'a world society' of international organizations and related transnational networks that share Western liberal norms and preferences. Fourth, in the making of these changes, science, scientific experts and the educational system constitute the central framework, agents and channels of change (Drori et al., 2003). As will soon be clear, this insight that connects 'norm diffusion' to 'science and rationalization' is critical to our understanding of the diffusion of regulatory agencies. Fifth, the high level of social, cultural and organizational isomorphism that exists today is far too great to be explicable solely in functionalist terms. Scientific knowledge 'constitute[s] the religion of the modern world' (Meyer et al., 1997:166). Consequently, some of what is usually portrayed as regulatory learning is sometimes mere regulatory emulation.

The emphasis of the WSA on the diffusion of norms may be more strongly entrenched by explicit reference to knowledge actors, namely, transnational networks of professionals and experts. Thus, our explanation here stands on a second pillar: transnational networks of professionals are the backbone of what might be labelled 'Global Civil Society' (Kaldor, 2003). These transnational networks of experts include both 'non-state actors' in the global system (Higgott, Underhill and Bieler, 2000) and intergovernmental networks of experts (Slaughter, 2004). Their importance is suggested to be increasing and following growing interaction across borders and the celebrated authority of scientific knowledge. The decline of trust in social institutions may also affect the sciences, though apparently less than other forms of authority. The rise of science and of professionalism is also enhanced by the 'end of ideology', as ideologies used to place some important constraints on scientific autonomy. Some of these transnational networks are civil in the sense that their members are autonomous from the state; but others – including (most importantly for our purpose) networks of regulators – are not (Slaughter, 2004). Regulators are increasingly professionals and this professionalism entails some autonomy. A simple dichotomy between intergovernmentalist and supranationalist networks might be misleading in our case. Networks of regulators are acting under two masters, their epistemic community and the particular sovereign of each of their states. As noted above, participation in networks makes regulators sensitive to their reputation among their peers; in addition, regulatory networks can develop common professional norms, which, as with most other groups, tend to value autonomy. The epistemic authority tends to be transnational, yet the political masters are usually national governments and follow their domestic logic of policy making. Institutional autonomy (following delegation to independent regulatory agencies) makes it easier for regulators to follow the policy preferences that are driven from their epistemic community and makes it more difficult for politicians to control regulators. Transnationalization therefore increases the power of some experts and some agents of the state and decreases the power of others. As noted above, the creation of networks of agencies at the EU level coordinated by European agencies might also be a sign of this trend.

We suggest that the authority of science as a force of convergence on 'Western rationality' as suggested by the WSA, the diffusion of new information through transnational networks, and the interest of knowledge actors in enhancing their autonomy may add up to a powerful explanation for the co-diffusion of privatization and regulatory agencies and its framing as policy learning. At the centre of such an explanation would stand the economics profession and its advocacy of the market for the efficient use of resources under the assumption of scarcity, while the formation of core ideas and high priests of knowledge rests with the universities, especially American ones (Dezalay and Garth, 2002; Bockman and Eyal, 2002; Kogut and Macpherson, 2003). Their advocacy of market instruments and of the work of global markets is essential for the advance of privatization policies, while their growing recognition of the importance of institutions explains the transformation of the independent regulatory agency from a peculiar institution of limited diffusion into global best practice. The knowledge-orientation nature of these networks creates authority patterns that are celebrated as policy learning. Yet policy learning is not divorced from power, and power comes into play in our account in two forms. First, the institutional platform for the authority of knowledge, the agency, is guaranteed through the delegation of authority and legal provisions that protect it from certain political controls (for instance, ministers and their staff). Second, expertise and knowledge are segmented into various branches of knowledge and in consequence 'professional competition' is one of the characteristics of the new order. In some cases, when market issues prevail, professionals such as lawyers or engineers find themselves less influential than economists.

The spread of privatization has many causes, but an important and probably necessary one was the widespread endorsement of it by the economics profession. At the same time we find that economists have been much more dominant in the new agencies regulating the utilities, supplanting, to some extent, the traditional role of engineers in these areas; moreover, the new regulators typically enjoy high academic qualifications. It is not uncommon to find that entry into the higher echelons of a regulatory agency requires a second or a third degree. What economists gained others lost, and the measure of their success is expressed not only in their dominance in the economic regulatory agencies but also in the failure of natural scientists and engineers to achieve similar autonomy in social arenas. The modest diffusion of the institution of the independent regulatory agency in the social arenas is therefore mainly due to the gap in professional prestige and the uneven resources of different experts, but also to the limited introduction of market mechanisms in such cases. Note that this theoretical perspective can also deal with the gaps in the diffusion of social regulatory institutions between Latin America and Europe, in so far as other professional communities, for example physicians and biologists, also gained strong scientific recognition in the European context, and were able to push for their own regulatory governance institutions.

CONCLUSION

We are now in a position to conclude the study of the diffusion of regulatory agencies in the context of the rise of the new global order of what we called 'regulatory capitalism'. We documented the diffusion of these agencies as they spread across regions and regulatory arenas. We then examined our four main patterns of variations and similarities in the diffusion of regulatory agencies, testing regional and sectoral variations against three theories of political and economic change. We first observed that new regulatory agencies have been established across both areas (economic and social regulation) and across both regions (Europe and Latin America) and suggest that this pattern is best explained by the professionalization of the world's elites and their growing interactions in transnational forums. By contrast, the regulatory competition argument, which emphasizes credibility, while it accords with the diffusion of regulatory agencies in the economic arena, cannot explain why agencies also spread in social regulation. Similarly, privatization is likely to be linked to agencies in utilities, but is surely unrelated to the establishment of social agencies. Europeanization, finally, has obviously little to say with respect to the diffusion of regulatory agencies in Latin America.

Second, we found that the spread of regulatory agencies in economic regulation has been faster than in social regulation. This observation is one of the main predictions of the regulatory competition argument: as countries compete for capital, they are more likely to create regulatory agencies to improve their credibility in domains where attracting private investment is important, that is, in economic regulation in general, but especially when markets in utilities are opened. In this context, privatization is an important predictor of agency creations. The 'transnational network of professionals' argument can in principle account for this trend if those networks are more powerful in economic than in social regulation, but we could not demonstrate this point empirically. Our evaluation is therefore undetermined, as further empirical work would be needed. As for Europeanization, the very limited development of European agencies in the economic domain (with the notable exception of the European Central Bank (ECB)) indicates that this thesis performs poorly as an explanation of the observed difference between economic and social regulation.

Third, we showed that the spread of regulatory agencies is greater in Europe than in Latin America. It should be noted that cross-regional differences arise with social regulation, since economic agencies have spread equally in both Europe and Latin America. Therefore, explaining differences between the two regions amounts to explaining why more social agencies have been established in Europe than in Latin America, which is our fourth observation. We thus discuss our third and fourth observations together. The regulatory competition thesis can explain the similarity between the regions, namely, that economic agencies have diffused everywhere. By contrast, it cannot explain the difference in social regulation. The regulatory competition thesis, which emphasizes credibility, simply cannot explain why agencies exist in social domains. Thus, from this perspective the puzzle is not why so few social agencies exist in Latin America, but why so many have been established in Europe. The regulatory competition thesis has no answer for this. The 'network of experts' hypothesis does better. As we have shown, such networks are more developed in Europe, notably thanks to the EU-level agencies that coordinate national authorities in the fields of pharmaceuticals, the environment and food safety. It thus appears that Europeanization also matters here, though not in its strong, hierarchical form. As a result, the 'network of experts' and Europeanization arguments appear embedded and cannot easily be separated empirically. However, taken together these two mechanisms seem capable of explaining why there are fewer social agencies in Latin America and, as a result (given that the number of economic agencies in the two regions is very similar), the spread of regulatory agencies is overall greater in Europe. There are reasons to believe that this difference is due to the gaps in the power of professionals in the two regions, which can in part be linked to the more developed institutional framework of social regulation at the EU level.

All in all, how well do the three theories fit the observations? From the regulatory competition perspective the diffusion of agencies in social regulation is highly puzzling, yet the theory explains quite well the spread of economic agencies in the two regions, as well as the fact that economic agencies are much more widespread than social ones. However, it does less well if one expects that the pressures for economic and institutional reform will be greater in Latin America, since European countries can shield themselves better from the pressures of globalization (fortress Europe). The approach thus has both considerable strengths and some important limitations. The 'networks of expertise' approach fills in the gaps left by regulatory competition, and can account for the wider spread of social agencies in Europe. In addition, it is the only theory that can account for our first observation, namely, that despite the existing variations regulatory authorities have spread in all the sectors and countries examined here. The regional integration approach, finally, is clearly the weakest. At best, integration promoted a differential in the spread of regulatory agencies in a very soft way, through the establishment of regulatory networks at the EU level. This channel of diffusion, however, can to a large extent be understood as policy learning in networks of expertise within the specific institutional milieu of regional integration; as a consequence, we find that the regionalization thesis cannot be completely disentangled from the WSA. In order to supply more robust answers to the questions that we have raised here, more research is required. We hope that future research will find this chapter useful.

NOTES

1. This chapter was prepared for the 'Privatisation and Market Development: Global Movements in Public Policy Ideas' workshop convened by Graeme Hodge. We would like to acknowledge and thank Graeme Hodge for the invitation to participate in the workshop as this paper wouldn't have been written without him.
2. On the distinction between structural and diffusion perspectives, see Elkins and Simmons (2005), Levi-Faur (2005).
3. Conventionally, regulation is termed 'economic' when it deals with the price, entry, exit and service of an industry, and 'social' when it concerns non-economic issues such as public health or environmental protection (Meier, 1985:3).
4. The date of establishment is the date of the creation of the agency, or of its reform in the event that autonomy was granted subsequently. Data on the establishment of agencies are taken from Jordana and Levi-Faur's (2004) database on regulatory agencies.
5. It is interesting to note that very little is known about the extent to which the establishment of regulatory agencies actually increases the credibility of regulatory policy.

6. Historically, in Latin America economic and political integration initiatives have been quite common since the nineteenth century, starting during the wars of independence. But most failed at a very early stage and none achieved a solid basis. More recently, during the second half of the twentieth century, many integration initiatives emerged, of very different kinds. Many were of a subregional nature, such as Mercosur (Argentina, Brazil, Uruguay and Paraguay) or the various attempts to create the Centro-American Union. Others were limited to trade issues, as for example the 1994 NAFTA (a free trade agreement between Mexico, the US and Canada). Yet perhaps the more active institutions for integration are in fact the development banks, such as the Inter-American Development Bank, which is now creating regional networks and promoting the diffusion of new governmental technologies.
7. Decision 2003/796/EC of 11 November 2003.
8. However, the pharmaceutical regulatory agency, probably an exception in the whole social sphere, has de facto obtained important regulatory capabilities in some areas (Feick, 2002).

REFERENCES

Bockman, J. and G. Eyal (2002), 'Eastern Europe as a laboratory for economic knowledge: the transnational roots of neoliberalism', *American Journal of Sociology*, **108**, 310–52.

Carruth, A., A. Dickerson and A. Henley (2000), 'What do we know about investment under uncertainty?', *Journal of Economic Surveys*, **14** (2), 119–53.

Dehousse, R. (1997), 'Regulation by networks in the European Community: the role of European agencies', *Journal of European Public Policy*, **4** (2), 246–61.

Dezalay, Y. and G.B. Garth (2002), *The Internationalization of Palace Wars: Lawyers, Economists and the Contest to Transform Latin American States*, Chicago, IL: University of Chicago Press.

Drori, G.S., J.W. Meyer, F.O. Ramirez and E. Schofer (2003) *Science in the Modern World Polity: Institutionalization and Globalization*, Stanford, CA: Stanford University Press.

Eberlein, B. (1999), 'Etat régulateur en Europe', *Revue française de science politique*, **49** (2), 205–30.

Elkins, Z. and B. Simmons (2005), 'On waves, clusters, and diffusion: a conceptual framework', *Annals of the American Academy of Political and Social Sciences*, **598**, 33–51.

European Commission (1999), *Fifth Report on the Implementation of the Telecommunications Package*, COM(1999)537, Brussels: EC.

European Commission (2001), *Sixth Report on the Implementation of the Telecommunications Package*, COM(2000)814, Brussels: EC.

European Commission (2002), *Eighth Report on the Implementation of the Telecommunications Package*, COM(2002)695, Brussels: EC.

Feick, J. (2002). 'Regulatory Europeanization, national autonomy and regulatory effectiveness: marketing authorization for pharmaceuticals', MPIfG discussion paper 02/6, Cologne.

Geradin, D. and J. McCahery (2004), 'Regulatory co-operation: transcending the regulatory competition debate', in Jacint Jordana and David Levi-Faur (eds), *The Politics of Regulation*, Cheltenham, UK and Northampton, MA, USA: Edward Elgar, pp. 90–123.

Gilardi, F. (2002), 'Policy credibility and delegation to independent regulatory agencies: a comparative empirical analysis', *Journal of European Public Policy*, **9** (6), 873–93.

Gilardi, F. (2005a), 'The institutional foundations of regulatory capitalism: the diffusion of independent regulatory agencies in Western Europe', *Annals of the American Academy of Social and Political Sciences*, **598**, 84–101.

Gilardi, F. (2005b), 'The formal independence of regulators: a comparison of 17 countries and 7 sectors', *Swiss Political Science Review*, **11** (4), 139–67.

Henisz, W.J. (2000), 'The institutional environment for multinational investment', *Journal of Law, Economics, and Organization*, **16** (2), 334–64.

Henisz, W.J. (2002), 'The institutional environment for infrastructure investment', *Industrial and Corporate Change*, **11** (2), 355–89.

Higgott, R., G. Underhill and A. Bieler (2000), *Non-State Actors and Authority in the Global System*, London: Routledge.

Jabko, N. (2004), 'The political foundation of the European regulatory state', in Jacint Jordana and David Levi-Faur (eds), *The Politics of Regulation*, Cheltenham, UK and Northampton, MA, USA: Edward Elgar, pp. 200–217.

Jakobsen, M.L. (2004), 'European electricity liberalisation: ideational globalisation or Europeanisation?', paper presented at the Second Pan-European Conference on EU Politics, Bologna, 24–26 June.

Jordana, J. and D. Levi-Faur (2005), 'Towards a Latin American regulatory state? The diffusion of autonomous regulatory agencies across countries and sectors', *Annals of the American Academy of Social and Political Science*, **598**, 102–24

Jordana, J. and D. Levi-Faur (2006), 'The diffusion of regulatory capitalism in Latin America', *International Journal of Public Administration*, **29** (4), 335–66.

Kaldor, M. (2003), 'The idea of civil society', *International Affairs*, **79** (3), 583–93.

Keck, M.E. and K. Sikkink (1998), *Activists Beyond Borders: Advocacy Networks in International Politics*, Ithaca, NY: Cornell University Press.

Kogut, B. and M.J. Macpherson (2003), 'The decision to privatize as an economic policy idea: epistemic communities, palace wars, and diffusion', paper presented at the International Diffusion of Political and Economic Liberalization Conference, Harvard University, 3–4 October.

Leibfried, S. and P. Pierson (eds) (1995), *European Social Policy: Between Fragmentation and Integration*, Washington, DC: Brookings Institution.

Levi-Faur, D. (1999), 'Governing the Dutch telecommunications reform: regulation, deregulation and re-regulation within the context of European policy regime', *Journal of European Public Policy*, **6** (1), 102–22.

Levi-Faur, D. (2002), 'Herding towards a new convention: on herds, shepherds, and lost sheep in the liberalization of the telecommunications and electricity industries', Nuffield College political papers series W6-2002, University of Oxford.

Levi-Faur, D. (2003), 'The politics of liberalisation: privatisation and regulation-for-competition in Europe's and Latin America's telecoms and electricity industries', *European Journal of Political Research*, **42**, 705–40.

Levi-Faur, D. (2004), 'Comparative research designs in the study of regulation: how to increase the number of cases without compromising the strengths of case-oriented analysis', in Jacint Jordana and David Levi-Faur (eds), *The Politics of Regulation*. Cheltenham, UK and Northampton, MA, USA: Edward Elgar, pp. 177–98.

Levi-Faur, D. (2005), 'The global diffusion of regulatory capitalism', *Annals of the American Academy of Political and Social Sciences*, **598**, 52–66.

Levi-Faur, D. and G. Sharon (2004), 'The rise of the British regulatory state: transcending the privatization debate', *Comparative Politics*, **37** (1), 105–24.

Levi-Faur, D., J. Jordana and F. Gilardi (2005), 'Regulatory revolution by stealth: on the citadels of regulatory capitalism and the rise of regulocracy', paper presented to the ECPR Conference, 8–10 September, Budapest.

Levy, B. and P.T. Spiller (1994), 'The institutional foundations of regulatory commitment: a comparative analysis of telecommunications regulation', *Journal of Law, Economics, and Organization*, **10** (2), 201–46.

Lindblom, C. (1977), *Politics and Markets: The World's Political Economic Systems*, New York: Basic Books.

Majone, G. (1994), 'The rise of the regulatory state in Europe', *West European Politics*, **17** (3), 77–101.

Majone, G. (1996), 'Temporal consistency and policy credibility: why democracies need non-majoritarian institutions', European University Institute working paper RSC no. 96/57, San Domenico di Fiesole.

Majone, G. (1997a), 'From the positive to the regulatory state: causes and consequences of changes in the mode of governance', *Journal of Public Policy*, **17** (2), 139–67.

Majone, G. (1997b), 'The new European agencies: regulation by information', *Journal of European Public Policy*, **4** (2), 262–75.

Majone, G. (2001), 'Nonmajoritarian institutions and the limits of democratic governance: a political transaction-cost approach', *Journal of Theoretical and Institutional Economics*, **157**, 57–78.

Majone, G. (2002a), 'The European Commission: the limits of centralization and the perils of parliamentarization', *Governance*, **15** (3), 375–92.

Majone, G. (2002b), 'Delegation of regulatory powers in a mixed polity', *European Law Journal*, **8** (3), 319–39.

Majone, G. (2002c), 'Functional interests: European agencies', in John Peterson and Michael Shackleton (eds), *The Institutions of the European Union*, Oxford: Oxford University Press, pp. 292–325.

McNamara, K. (2001), 'Where do rules come from? The creation of the European Central Bank', in Alec Stone Sweet, Wayne Sandholtz and Neil Fligstein (eds), *The Institutionalization of Europe*, Oxford: Oxford University Press, pp. 155–70.

Meier, K.J. (1985), *Regulation: Politics, Bureaucracy, and Economics*, New York: St. Martin's Press.

Meyer, J.W. and R. Brian (1977), 'Institutionalized organizations: formal structure as myth and ceremony', *American Journal of Sociology*, **83** (2), 340–63.

Meyer, J.W. and B. Rowan (1977), 'Institutionalized organizations: formal structure as myth and ceremony', *American Journal of Sociology*, **83**, 340–63.

Meyer, J.W., J. Boli, G. Thomas, and F. Ramirez (1997), 'World society and the nation-state', *American Journal of Sociology*, **103** (1), 144–81.

Michalis, M. (2003), 'The governance of European telecommunications: towards soft-policy coordination', paper presented at the ECPR General Conference, 18–21 September, Marburg.

Muegge, D. (2004), 'Financial Liberalization and the European Integration of Financial Market Governance', unpublished manuscript, ASSR, University of Amsterdam.

Müller, W.C. and V. Wright (1994), 'Reshaping the state in Western Europe: the limits to retreat', *West European Politics*, **17** (3), 1–11.

North, D. (1990), *Institutions, Institutional Change, and Economic Performance*, Cambridge: Cambridge University Press.

Poulantzas, N. (1969), 'The problem of the capitalist state', *New Left Review*, **58**, 67–78.

Radaelli, C.M. (2004), 'The puzzle of regulatory competition', *Journal of Public Policy*, **24** (1), 1–23.

Slaughter, A.M. (2004), *A New World Order*, Princeton, NJ: Princeton University Press.

Spiller, P.T. (1993), 'Institutions and regulatory commitment in utilities privatization', *Industrial and Corporate Change*, **2** (3), 387–450.

Stone, D. (2003), 'The knowledge bank and the global development network', *Global Governance*, **9** (1), 43–61.

Stone, D. (2004), 'Transfer agents and global networks in the transnationalisation of policy', *Journal of European Public Policy*, **1** (3), 545–66.

Tiebout, C. (1956), 'A pure theory of local expenditures', *Journal of Political Economy*, **64** (5), 416–24.

Vogel, S. (1996), *Freer Markets, More Rules*, Ithaca, NY: Cornell University Press.

Williamson, O. (2000), 'The new institutional economics: taking stock, looking ahead', *Journal of Economic Literature*, **38**, 595–613.

8. Prospects for the global regulation of markets

George Gilligan

INTRODUCTION[1]

This chapter considers developments regarding approaches to regulating markets in an era of globalization[2] and increasing privatization (the latter generally occurring in more developed jurisdictions). The issue of global regulation of markets, whether it is feasible, and if so how, is one that is increasing in strategic importance, as evidenced by the upward trend over the last 25 years in the numbers, intensity and impact of multilateral regulatory agreements and models. Examples of this trend include amongst many others: the World Trade Organization (WTO),[3] the Financial Action Task Force (FATF)[4] and the World Intellectual Property Organization (WIPO).[5] It is likely that the strategic significance of multilateral regulatory agreements and models will increase as nation states, regional groupings, international organizations and private sector actors (whether transnational corporations, local firms, professional associations, organized labour, various interest groups, individuals or others) seek to manage the tensions and potentials for conflict that inevitably accompany trading contexts. The pressure around the world is intensifying to find and maintain workable regulatory arrangements within which countries and those industry sectors that are becoming more global in their character can continue to grow and provide trickle-down wealth effects to their related communities. It is difficult to over-estimate the importance of finding regulatory models that can help not only to avoid war and other types of conflict, but also to assist in countering the threats posed by factors such as terrorism and organized crime, and to facilitate efforts to reduce the devastating effects of poverty and lack of productive capacity that blight so many countries and millions of people around the world, especially in Africa.

The issues of poverty and hunger are obviously not new, but what has changed in recent years is the increasing interaction and economic interdependence between countries as the processes of globalization evolve. It is no longer really feasible for individual nation states to act as independently of other nation states as they might have done in the past, as developments in information technology and liberalization of markets gather pace. These factors have helped to prompt increases in the extent and impact of networked governance, not only in the public sector, but also in business arenas both locally and internationally. Amongst the effects of these developments is the reality that constantly permeating within political and business discourses (and regarding certain matters sometimes these separate discourses can merge) are issues such as:

- Can global markets be regulated and, if so, who decides who, or what, regulates such markets?
- Are multilateral modes of regulating markets desirable and can they be legitimated?
- What are the relative advantages of regulation and deregulation, and correspondingly, the relative strengths/weaknesses of existing relevant international protocols, which include mechanisms such as treaties, conventions and frameworks of understanding?
- What should be the appropriate roles of national, regional and international regulatory actors?
- What are the potentials of both private and public sector organizations, and of non-governmental organizations (NGOs) to act as regulatory actors in different industries?
- What are the realities of regulatory capacity for both developed and less developed economies?
- Can the inevitable effects of self-interest on both regulated and regulating actors be identified, balanced and incorporated into models of regulating global markets that can work relatively well?

These are huge questions requiring conceptual and empirical analysis way beyond the scope of a single chapter, or one suspects a single book. However, the approach that this chapter takes in order to throw light on at least some of the issues associated with the global regulation of markets is to engage in three case studies of different sectors: financial services, intellectual property and pharmaceuticals. Not all contemporary industries are global in character, for example housing or utilities, but a growing number are becoming increasingly so, and these include financial services, intellectual property and pharmaceuticals.

This chapter discusses whether there are common patterns of multilateral regulatory development emerging across these three industries that might be generalized across other sectors of the global economy. Of particular interest is the potential of legitimacy-based approaches for understanding how models and processes of multilateral regulation emerge and are sustained. An analysis grounded in legitimacy is useful when analysing how regulatory regimes evolve because norms and standards in regulation can be local, national or international phenomena. These regulatory norms and standards can interact at a number of levels in different ways. Of particular importance is the political reality that as regulatory space and discourse become both more congested, and more contested, struggles for regulatory supremacy intensify. Thus, regulatory knowledge and expertise can become resources to be employed strategically in regulatory disputes, whether these disputes are local, regional or global in nature (Dezelay, 1993). A legitimacy-based approach can work well as a window on the regulation of intensely competitive environments such as financial services, intellectual property and pharmaceuticals. In industries such as these private, corporate and state forces intermingle as regulatory control is sculpted by negotiated and symbiotic relationships. The process is not static, but one of continuing political adaptation within a regulatory setting, in which actors can erode existing regulation, lobby for change and take advantage of competition between different regulatory regimes. Deconstructing these forces at work can be a devilishly difficult task, but an emphasis on notions of social construction, and acknowledgement of the practical reality that multiple maps of meaning are available to, and can be utilized by, people, and/or, organizations, can help to identify emerging trends in regulation.

It is my contention that analysis grounded in legitimation theory possesses interpretative potential for evaluating this somewhat cloudy world of regulatory praxis. However, there are a few features which must be emphasized before utilizing the explanatory tool that is legitimacy. First, legitimacy is not a given, but rather an elastic and complex phenomenon. Second, legitimacy influences the composition of power relations, and throws light on systems of power, not only how power functions as an ongoing process, but also how power relations originate. These are what Beetham (1991) refers to as the developmental and self-confirming stories of power and legitimation. Third, legitimacy is integral to any body of knowledge or system of regulation (Tyler, 1990), and can be highly complex in its form involving not only beliefs, but also consent, both active and passive, as well as other factors such as legality, judicial determination and an inherent potential for differential interpretation. It should be clear to the reader now that understandings of legitimacy can be highly fluid and so it can be helpful to perceive of legitimacy as a continuum of belief and evaluation. A useful model is Suchman's (1995) three-tier hierarchy of organizational legitimacy. At its base is pragmatic legitimacy, which is rooted in self-interested calculation, with an emphasis on notions of exchange and value; the central tier is moral legitimacy, where normative evaluations are crucial, with an emphasis on notions of consequence, procedure, structure and personality; and at the apex of the legitimacy hierarchy is cognitive legitimacy when comprehensibility is crucial, with an emphasis on notions of predictability and plausibility. When people, either as individuals, or as members of organizations, assess the relative validity of institutions, sets of rules and practices such as how much they should comply with multilateral regulatory initiatives, they are making decisions in relation to how, why and where, such institutions, rules and practices are situated on this continuum of legitimacy. This chapter employs this explanatory model to evaluate developments in the multilateral regulation of the three selected sectors: financial services, intellectual property and pharmaceuticals.

FINANCIAL SERVICES

Throughout history almost as long as there has been trade in commodities or services, in the majority of situations at some stage financial services expertise has been utilized. Historically conflict often has been a feature of trading contexts and so (as stated earlier) in recent times as the momentum of globalization has grown, there has been a trend towards increased multilateral regulatory protocols to act as circuit-breaker mechanisms that can help to mediate trade tensions. Consequently given both its international character and its strategic trading importance, the financial services sector, unsurprisingly (as indicated below in Table 8.1), has seen a substantial number of multilateral regulatory initiatives.

The organizations and agreements in Table 8.1 do not comprise an exhaustive list of multilateral regulatory activity in financial services, but they do indicate its deepening and intensifying influence. Trade conflicts occur in most industries at some time, but the financial services sector has become a site of particular tensions and conflicts, partly as a result of it being one of the most integrated elements of the contemporary global economy. For example, in recent times in some international forums there has been growing tension regarding the levels of transparency and international cooperation provided by certain jurisdictions. It is quite possible that some of these contemporary tensions in financial services are likely to be reproduced in other areas of global trade in the future as part of ongoing trade-offs and interaction between a globalizing economy, the need to counter terrorism in a post-September 11 world,[6] the rise of networked governance and legitimate jurisdictional self-interest. Of special interest for this paper is the growing push for increased transparency and exchange of information in financial services from multilateral organizations such as the Organisation for Economic Co-operation and Development (OECD),[7] the FATF and the European Union (EU).[8] In particular, as a case study in emerging styles of global regulation production, this chapter focuses on the activities in recent years of the OECD with regards to what it terms *harmful tax practices* and the ramifications of its initiatives in

Table 8.1 Key initiatives within global financial markets

Year	Initiative	Nature	Primary drivers of initiative
1930	Bank for International Settlements	International financial regulator	US, UK and France
1944	Bretton Woods Agreement	International financial regulator	G10 countries[a]
	World Bank (WB)		G10 countries
1945	International Monetary Fund (IMF)	International monetary regulator	G10 countries
1947[b]	General Agreement on Tariffs and Trade (GATT)	Multilateral agreement on trade in goods	US
1960	Organisation for Economic Co-operation and Development (OECD)	International cooperative body	
1962[c]	Group of Ten Central Bank Governors (G10)	International banking regulator	G10 countries
1963[d]	Model Tax Convention on Income and on Capital	Multilateral agreement on taxation	OECD
1971[e]	Eurocurrency Standing Committee (ECSC) (renamed Committee on the Global Financial System (CGFC) in 1999)	International cooperative body	G10 countries
1973	International Accounting Standards Committee (IASC) (renamed International Accounting Standards Board (IASB) in 2001)		
1974	Committee on Banking Supervision (Basle Committee (BS))	International banking regulator	UK
	Interamerican Association of Securities Commissions and Similar Organizations (IAASCSO) (renamed International Organization of Securities Commissions (IOSCO) in 1984)[f]	International cooperative body	
1975	Basle Concordat[g]	Multilateral agreement	
	Group of 7 (G7)[h]	International policy group	
1983	Principles for the Supervision of Banks' Foreign Establishments (Basle Concordat)[i]	Multilateral agreement	
1986–1994[j]	Uruguay Round	Multilateral negotiations	US, EU, Japan and the private sector

Year		Type	
1988	International Convergence of Capital Measurement and Capital Standards (Basle Committee)[k]	Multilateral agreement	
1989	Second Banking Directive[l]	Regional agreement	European community
	Financial Action Task Force[l]	Intergovernmental body	US
1992	International Association of Insurance Supervisors (IAIS)	International organization	
1995	General Agreement on Trade in Services (GATS)	Multilateral agreement	India and Brazil[m]
1999[n]	Financial Stability Forum	International cooperative body	G7
	Group of 20 (G20)[o]	International cooperative body	G7
2001–06	Basel II: International Convergence of Capital Measurement and Capital Standards: A Revised Framework	Multilateral agreement	
2005	Savings Tax Directive	Regional agreement	EU

Notes:

a. In 1962 the G10 comprised the following member countries: Belgium, Netherlands, Canada, Sweden, France, Germany, United Kingdom, Italy, United States and Japan. Despite Switzerland being added to the Group of 10 in 1964, the Group continued with its initial name (IMF, 2003)
b. Drahos (2001)
c. Porter (2002)
d. OECD
e. Porter (2002)
f. Porter (1993)
g. Basle Committee (1997)
h. Members of the G7 are as follows: Canada, Japan, France, United Kingdom, Germany, United States and Italy (IMF, 2003)
i. Basle Committee (1983)
j. WTO (2004)
k. Basle Committee (1997)
l. FATF (2004)
m. Bhagwati (1988)
n. Porter (2002)
o. The G20 group comprises the following member countries and the European Union: Argentina, France, Japan, South Africa, Australia, Germany, Korea, Turkey, Brazil, India, Mexico, United Kingdom, Canada, Indonesia, Russia, United States, China, Italy, Saudi Arabia (IMF, 2003)

this area (hereafter referred to as the OECDHTPI). The OECD's work in this area has been carried largely through its Forum on Harmful Tax Practices which is a subsidiary body of the OECD's Committee on Fiscal Affairs (OECD, 2004).

Of course the interconnected realities of governance in contemporary life in general, and in trade in particular, mean that no multilateral regulatory initiative can act in isolation from the effects of other multilateral regulatory activity and reactions to such activity. Nevertheless as can be seen in the discussion below, by using the OECDHTPI as a window on current multilateral regulatory discourse in relation to financial services, an emerging issue seems to be whether erosion of sovereignty is becoming a price to be paid by at least some of those jurisdictions that want to participate in the global market for financial services. Sovereignty itself is very much a disaggregated phenomenon which operates at a range of levels and can be difficult to quantify (Jackson, 2003). Consequently, contemporary understandings regarding what constitutes sovereignty and how much sovereignty is appropriate can be in continuing flux. These fluctuations feed into the development of regulatory structures and processes that are more internationalized and also into a variety of emerging modes of governance that have a capacity for impacts of broad international scope. However, if there is a trend towards levels of jurisdictional sovereignty being linked to levels of participation in multilateral regulatory protocols, then it raises interesting issues of legitimacy and how prevailing sets of power relations will manifest within both national and international regulatory infrastructures of financial services, and indeed of other sectors.

As international organizations such as the FATF and the OECD assume a higher profile in how international regulatory financial infrastructures are constructed there is an increasing emphasis on the legitimacy of the specific processes involved. This is especially the case regarding who actually participates in the relevant decision making and their relative levels of influence on decisions that are made. As can be seen in the brief history below of the OECDHTPI, it is this issue of perception of legitimacy that has been crucial in how the discourse and regulatory struggle has unfolded over the last five years.

In May 2000, the OECD declared that the following 34 jurisdictions met the OECD's technical criteria as tax havens: Andorra, Anguilla, Antigua and Barbuda, Aruba, Bahamas, Bahrain, Barbados, Belize, British Virgin Islands, Cook Islands, Dominica, Gibraltar, Grenada, Guernsey/Sark/Alderney, Isle of Man, Jersey, Liechtenstein, Liberia, Maldives, Marshall Islands, Monaco, Montserrat, Nauru, Netherlands Antilles, Nieue, Panama, Samoa, Seychelles, St Lucia, St Christopher & Nevis, St Vincent and the Grenadines, Tonga, Turks and Caicos, US Virgin Islands and Vanuatu (OECD, 2000). In April 2002, the OECD published its second blacklist and classified as *Uncooperative Tax*

Havens: Andorra, Liberia, Liechtenstein, Marshall Islands, Monaco, Nauru, and Vanuatu (OECD, 2002). In May 2003, the list was revised to remove Vanuatu (OECD, 2003a). The list was further revised in December 2003 to remove Nauru (OECD, 2003b). In March 2004, in its Progress Report the OECD (2004) confirmed that it still considered Andorra, Liberia, Liechtenstein, the Marshall Islands and Monaco as Uncooperative Tax Havens. Unsurprisingly the blacklisting process attracted criticism from affected jurisdictions, in particular from the Caribbean Community (CARICOM) (2000:8–9) which condemned the OECDHTPI as:

> activities, which are unilateral and inconsistent with international practice, are designed to impair the competitive capacity of Caribbean jurisdictions in the provision of global financial services . . .
>
> Heads of Government took note that each of the reports, was prepared by bodies in which the Caribbean has no representation and was based on incomplete information and on standards set unilaterally by these bodies. They deplored the fact that the lists were published with the objective of tainting jurisdictions in the eyes of the investment community and the international financial market. They condemned the actions of the OECD . . . as contrary to the tenets of a global market economy promoted by G7 countries. They reiterated that the proposed OECD actions have no basis in international law and are alien to the practice of inter-state relations.

Mr Owen Arthur, Prime Minister and Finance Minister of Barbados, was scathing of what he saw as the OECD's 'institutional imperialism' and its 'use of crude threats and stigmas' (tax-news.com, 2000). The basis of the arguments of these critics is an attack on the legitimacy, and therefore the credibility, of the initiatives of the OECD. Since the first protests by Caribbean leaders in 2000 a loose coalition opposed to the OECDHTPI has emerged. It includes the Secretariat of the International Tax and Investment Organization (ITIO),[9] which has questioned whether OECD members and other developed economies are: 'prepared explicitly to confirm their intention of abiding by the standards demanded of small and developing economies (tax-news.com, 2001). As part of its campaign to de-legitimate the OECDHTPI, the ITIO in conjunction with the Society of Trust and Estate Practitioners (STEP),[10] commissioned the international law firm Stikeman Elliott (2000) to produce a critique of the review procedures engaged in by the OECD regarding the OECD's strategy. Other high-profile pressure groups such as the National Taxpayers Union (NTU), and the Center for Freedom and Prosperity (CFP), have emerged to argue strongly against the overall legitimacy of the OECDHTPI. Both the NTU and the CFP are based in Washington, DC, and have lobbied fiercely to members of the US Congress and the White House Administration of President Bush to persuade them to oppose the OECDHTPI (Mitchell, 2001). Also, the Commonwealth Secretariat (2000:9) has been critical of the OECD:

> While the OECD has called for transparent and open tax regimes from offshore
> finance centres, its own process for seeking international cooperation has been less
> than transparent and inclusive. Multi-lateralisation of this process would be desirable.

In addition, the legitimacy of the OECD's position has been hurt by the fact
that there is discord on the issue within its own membership. For example,
Belgium and Portugal abstained from the 2001 Progress Report; Luxembourg
recalled its abstention to the OECD's 1998 Report *Harmful Tax Competition:
An Emerging Global Issue* and applied that abstention to the 2001 Progress
Report; and Switzerland applied its 1998 abstention to any follow-up
work undertaken since 1998 (OECD, 2001). The continuing abstention of
Luxembourg and Switzerland was acknowledged in the 2004 Progress Report
(OECD, 2004). Inevitably this undermines to a certain extent the legitimacy of
the OECD and subsequent impact of the OECDHTPI. The concerted efforts of
opponents to the OECDHTPI to position as central to the debates on tax
competition issues relating to the legitimacy of process and mission, and in
particular the notion of a level playing field in tax competition for all jurisdictions has had a considerable impact. Overall the OECDHTPI has had a significant galvanizing effect, but the OECD has been forced to change tack or
else risk seeing its broader efforts on tax competition founder. In cooperation
with opponents to the OECDHTPI, now more gently referred to by the OECD
as Non-OECD Participating Partners (NOPPs), the OECD has established the
Global Forum on Taxation. The Global Forum met in Ottawa in October 2003
and again in Berlin in June 2004, where it produced a policy document to
advance efforts towards achieving a level playing field in tax competition
(Global Forum on Taxation, 2004). The Global Forum is increasing in its
strategic importance and seems to represent an acknowledgement by the
OECD that coordinated actions against harmful tax practices require broad-
based legitimacy and the capability for differential levels of implementation.
As such the OECD might be said to have been challenged relatively successfully by its opponents. The challenge for the OECD is to prove that the
OECDHTPI can make the leap from merely pragmatic legitimacy to the
higher tiers of moral and cognitive legitimacy in Suchman's model of organizational legitimacy. To date it seems fair to say that the OECD has not
achieved that goal and it is not clear yet whether it can.

The saga that is the OECDHTPI thus far, illustrates competing social
constructions of legitimacy being used to explain differing perspectives and
evaluations of the same social phenomena. The lack of support for the listing
processes by many of those listed is not surprising and typifies what some
legitimacy theorists might refer to as *a lack of compliance pull*. Under this
construct of compliance pull, the more legitimate a rule or set of rules, initiative or regulatory framework is perceived to be by those who are subject to its

effects, the greater the level of compliance they will be accorded. Similarly, the lower the levels of legitimacy accorded to specific rules, the lower will be the levels of compliance accorded. Interestingly the compliance pull–legitimacy relationship is an interactive one, so that increasing levels of compliance pull will strengthen the legitimacy and compliance levels achieved by rules/initiatives etc, and decreasing levels of compliance pull will have the opposite effect (Raustalia and Slaughter, 2002). The interactive compliance pull–legitimacy relationship is crucial to any ultimate success that might be achieved by the OECDHTPI. Indeed it is likely that this compliance pull–legitimacy relationship will be crucial to most protocols of global regulation that do emerge and certainly similar pressures can be observed regarding multilateral regulatory initiatives in other sectors, such as intellectual property and pharmaceuticals.

INTELLECTUAL PROPERTY

Intellectual property (IP), represents intangible personal property, that as forms of abstract objects, has a long history of regulation which has traditionally focused on two forms of IP rights – industrial rights, including patents, designs and trademarks, and artistic/creative rights, encompassing copyright (Maskus, 1997). The creation of new types of IP rights, including areas such as plant breeders' rights and the patenting of micro-organisms has seen

> the global architecture of the IPRs [Intellectual Property Rights] regime become increasingly complex, and includes a diversity of multilateral agreements, international organizations, regional conventions and instruments, and bilateral agreements (UNCTAD-ICTSD, 2003:43).

Table 8.2 shows that there have been specific forms of IP regulation at the international level for over a century.

However, the evolution of IP's global regulatory architecture may be traced back to medieval Europe, consolidating on well-engineered national and regional frameworks (Braithwaite and Drahos, 2000). During the period of the Industrial Revolution, the spread of patent and trademark law through Europe gave rise to more comprehensive national regulatory structures (Machlup and Penrose, 1950), culminating in legal protection through both the parliaments and the courts (Ladas, 1975). The nineteenth century saw the shift from chaotic independent, national regulation underpinned by national protectionism towards regional regulation, primarily through bilateral arrangements (Ricketson, 2000). By 1883 approximately 69 agreements covering IP rights, the majority of which were bilateral, were in force (UNCTAD-ICTSD, 2003; Ladas, 1975).

Table 8.2 Key initiatives within global intellectual property market[a]

Year	Initiative	Nature	Primary drivers of initiative
1883	Paris Convention for the Protection of Industrial Property	Multilateral agreement	Argentina, Bolivia, Brazil, Chile, Paraguay, Peru and Uruguay
1886	Berne Convention for the Protection of Literary and Artistic Works	Multilateral agreement	
1889[b]	Montevideo Convention	Regional agreement	
1891	Madrid Agreement (Marks)	Multilateral agreement	
	Madrid Agreement (Indication of Source)	Multilateral agreement	
1893[c]	United International Bureaux for the Protection of Intellectual Property (BIRPI)	International organization	
1925	Hague Agreement	Multilateral agreement	
1947	General Agreement on Tariffs and Trade (GATT)	Multilateral agreement on trade in goods	US
1961	International Convention for the Protection of New Varieties of Plants	Multilateral agreement	
1967[d]	Stockholm Protocol	Multilateral agreement	Developing countries, especially India
	World Intellectual Property Organization	Multilateral organization	United Nations
1970	Patent Cooperation Treaty	Multilateral treaty	
1973–79[e]	GATT Tokyo Round	Multilateral trade negotiations	US and EU

Year	Agreement	Type	Proponents
1980s	Bilateral Investment Treaty (BIT)	Bilateral treaty	US
1983[f]	Caribbean Basin Initiative (CBI)	Regional agreement	US
1986–94	Uruguay Round	Multilateral negotiations	US, EU, Japan and the private sector
1993	North American Free Trade Agreement	Regional agreement	US
1995[g]	World Trade Organization	Multilateral trade body	
	Entry into force of the WTO Agreement on Trade-Related Aspects of Intellectual Property (TRIPS Agreement)	Multilateral trade treaty (global regulatory device![h])	US, EC and Japan
1996	WIPO Copyright Treaty (WCT)	Multilateral treaty	
	WIPO Performers and Phonograms Treaty (WPPT)	Multilateral treaty	
2000	Patent Law Treaty (PLT)	Multilateral treaty	
2001	Doha Declaration on TRIPS	Multilateral negotiations	Least developed countries including Brazil and a number of African countries

Notes:

a. Sources include: UNCTAD-ICTSD (2003); Drahos (2001); Maskus (1997); Caslon Analytics (2004); Barton (2004)
b. Ladas (1975)
c. Bogsch (1992)
d. Sacks (1969)
e. UNCTAD-ICTSD (2003)
f. Drahos, 2001
g. Drahos, 2001
h. Maskus 1997

Table 8.3   International intellectual property regulation[a]

Key international regulatory bodies
* World Intellectual Property Organization (WIPO)
* World Trade Organization (WTO)

Key intellectual property protection treaties
* Berne Convention for the Protection of Literary and Artistic Works (1886)
* Brussels Convention Relating to the Distribution of Programme-Carrying Signals Transmitted by Satellite (1974)
* Convention for the Protection of Producers of Phonograms Against Unauthorized Duplication of Their Phonograms (1971)
* Madrid Agreement for the Repression of False and Deceptive Indications of Source on Goods (1891)
* Nairobi Treaty on the Protection of the Olympic Symbol (1981)
* Paris Convention for the Protection of Industrial Property (1883)
* Patent Law Treaty (PLT) (2000)
* Rome Convention for the Protection of Performers, Producers of Phonograms and Broadcasting Organizations (1961)
* Trademark Law Treaty (1994)
* Treaty on the International Registration of Audiovisual Works (Film Register Treaty) (1989)
* Washington Treaty on Intellectual Property in Respect of Integrated Circuits (1989)
* WIPO Copyright Treaty (WCT) (1996)
* WIPO Performances and Phonograms Treaty (WPPT) (1996)

Key global protection systems treaties:
* Budapest Treaty on the International Recognition of the Deposit of Microorganisms for the Purposes of Patent Procedure (1977)
* Hague Agreement Concerning the International Deposit of Industrial Designs (1925)
* Lisbon Agreement for the Protection of Appellations of Origin and their International Registration (1958)
* Madrid Agreement Concerning the International Registration of Marks (1891)

Key classification treaties
* Locarno Agreement Establishing an International Classification for Industrial Designs (1968)
* Nice Agreement Concerning the International Classification of Goods and Services for the Purposes of the Registration of Marks (1957)
* Strasbourg Agreement Concerning the International Patent Classification (1971)
* Vienna Agreement Establishing an International Classification of the Figurative Elements of Marks (1973)

Note:
a.   Adapted from: 'Treaties and Contracting Parties' (WIPO, 2004), www.wipo.int/treaties/en/

The emergence of a coherent international regulatory framework for IP did not occur until the concluding period of the nineteenth century. This shift towards greater harmonization and mutual recognition was driven by the economics of international trade and the underdeveloped nature of rights attached to IP (Maskus 1997). For Braithwaite and Drahos (2000:59) international harmonization 'arrived in the form of two multilateral pillars', the 1883 Paris Convention for the Protection of Industrial Property (Paris Convention) and the 1886 Berne Convention for the Protection of Literary and Artistic Works (Berne Convention) (refer Table 8.2 and Table 8.3). These pivotal agreements on patents and copyright respectively provided for reciprocal protection and harmonization between national IP regimes, thereby shifting away from the traditional bilateral nature of IP regulation. Initially narrow in focus, both conventions have been amended numerous times to encompass the evolutionary nature of IP, with most nations now signatories to both (Caslon Analytics, 2004).[11] The Paris and Berne multilateral conventions guided the global system of IP regulation into a distinctly superior market, further advanced by the implementation of complementary agreements, as illustrated by Tables 8.2 and 8.3.

Parallel to the development of multilateral and bilateral agreements was the creation of international organizations to administer the various agreements within the global IP architecture. The Paris and Berne conventions provided for the formation of the United International Bureaux for the Protection of Intellectual Property (BIRPI) (Bogsch, 1992). However, it was not until the organization was superseded by a specialized IP agency – the World Intellectual Property Organization (WIPO) established by treaty in 1967 – that there was a markedly stronger shift towards international cooperation (Doern, 1999). As a specialist agency of the United Nations, WIPO's vision is focused on the 'maintenance and further development of the respect for intellectual property throughout the world' (WIPO, 2004). Within the modern context, WIPO signifies the incremental push for greater harmonization within the IP regulatory framework. It is arguable however that whilst the WIPO has provided a foundation for greater harmonization for IP regulation between nation states, its true potential could not be realized. This is predominantly due to WIPO having jurisdiction over only the treaties that it administers, thereby lacking wider enforcement and dispute resolution powers within the global IP regulatory architecture. A lack of enforcement of multilateral IP agreements thereby underpinned many of the developments within the global market during the mid-twentieth century (Braithwaite and Drahos, 2000). Consequently, maturation of the Australian IP protection framework has been analogous to the experience of many developed countries, undergoing incremental legislative development over a century. The first legislative recognition in Australia of industrial property rights occurred with the implementation of the Patents Act 1903 (Commonwealth), with subsequent legislative enactments and amendments encompassing ongoing international legal developments and technological advances (Ricketson, 2000). This need for national statutory underpinning highlights the ongoing legitimacy deficit at the heart of various attempts over the years to regulate intellectual property in multilateral frameworks.

Strengthening of the international IP regulatory framework occurred through the overarching framework of the Agreement on Trade Related Intellectual Property Rights (TRIPS) (see for example Gervais, 1998; Primo Braga, 1996; May, 2000),[12] principally through its ability to 'affect the greatest number of countries' (UNCTAD-ICTSD, 2003:43). The evolution of the TRIPS Agreement as a global regulatory device can be traced essentially to the expansion of trade laws and its subsequent linkage to IP internationally by the US during the 1973–79 General Agreement on Tariffs and Trade Tokyo Round (Doremus, 1996) and domestically during the 1980s and early 1990s (Braithwaite and Drahos, 2000). Requiring stronger standards of protection and enforcement within the IP sector, the US (and its many transnational companies) pressured developing countries to strengthen their legal and enforcement regimes for IP through the application of regional trade agreements such as the North American Free Trade Agreement (NAFTA). A failure to act on provisions for strengthening IP protection within the developing country had the potential to result in US-initiated trade restrictions against the weaker state (Getlan, 1995). The strategy to characterize IP protection as a trade-related problem underpinned not only the US's position at the Uruguay Round, but also that of the EU and Japan (UNCTAD-ICTSD, 2003).

As illustrated by the TRIPS negotiations during the Uruguay Round (1986–93), the US, EU and Japan were predisposed to committing developing nations to global 'minimum standards' through ongoing regulatory standards and compliance monitoring (Maskus, 1998). Their focus on enforcement, a mechanism lacking under WIPO, thereby became the means of implementing greater harmonization between developing and developed nations. With mandate in mind, the broad trade negotiations of the Uruguay Round provided for strong trading countries such as the US to sacrifice trade concessions to developing countries within the multilateral trade body, the World Trade Organization (WTO), in return for extensive IP reform. Constructed as a single package, the Final Act of the Uruguay Round encompassed the agreement for the creation of the WTO and the TRIPS agreement, thereby enforceable on all member states within specific transition periods (WTO, 2004). The economic imperative created by the broad trade negotiations for many countries ensured that 'there was no way for a state which wished to become or remain a member of the multilateral trading regime [WTO] to sidestep TRIPS' (Braithwaite and Drahos, 2000:63). As late modern capitalism continues to develop under conditions of globalization, and as a higher proportion of wealth creation in global GDP is in areas associated with intellectual property, then the strategic importance of TRIPS in global trading infrastructures will become more apparent. The enactment of the TRIPS Agreement thereby theoretically provided the catalyst for increased multilateralism in favour of the more traditional regional agreements. However, international differences in regulating the minimum 'standards framework' prescribed under the TRIPS Agreement have ensured that some countries, such as the US – a major force within the Uruguay Round negotiations – have continued to embrace regional, bilateral agreements over global approaches. This follows something of a pattern because the US has favoured bilateral over global approaches in other areas as well, for example taxation (Gilligan, 2003). Since 1995 Drahos (2001:3) notes that

> there has been no apparent decline in US bilateral activity on intellectual property since the signing of TRIPS . . . [rather] . . . the level of bilateral activity by the US has increased.

For Maskus (1998), the regional/bilateral approach adopted by the US is indicative of its broader trade goals. Phrases such as 'TRIPS plus', 'Section 301[13] surveillance' and the 'US Bilateral Investment Treaty Program' (Drahos, 2001) appear indicative of the US's mandate to procure intellectual property benefits for its domestic market. In the view of Drahos, the extensive use of regional/bilateral trade agreements by the US within developing countries has emasculated many of the protections provided by the transitional period of the TRIPS schedule, enabling the US to entrench more extensive IP protection regimes in developing economies (Drahos, 2001). A similar approach appears to have been adopted by the EU, prompting Maskus (1997:693) to note that 'a system is emerging in which regional protection for intellectual property could be stronger than global norms'. The self-interest of nation states and regional blocs influences what stance they favour. Consequently, nations who are relatively weaker or more exposed in global trading contexts such as Australia, have tended, unsurprisingly, to favour a multilateral approach to IP regulation and protection, as opposed to the regional and bilateral emphases preferred by the US and the EU. This utilitarian approach towards global, regional or bilateral agreements is to be expected and contributes to the complex architecture of the global IP protection regime. For example, Figure 8.1 illustrates the increasingly multi-tiered framework of the US's system of IP regulation in the post-TRIPS era.

At the very minimum, the four layers of regulation – multilateral, regional, bilateral and domestic – would appear to demand extensive cooperation and harmonization of numerous agencies and institutions if the goal of 'adequate and effective protection for intellectual property' (Drahos, 2001:5) is to be

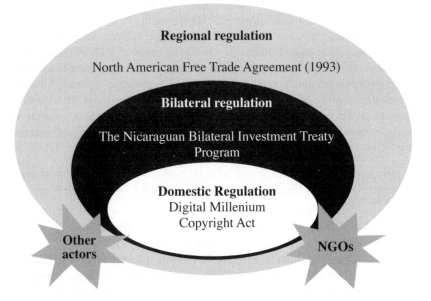

Multilateral Regulation
TRIPS Agreement (1995) and
WIPO Copyright Treaty (1996)

Regional regulation

North American Free Trade Agreement (1993)

Bilateral regulation

The Nicaraguan Bilateral Investment Treaty
Program

Domestic Regulation
Digital Millenium
Copyright Act

Other
actors

NGOs

Source: Text/info taken from Caslon Analytics intellectual property guide (2004),
http://www.caslon.com.au/ipguide.htm

*Figure 8.1 An example of multi-tiered regulatory structure of intellectual
property in the United States of America*

achieved. This multi-tiered framework approach adopted by the US is analogous to that of many stronger systems within advanced economies, including Japan, Australia and many member states of the EU. The question of costs associated with the continuous monitoring and compliance under these complex multilateral approaches to regulating global markets in IP markets remains uncertain, as does the issue to whom the potential trade benefits accrue of existing global IP regulatory arrangements (Maskus, 1997). These uncertainties hint at how difficult it might be to draw up a definitive list of variables against which one might best evaluate efforts to regulate a global sector such as intellectual property. However, it is likely that there will be continuing debate and conflict about not only what these specific variables should be, but also just how legitimate in reality TRIPS and other international protocols actually are. Different jurisdictions and interest groups are likely to rank them in different tiers of the organizational legitimacy hierarchy, and these decisions are likely to be highly influenced by prevailing political and economic realities.

THE PHARMACEUTICAL SECTOR

Pharmaceuticals are a highly regulated sector and most countries have an identifiable regulatory infrastructure within their national legislative framework (Harris, 1994). Although methods of regulation may differ markedly between countries (Wright, 2002), there has been an overarching trend for extensive pharmaceutical regulation due to the need to ensure quality, safety and therapeutic efficacy. There is considerable ambiguity regarding the position and motives of the state in the development of pharmaceutical regulation however, given the state's various roles as regulator, consumer and health policy maker. This mix of responsibilities has stimulated an active regulatory history, prompting Braithwaite and Drahos (2000:360) to comment that 'the history of the pharmaceutical industry is the history of its regulation'. This is testament to how lightly many other industries have been regulated in comparison with pharmaceuticals.

Table 8.4 illustrates that market development of the pharmaceutical sector is increasingly complex, but remains dominated by regional harmonization in preference to global regulatory protocols. Whilst this framework is gradually changing in light of the 1995 TRIPS agreement, the 2001 Doha Declaration and the 2003 Cancun meeting, Wiktorowicz (2003:616) notes that global harmonization has been slow to progress due to the 'unwillingness on the part of states to relinquish national authority in an area so central to health safety, and industrial competitiveness'. This reflects the perennial tension in multilateral contexts between issues of national sovereignty and self-interest and global regulatory ambitions. Market power and policy development within the sector has been dominated by actors in Japan, western Europe and the United States, rather than any global process (Braithwaite and Drahos, 2000). So, despite the World Health Organization's (WHO) attempt to promote global harmonization during the 1970s on the foundation of market efficiency (Nightengale, 1981), the pharmaceutical industry remained characterized by the trade goals of its more powerful transnational conglomerates. However, the 1980s did result in a shift in the regulatory architecture towards increased harmonization in which:

> trade, international market competition and the structural interests of the pharmaceutical industry ... [were], and remain, key motivating factors (Abraham and Reed, 2001:115).

For the US, initial international harmonization in pharmaceuticals was effected within an economic context. This initial period of harmonization in

Table 8.4 Key initiatives within global pharmaceutical market[a]

Year	Initiative	Origin	Primary drivers of initiative
1883	Paris Convention for the Protection of Industrial Property	Multilateral agreement	US
1947	General Agreement on Tariffs and Trade (GATT)	Multilateral agreement on trade in goods	
1948	World Health Organization (WHO)	International organization	
1965	EC Directive on Medicinal Products	Regional agreement	European Community
1975	Committee for Proprietary Medicinal Products (CPMP)	Regional agreement	European Community
1980s	European Community's Single Market in Pharmaceuticals	Regional agreement	European Community (now the EU)
1986–94	Uruguay Round	Multilateral negotiations	US, EU, Japan and the private sector
1990	International Conference on Harmonisation of Technical Requirements for Registration of Pharmaceuticals for Human Use (ICH)	International organization	Europe, Japan and US
1993	European Medicines Agency (EMEA)	Regional organization	EU
1993	North American Free Trade Agreement	Regional agreement	US
1995[b]	World Trade Organization	Multilateral trade body	
	Entry into force of the WTO Agreement on Trade-Related Aspects of Intellectual Property (TRIPS Agreement)	Multilateral trade treaty (global regulatory device![c])	US, EC and Japan
2001	Doha Declaration on TRIPS	Multilateral negotiations	Least developed countries including Brazil and a number of African countries
2003	Cancun Conference	Multilateral negotiations	US

Notes:
a. Source: ICH (2004); Barton (2004); EMA (2004); WHO (2004); Drahos (2001); Maskus (1997)
b. Drahos, 2001
c. Maskus, 1997

1985 saw the US government opting to engage in bilateral agreements with the Japanese government (Ferris, 1992), in which the primary goal was to obtain access to one of the world's most highly concentrated pharmaceutical markets (Reed-Maurer, 1994). Driven by international trade goals and fear of a decreasing market share under the US–Japan alignment, the EU began to implement a regulatory framework to promote regional harmonization with a 'single market' EU market in pharmaceuticals (Wyatt-Walter, 1995; Abraham and Reed, 2001). These developments reflect the familiar pattern of jurisdictions or regional groupings seeking to protect and/or stimulate market share through strategies to influence emerging regulatory infrastructures.

Despite the push for regional harmonization, the increasing transnational basis of the contemporary pharmaceutical company has dictated an increasing need for greater global cooperation (Wiktorowicz, 2003). This is the pragmatic reality of contemporary regulatory praxis being required to reflect the composition of relevant markets and the agendas of power players in those markets. The needs and priorities of these forces is evident in the initiation of trilateral meetings between the EU, Japan and the US in early 1990. Formalization of the meetings occurred in April 1990 through the International Conference on Harmonisation of Technical Requirements for Registration of Pharmaceuticals for Human Use (ICH). As a joint initiative between six parties, involving both regulators (of the EU, Japan and US) and industry (ICH, 2004),[14] Anon (2000) argues that the ICH is the first stage in global harmonization for the world's largest pharmaceutical markets. With a mandate constructed on the 'need to harmonise' (ICH, 2004), the ICH has developed a series of 'guidelines on drug safety for new drug approval, which the government regulatory agencies of the EU, Japan and US invariably adopt' (Abraham and Reed, 2001:114). Consisting of only guidance material and policy frameworks at this stage, it appears significant in respect to the global regulatory framework that the WHO is enthusiastic about adopting a number of revised ICH guidelines as part of its own guidance material (Anon, 1992).

In contrast to the potential development of 'soft law' through the ICH framework, the implementation of the TRIPS agreement in 1995 has resulted in the firmer product of a comprehensive multilateral trade agreement between 180 countries. Key proponents for the TRIPS agreement included pharmaceutical transnationals who were fighting for higher standards within global intellectual property regulations (UNCTAD-ICTSD, 2003). As part of the agreement, patents for pharmaceutical products are included within the framework, and thereby drug access within developing countries (Barton, 2004). Despite the TRIPS agreement being clearly 'unfinished business' as illustrated by the Doha Declaration (2001) and Cancun Conference (2003), the extensive multilateral framework for future global harmonization for pharmaceutical regulation has been constructed.

Notwithstanding this gradual transition to a more complex global regulatory framework, harmonization of the pharmaceutical industry remains more highly evolved at the regional level (Wiktorowicz, 2003). This is arguably best illustrated by the EU's attempts create a 'single market' for pharmaceutical products. Under the EU's legislative framework, Kanavos and Mossialos (1999) note, the European Medicines Evaluation Agency (EMEA) has achieved uniform agreement on a number of common industry practices, including classification, manufacturing and marketing. The rationale for EMEA is that costs are thereby decreased by avoiding unnecessary duplication, whilst increasing efficiency (Makinen et al., 2002). However, the existence of multiple national markets across the EU, underpinned by a lack of uniform legislation, has provided a number of barriers to the EU's 'single market' policy for model regional harmonization (Makinen et al., 2002). Whilst Kanavos and Mossialos (1999) maintain that substantial progress has been made towards regional harmonization, state supremacy over all facets of health policy remains problematic for the harmonization goal. Only if, and when, a number of trade-offs are made between member states will full regional harmonization occur. The continuing push by the European Commission towards a single market in form, as well as in function, remains a key driver in emerging modes of pharmaceuticals regulation, but specific national interests are still very much in play. So, as with financial services and IP, pharmaceuticals is a sector in which continuing legitimacy struggles are likely regarding multilateral regulatory initiatives. However, unlike financial services that has literally thousands and thousands of players, pharmaceuticals is a sector dominated by a relatively small number of transnational firms. This concentration of dominant commercial actors means that struggles for regulatory legitimacy are likely to be even more emotive in pharmaceuticals given its inextricable linkages to the health and well-being of citizens around the world.

CONCLUSION

What conclusions might one draw from this discussion? First, no template for regulating global markets is yet clear. However, what is abundantly apparent is that in an era of globalization, economic and political ties between many jurisdictions are deepening and jurisdictions increasingly are playing a mediating role regarding the interests of much business that may be conducted within and around their spheres of influence. These developments are affecting the sovereignty of jurisdictions as local political priorities become more intertwined with international politics and the requirements of international business. The evolution of these structures and processes can be something of an international power-play, whether in a global context such as the OECDHTPI, or a more regionally oriented performance (Gilligan, 2003). However, as we have seen with the OECDHTPI, the sovereignty and relative power of the nation state remain strong forces in global regulatory praxis and have the capacity to emasculate multilateral regulatory protocols initiatives that do emerge.

Second, it is important to remember that different jurisdictions have different perceptions about what are their respective legitimate interests. Allied to this is the reality that there can be substantial differences between both the functional capacity and prescribed mission of comparable regulators in different jurisdictions. The political, social and economic implications of this asymmetry are substantial. Domestic statutory legislation and/or external political pressure will not automatically promote the objectives of multilateral regulatory initiatives. Significant levels of formal harmonization may occur, but the substantive reality in terms of regulatory compliance and/or action may be a different story altogether. It is more likely that in many cases it may be the combined effects of both the supporting regulatory infrastructures, and prevailing levels of commitment to specific standards of behaviour within both the political and the business environments that emerge as the key factors. Nurturing the latter is usually more problematic and arguably the greatest challenge for both domestic and international regulatory development.

Normative issues are crucial when seeking to understand issues of compliance, whether at the local, national or international level. Franck (1988) in his efforts to produce a general theory of compliance stressed that levels of compliance are shaped substantially by how legitimate the relevant rules are considered to be by those communities supposedly subject to them. Indeed there is growing empirical evidence of 'a linear relationship between legitimacy and compliance, as legitimacy increases, so does compliance' (Tyler, 1990:57). Tyler (1990) found that issues of procedural justice are a crucial mediating factor in deciding whether people perceive legal processes as legitimate, and they can provide a valuable cushion for law enforcement agencies when they hand down unfavourable outcomes. There is every reason to believe that similar forces operate in most sectors and could even be more influential given the less secure mandate that regulatory agencies and international organizations possess in comparison with the vast majority of local police forces and courts. Most people believe that laws should be obeyed and it is this broader normative commitment to compliance as a general principle amongst those regulated which is perhaps the greatest asset that regulators and international organizations can access when developing multilateral regulatory initiatives.

The discussion above of financial services, IP and pharmaceuticals shows unsurprisingly that moves towards global regulatory initiatives in different sectors achieve differential levels of legitimacy, and this pattern is likely to be repeated across other sectors as globalization progresses. The elusive holy grail of successful international regulation, whether global or more regional in nature, is at heart an issue of balance. Consequently issues of inclusiveness and sovereignty need to be factored heavily into the development of international initiatives, and the input of affected jurisdictions sought, in order that multilateral regulatory efforts may have a realistic hope of success. The promotion of technocratic strategies that are the engine of most multilateral initiatives can only really be credible if they win the trust of affected groups, whether regulators, producers, consumers or others. It is not enough to pronounce objectives such as accountability and transparency as universal goods, because as the earlier discussion shows, such a strategy is unlikely to prompt sufficient levels of trust by rational actors in relevant regulatory institutions and processes, unless such initiatives rank well in a continuum of organizational legitimacy. Achieving adequate levels of legitimacy can be extremely difficult but there may be utility for those promoting multilateral regulatory initiatives in emphasizing demand side strategies based on incentive models that aim simultaneously not only to decrease regulatory burdens in all countries, but also promote optimal levels of social capital creation. This is especially important in trying to foster meaningful development in less developed jurisdictions and effective integration of all jurisdictions into the global and regional economies. All this as they say is *a big ask*. Indeed it may be impossible to achieve in practice in some contexts, but pursuing such goals offers some potential for regulatory innovation to help mediate and manage tensions in global markets.

NOTES

1. I would like to acknowledge the research assistance of Ms Diana Bowman in the preparation of this chapter.
2. It is not possible within the confines of this paper to canvass the debates regarding the utility of various definitions of globalization and how best to assess its impacts. There are many texts that discuss globalization including: Bordo, M., M. Taylor and J.G. Williamson (2003), *Globalization in Historical Perspective*, Chicago, IL: University of Chicago Press; Hirst, P. and G. Thompson (1998), *Globalization in Question: The International Economy and the Possibilities of Governance*, Cambridge: Polity Press; and Stiglitz, J. (2003), *Globalization and its Discontents*, New York: W.W. Norton & Company.
3. The WTO was established in 1995 and has built on the work of the General Agreement on Tariffs and Trade (GATT). The WTO's brief is to deal with the rules of trade at a global or near global level by: administering trade agreements; acting as a forum for trade negotiations and the settlement of trade disputes; cooperating with other international organizations; and providing technical assistance and training for developing countries. For further information see: http://www.wto.org/english/thewto_e/whatis_e/whatis_e.htm. As at 23 March 2005, the WTO has 148 members. See: http://www.wto.org/english/thewto_e/whatis_e/tif_e/org6_e.htm.

4. The Financial Action Task Force on Money Laundering (FATF) is an inter-governmental organization that seeks to develop and promote policies at both national and international levels to combat money laundering. The FATF was established following the G7 Summit held in Paris in 1989. G7 members are: Canada, France, Germany, Italy, Japan, the United Kingdom (UK) and the United States (US). Initially, the FATF was convened from the G7 member states, the European Commission (EC) and eight other countries, but it now has a membership of 31 jurisdictions, with the EC and the Gulf Cooperation Council as member international organizations. The 31 member jurisdictions are: Argentina, Australia, Austria, Belgium, Brazil, Canada, Denmark, Finland, France, Germany, Greece, Hong Kong, Iceland, Ireland, Italy, Japan, Luxembourg, Mexico, Netherlands, New Zealand, Norway, Portugal, Russian Federation, Singapore, South Africa, Spain, Sweden, Switzerland, Turkey, the United Kingdom (UK) and the United States (US). The FATF has a small Secretariat that is housed in the headquarters of the OECD in Paris, but the FATF is a separate international body and not part of the OECD. For more background information regarding the FATF, see: http://www.oecd.org/fatf/AboutFATF_en.htm.

5. The WIPO is an international organization dedicated to promoting the use and protection of intellectual property. The WIPO is based in Geneva and is one of the 16 specialized agencies of the United Nations system of organizations. The WIPO administers 23 international treaties dealing with different aspects of intellectual property protection. For further information see: http://www.wipo.int/index.html.en. As at 23 March 2005, the WIPO has 182 member states. See: http://www.wipo.int/about-wipo/en/members/member_states.html.

6. The consequences of the al-Qaeda attacks in the US on 11 September 2001 have been immense and have affected most countries in significant ways. There have been particular ramifications for the financial services sector both globally and more locally, as governments around the world seek to impact upon the funding of terrorist organizations. This concerted anti-terrorist push has influenced not only how different multilateral initiatives are perceived, but also has affected their prospects for successful implementation.

7. The OECD is based in Paris and comprises 30 member countries with the European Commission as a member international organization. The 30 member countries are: Australia, Austria, Belgium, Canada, Czech Republic, Denmark, Finland, France, Germany, Greece, Hungary, Iceland, Ireland, Italy, Japan, Korea, Luxembourg, Mexico, Netherlands, New Zealand, Norway, Poland, Portugal, Slovak Republic, Spain, Sweden, Switzerland, Turkey, the United Kingdom (UK) and the United States (US). All members share a stated commitment to democratic government and the market economy. The OECD has active relationships with 70 other countries and seeks to foster good governance in the public service and in corporate activity. For more information regarding the OECD, see: http://www.oecd.org/EN/about/0,,EN-about-0-nodirectorate-no-no-no-0,00.html.

8. The European Union grew from the European Economic Community, which initially consisted of just six countries: Belgium, Germany, France, Italy, Luxembourg and the Netherlands. Denmark, Ireland and the United Kingdom joined in 1973, Greece in 1981, Spain and Portugal in 1986, Austria, Finland and Sweden in 1995. In 2004 the biggest ever enlargement took place with Cyprus, the Czech Republic, Estonia, Hungary, Latvia, Lithuania, Malta, Poland, Slovakia and Slovenia joining. For further information see: http://europa.eu.int/abc/index_en.htm.

9. Members of the ITIO are: Anguilla, Antigua and Barbuda, Bahamas, Barbados, Belize, British Virgin Islands, Cayman Islands, Cook Islands, Malaysia, St Kitts and Nevis, St Lucia, Turks and Caicos and Vanuatu. Organizations that have formal observer status with the ITIO include: the CARICOM Secretariat, the Commonwealth Secretariat and the Pacific Islands Forum Secretariat.

10. STEP has branches in 26 jurisdictions and a membership of more than 8000 who are drawn largely from the legal, accountancy, corporate trust, banking, insurance and related professions.

11. By 1993, 100 nations had signed up to the Berne Convention. Interestingly, it was not until 1993 that the US became signatory to this Convention (Caslon Analytics, 2004).

12. For more in-depth review and analysis of the WTO and TRIPS Agreement, see: Gervais, D. (1998), *The TRIPS Agreement: Drafting History and Analysis*, London: Sweet and Maxwell;

Primo Braga, C.A. (1996), 'Trade-Related Intellectual Property Issues: The Uruguay Round Agreement and its Economic Implications', in Will Martin and L. Alan Winters (eds), *The Uruguay Round and the Developing Countries*, Cambridge: Cambridge University Press; or May, C. (2000), *A Global Political Economy of Intellectual Property Rights: The New Enclosures?*, London: Routledge.

13. Section 301 is part of the US Trade Act.

14. The 'Six Pack' members are: European Commission – European Union (EU), European Federation of Pharmaceutical Industries and Associations (EFPIA), Ministry of Health, Labor and Welfare, Japan (MHLW), Japan Pharmaceutical Manufacturers Association (JPMA), US Food and Drug Administration (FDA) and the Pharmaceutical Research and Manufacturers of America (PhRMA). In addition to these six members, the ICH also has a number of 'Observers', who are non-ICH countries and regions. These include the World Health Organization, the European Free Trade Area and Health Canada (ICH, 2004).

REFERENCES

Abraham, J. and T. Reed (2001), 'Trading risks for markets: the international harmonisation of pharmaceuticals', *Health, Risk and Society*, **3** (1), 113–28.

Anon (1992), 'ICH Progress So Far', *Scrip*, **1708**, 14–15.

Anon (2000), 'ICH progress on single dossier', *Scrip*, **2522**, 17.

Barton, J. (2004). 'TRIPS and the global pharmaceutical market', *Health Affairs*, **23** (3), 146–54.

Basle Committee for Banking Supervision (1983), *Principles for the Supervision of Banks Foreign Establishment (Basle Concordat)*, Basle: Bank for International Settlements.

Basle Committee for Banking Supervision (1997), *History of the Basle Committee and its Membership*, Basle: Bank for International Settlements.

Beetham, D. (1991), *The Legitimation of Power*, London: Macmillan.

Bhagwati, J.N. (1988), 'Trade in services: developing country concerns', *Economic Impact*, **62**, 58–64.

Bogsch, A. (1992), *Brief History of the First 25 Years of the World Intellectual Property Organization*, Geneva: World Intellectual Property Organization.

Braithwaite, J. and P. Drahos (2000), *Global Business Regulation*, Melbourne: Cambridge University Press.

Caribbean Community (CARICOM) (2000), 'Communiqué issues on the conclusion of the 21st meeting of the conference of heads of government of the Caribbean Community', 2–5 July, Canouan, St. Vincent and the Grenadines.

Caribbean Community (CARICOM) (2000), conference of heads of government, Canouan, St. Vincent and the Grenadines, 2–5 July, accessed at www.caricom.org/pres91_00.htm, pp. 8–9.

Caslon Analytics (2004), 'Intellectual property guide', accessed 27 August at www.caslon.com.au/ipguide.htm.

Commonwealth Secretariat (2000), *The Implications of the OECD Harmful Tax Competition Initiative for Offshore Finance Centres*, London: Commonwealth Secretariat.

Dezelay, Y. (1993), 'Professional competition and the social construction of transnational regulatory expertise', in J. McCahery, S. Picciotto and C. Scott (eds), *Corporate Control and Accountability*, Oxford: Clarendon Press, pp. 203–16.

Doern, B. (1999), *Global Change and Intellectual Property Agencies: An Institutional Perspective*, London: Pinter.

Doremus, P. (1996), 'The externalization of domestic regulation: intellectual property rights reform in a global era', *Global Legal Studies Journal*, **3** (2), 341–74.

Drahos, P. (2001), 'Bilateralism in intellectual property', paper prepared for Oxfam BG, London.

European Medicines Agency (2004), 'About us', accessed 23 August at www.emea.eu.int/.

Ferris, M.J. (1992), 'A review of the Japanese regulatory system', in J.P. Griffin (ed.), *Medicines: Regulation, Research and Risk*, Belfast: Queen's University Press.

Financial Action Task Force (FATF) (2004), 'About the FATF', accessed 23 August at www.fatf-gafi.org/pages/0,2987,en_32250379_32235720_1_1_1_1_1,00.html.

Franck, T.M. (1988), 'Legitimacy in the international system', *American Journal of International Law*, **82** (4), 705–59.

Gervais, D. (1998), *The TRIPS Agreement: Drafting History and Analysis*, London: Sweet & Maxwell.

Getlan, M. (1995), 'TRIPS and future of Section 301: a comparative study in trade dispute resolution', *Columbia Journal of Transnational Law*, **34**, 173–218.

Gilligan, G. (2003), 'Whither or wither the European Union Savings Tax Directive? – A case study in the political economy of taxation', *Journal of Financial Crime*, **11** (1), 56–72.

Global Forum on Taxation (2004), 'A process for achieving a global level playing field', http://www.oecd.org/dataoecd/13/0/31967501.pdf.

Harris, A.H. (1994), 'Economic appraisal in the regulation of pharmaceuticals in Australia', *Australian Economic Review*, second quarter, 99–104.

International Conference on Harmonisation of Technical Requirements for Registration of Pharmaceuticals for Human Use (ICH) (2004), 'Structure: history and function', accessed 27 August at www.ich.org/UrlGrpServer.jser?@_ID=276&@_TEMPLATE=254.

International Monetary Fund (IMF) (2003), 'A guide to committees, groups and clubs: a fact sheet', accessed 23 August, 2004 at www.imf.org/external/np/exr/facts/groups.htm#G10.

Jackson, J.H. (2003), 'Sovereignty modern: a new approach to an outdated concept', *American Journal of International Law*, **97**, 728–802.

Kanavos, P. and E. Mossialos (1999), 'Outstanding regulatory aspects in the European pharmaceutical market', *Pharmacoeconomics*, **15** (6), 519–33.

Ladas, S.P. (ed.) (1975), *Patents, Trademarks, and Related Rights: National and International Protection*, Cambridge, MA: Harvard University Press.

Machlup, F. and E. Penrose (1950), 'The patent controversy in the nineteenth century', *Journal of Economic History*, **10** (1), 1–29.

Makinen, M., P.T. Rautava and J.J. Forsstrom (2002), 'Restrictions on imports of drugs for personal use within the European single market', *European Journal of Public Health*, **12** (4), 244–48.

Maskus, K.E. (1997), 'Implication of regional and multilateral agreements for intellectual property', *World Economy*, **20** (5), 681–94.

Maskus, K.E. (1998), 'The international regulation of intellectual property,' *Weltwirtschaftliches–Archiv*, **123** (2), 186–208.

May, C. (2000), *A Global Political Economy of Intellectual Property Rights: The New Enclosures?*, London: Routledge.

Mitchell, D.J. (2001), 'CFP strategic memo, 16 June, to leaders of low-tax jurisdictions and supporters of tax competition, financial privacy, and fiscal sovereignty, Washington, DC, accessed at www.freedomandprosperity.org/Papers/m06-16-01/m06-16-01.shtml.

Nightengale, S. (1981), 'Drug regulation and policy formulation', *Milbank Memorial Fund Quarterly Health and Society*, **59** (3), 412–44.

Organisation for Economic Co-operation and Development (OECD) (2000), *Towards Global Tax Co-operation. Report to the 2000 Ministerial Council Meeting and Recommendations by the Committee on Fiscal Affairs, Progress in Identifying and Eliminating Harmful Tax Practices*, Paris: OECD.

Organisation for Economic Co-operation and Development (2002), *The OECD Issues the List of Unco-operative Tax Havens*, Paris: OECD.

Organisation for Economic Co-operation and Development (2001), *The OECD's Project on Harmful Tax Practices: The 2001 Progress Report*, Paris: OECD.

Organisation for Economic Co-operation and Development (2003a), 'Vanuatu makes commitment and is removed from list of uncooperative tax havens', 25 May, accessed at www.oecd.org/document/41/0,2340,en_2649_33745_2512553_1_1_1_37427,00.html.

Organisation for Economic Co-operation and Development (2003b), 'Nauru is removed from list of uncooperative tax havens', 12 December, accessed at www.oecd.org/document/31/0,2340,en_2649_33745_21863583_1_1_1_37427,00.html.

Organisation for Economic Co-operation and Development (2004), *The OECD's Project on Harmful Tax Practices: The 2004 Progress Report*, Paris: OECD.

Porter, T. (1993), *States, Markets and Regimes in Global Finance*, Basingstoke: Macmillan.

Porter, T. (2002), 'Politics, institutions, constructivism and the emerging international regime for financial regulation', *Review of Policy Research*, **19** (1), 53–79.

Primo Braga, C.A. (1996), 'Trade-related intellectual property issues: the Uruguay Round Agreement and its economic implications', in Will Martin and L. Alan Winters (eds), *The Uruguay Round and the Developing Countries*, Cambridge: Cambridge University Press.

Raustalia, K. and A.M. Slaughter (2002), 'International law, international relations and compliance', in W. Carlsnaes, T. Risse, B. Simmons and T. Risse-Kappen (eds), *Handbook of International Relations*, London: Sage, pp. 538–58.

Reed-Maurer, P. (1994), 'Restructuring the Japanese pharmaceutical industry', *Scrip*, **5**, 38–40.

Ricketson, S. (2000), *Intellectual Property Administration and Policy in Australia: An Examination of the Australian Situation, Past and Present, and Recommendations for Future Change*, Melbourne: Faculty of Law, Monash University.

Sacks, H. (1969), 'Crisis in international copyright: the protocol regarding developing countries', *Journal of Business Law*, **26**.

Stikeman, Elliott (2000), *Towards a Level Playing Field – Regulating Corporate Vehicles in Cross-Border Transactions*, London: Society of Trust and Estate Practitioners and the International Tax and Investment Organisation.

Suchman, M.C. (1995), 'Managing legitimacy: strategic and institutional approaches', *Academy of Management Review*, **20** (3), 571–610.

Tax-news.com (2000), 'Caribbean havens fight back', 6 June, accessed at www.tax-news.com/html/oldnews/st_BISAGM_09_06_00.htm.

Tax-news.com (2001), 'Offshore jurisdictions give guarded welcome to OECD report', 16 November, accessed at www.tax-news.com/.

Tyler, T.R. (1990), *Why People Obey the Law*, New Haven, CT: Yale University Press.

United Nations Conference on Trade and Development (UNCTAD) and International Centre for Trade and Sustainable Development (ICTSD) (2003), *Intellectual Property Rights, Implications for Development Policy Discussion Paper*, Geneva: UNCTAD and ICTSD.

Wiktorowicz, M.E. (2003), 'Emergent patterns in the regulation of pharmaceuticals: institutions and interests in the United States, Canada, Britain, and France', *Journal of Health Politics, Policy and Law*, **28** (4), 615–58.

World Intellectual Property Organization (WIPO) (2004), 'Treaties and contracting parties', 29 August, accessed at www.wipo.int/treaties/en/.

Wright, D.J. (2002), *The Drug Bargaining Game: Pharmaceutical Regulation in Australia*, Sydney: University of Sydney Faculty of Economics and Business.

World Health Organization (WHO) (2004), 'About WHO', 23 August, accessed at www.who.int/en/.

World Trade Organization (WTO) (2004), 'Frequently asked questions about TRIPS in the WTO', accessed 2 September at www.wto.org/english/tratop_e-trips_e/tripfq_e.htm.

Wyatt-Walter, A. (1995), 'Globalisation, corporate identity and European technology policy', *Journal of European Policy*, **2**, 427–46.

9. Conclusions: spreading the privatization family business

Graeme Hodge

INTRODUCTION

The privatization story was always bigger than simply a political initiative under Margaret Thatcher in the United Kingdom. As we said earlier, it was more a long-standing war over centuries on the battlefields of philosophy, service delivery and capital interests against those of labour. And it went on to become a global movement. There is still much heat in the privatization debates of today, and this observation itself is testament to the long-standing experience of winners and losers from the reform.

Looking back, it is easy to see how the family of privatization reforms, that is, enterprise sales, contracting-out government services, public–private partnerships and private sector strategy, was supported by a confluence of other reforms. Each member of the family was supported, for instance, by the two-decades-long introduction of New Public Management (NPM) techniques. Both the progressive contractualization and the vastly increased focus, even fanaticism if we examine the arguments from many of today's public service reformers, on better performance measurement in all areas of government have strengthened privatization reforms. And once government activities were privatized, citizens became part of another new story – that of the re-regulated state. Or as Guttman (2003) called it 'government by third party'. Interpreted through another lens, citizens in many countries have found themselves within a new and complex network of public accountability institutions. The regulators general, consumer commissions, auditors and compliance inspectors all now rule in the privatized state. It has become increasingly complex, increasingly technical and because it has been founded on the increased contractualization of activities, increasingly legal. In this closing chapter, we will firstly reconsider the central policy questions posed at the outset, before we then draw together the bigger themes that have evolved throughout the book. Last, we will close by contemplating issues for the future.

POLICY ARENAS

This book aimed to bring together a range of contributions, with two purposes. First, we wanted to trace how the privatization idea had grown in application and spread to become a central policy idea, and even a 'solution' to some governance concerns. It also aimed to bridge the divide between developed economies and developing economies and provide space for reflection and thought on the importance of these policy ideas.

In discussing the first thrust of this book, we initially asked a series of questions concerning the four components of the privatization family:

1. What is the policy idea, and what has it now become?
2. How has the idea spread, why and through whom?
3. How effective has the policy idea been based on empirical evidence to date?
4. How can the effectiveness of this idea be improved now?

We were also interested in assessing which lessons are being learned internationally now, and which are not, as privatization ideas continue to spread globally.

In the second thrust of the book, we were wanting to examine some of the relevant issues visible as markets develop in a privatized state. Again, a series of questions were posed:

5. Given the observation that 'change in government' has today become a global business, to what degree are governments now dependent on business advice and business leadership? And should governments be reducing their dependence on buying such advice?
6. We have witnessed a global diffusion of common regulatory practices and institutional frameworks. But how have governments themselves come to apply such regulatory notions, and to what extent has such re-regulation been successful from experience to date?
7. As well, the international availability of finance has lubricated global markets and governing such global markets has become an increasingly important dimension today. But what are the multilateral mechanisms being adopted for governance here, where have these policy ideas come from, and how effective are they in meeting the needs of global citizens?

So, after the debate has subsided, how might we reinterpret the privatization family and its spread? And how has each of the privatization components performed?

INSIGHTS AND LEARNINGS ON PRIVATIZATION AND MARKET DEVELOPMENT

These chapters have provided many insights on the record of the privatization family, and the journey has covered a wide terrain. Looking over the essays, several points are worthwhile making.

First, there is little doubt that think tanks such as the Institute of Economic Affairs (IEA) and the Adam Smith Institute (ASI) were highly influential on senior ruling UK politicians such as Margaret Thatcher, Nicholas Ridley, Nigel Lawson and Sir Keith Joseph, as well as on 'shifting thinking within the Conservative Party, and also within industry and the media, to favour private over state enterprise' as Parker put it in Chapter 2. And whilst there was never a formal detailed privatization plan per se, and British privatizations were 'partially planned and partly opportunistic', the technique of privatizing state-owned enterprises arose through a combination of economic principles (property rights and public choice), immediate budgetary needs and ideology. There is also little doubt that the apparent success of privatization in the UK led directly to global influence through mass privatization programmes in central and eastern Europe, and the International Monetary Fund (IMF) shaping its structural adjustment loans to be increasingly conditional on economic reforms including privatization. The attraction of the British privatization model was clearly promoted in the work of British think tanks through activities such as training courses, and publications in conjunction with North American organizations such as the Fraser Institute, the Heritage Foundation and the Cato Institute. All this was as well of course fanned along by growing evidence of government failure and government waste and corruption in developing countries. So, whilst the enterprise sales model was more than solely an initiative of Margaret Thatcher's UK reign (given the West German and Taiwanese programmes in the 1960s) and the 1990s sales proceeds of some countries such as Portugal (where proceeds were equivalent to 25 per cent of its GDP) dwarfed the UK figure (at 7 per cent), there is nonetheless little doubt as to the central place of the UK in influencing global privatization ideas over the past quarter of a century.

Second, Parker's performance conclusion on the global spread of the enterprise sales model of privatization was interesting as well. After global receipts of almost $US937 billion, his assessment was surprisingly guarded; that 'privatization was . . . good in parts'. His judgement was that it enabled industry management to break away from stifling state bureaucracy, governments to raise funds, companies to access new private capital and for capital markets to develop. At the same time, though, he remarked on the unequal distribution of benefits, the probable accelerated demise of some industries, and bailouts having occurred as was the case for instance with British Railtrack. Whilst services may have improved on average, this was also unlikely to have been solely the result of ownership changes; larger customers and industry benefited whilst poorer income groups did not; wage differentials widened; and job losses occurred whilst managers won handsome salary increases. Additionally, investor gains were, in effect, subsidized by taxpayers (despite some recent clawbacks) whilst banks, lawyers and consultants all saw their earnings rise and become 'substantial'. Parker's overall lesson here was that 'privatizations by efficient and non-corrupt governments; into competitive product markets or with effective and efficient state regulatory bodies; and where there will be ongoing scrutiny of management behaviour by a competitive capital market, . . . [stand the] best chance of raising economic performance'. The paradox, as Parker makes clear, is that whilst privatization played such a central role in Thatcher's war to 'roll back the state', there is in reality a strong possibility that the privatization era in the UK will be remembered not for leading to less government but leading 'to more effective government'.

A third insight from these chapters builds on the earlier theme that privatization family reforms such as contracting-out have been imbedded within other, bigger movements. As Dudley and Bogaevskaya point out in Chapter 3, this imbeddedness has been both in terms of time, if we recall the adoption of contracting as a tool of the Achaemenid Empire five centuries BC to collect taxes, or to hire mercenaries to fight or build public works, and in terms of space, looking at public sector operations in different countries today. They review contracting reforms over many countries and comment that the role of international organizations such as the OECD was crucial, given that their 'reform guidelines took hold, became ideologically dominant, and diffused all over the world'. Looking at multiple countries over the globe, they saw reformers as being initiators (mostly Anglo-American), cautious (e.g. Nordic countries, Netherlands, Continental Europe and Canada), devolvers (some Asian reformers), central controllers (Latin American countries and central and eastern Europe), and isomorphic (some Asian and African countries). The characteristics of each of these groups have been the different drivers of contracting reforms. To Dudley and Bogaevskaya, the Anglo-American reformers were the most advanced and were driven by the desire to implement New Public Management reforms under a neoliberal ideology 'which prioritizes market over the state', and 'run[s] government like a business'. The result to their mind has been a 'new contractualism' whether between government and ministers, or between the state and the private sector. The cautious reformers were less convinced of the superiority of NPM reforms, and for a range of reasons questioned the legitimacy of contracting-out as a policy preference. Devolving Asian reformers, on the other hand, experienced the 1990s economic crisis and in line with the Anglo-American reform model, pushed national governments (such as South Korea, Thailand, Malaysia and

Market development

Singapore) to initiate contracting-out. Examples here included the South Korean government which aimed to cut down its manpower by 20 per cent as a target and Singapore, which implemented 'budgeting for results'. Other 'central controllers' sold off state companies and created distinct policy-making ministries and autonomous agencies operating under management contract. Lastly, isomorphic reformers, under pressure from international organizations such as the World Bank and the IMF sold natural monopolies, infrastructure and utilities. They point out in this context that some developing country governments can spend huge amounts on hiring external expertise (up to 20 per cent of their annual budgets) and that contracting-out regulatory functions, for instance, not only provides much needed capacity and competence, but also improves the credibility of resulting regulation, fosters independence in the regulatory process from political capture and attracts foreign investors.

Having said all this, there has not, in Dudley and Bogaevskaya's judgement, been any one consistent contracting-out reform model observed, aside from the remark that contracting reforms have, worldwide, increased the interdependence among organizations and that 'today, it is virtually impossible to identify any public programme that a single government agency can manage on its own without relying on some partnership with other public agencies, or private, or non-profit organizations'. This, we might reflect not only increases the complexity of delivering and managing the delivery of public sector services, but also affects matters of accountability – particularly public accountability. On this issue, these authors agree with Parker's earlier observation that a troubling aspect of both the two privatization family reforms so far has been the lack of success expected in the absence of effective market mechanisms, competition, business ethics and contract law. Unfortunately, few of these are well developed in typical developing economies.

The next component of the privatization family, public–private partnerships (PPPs) is as Greve says in Chapter 4, 'the talk of the (global) town these days'. Our fourth set of insights concerns this phenomenon, its ascendancy to centre stage and the identification of those supporting it. Using the 'Multiple Streams Framework' of Kingdon (1995), Greve suggests that PPPs burst onto the agenda by providing a timely policy solution for a specific UK problem within a broader political context. In essence, he argues that both a finance pressure (i.e. the inability to borrow public funds) in conjunction with widespread disappointment with traditional contracting amidst a widening gap between purchasers and providers was the ground on which the PPP solution was to take root and flower. The PPP policy provided a clear financial model, but with the attractions of a gloriously ambiguous and warm label that, in fact, had already been quietly road tested through its use in the background for decades. The broader context of politics comprising the national mood, pressure group campaigns and reform fashion all seemed to swing in favour of PPPs. The advocacy of the Blair government when it came to power was seen as a further positive, and through many of the same privatization advisers and consultants who had surfed the previous enterprise sales wave, Britain again came to be regarded as the world leader in public sector innovation. In the 1990s, therefore, the policy window had opened. And partnerships are now being implemented in Nordic countries, across the European Union, as well as in Australia and elsewhere. Importantly, Greve argues that the PPP policy enjoyed a very widely based pro-partnership coalition of support, from government departments, private sector actors (bankers, accountants, economists and private sector CEOs), pressure groups, consultants, construction companies and commercial experts, all of whom got a piece of the action, whilst potential losers, such as current and future taxpayers, tended to be left out of the direct picture and were less sure of their veracity. This is a sobering analysis, and one that challenges current rhetoric of many governments as to how, exactly, the public interest is being guaranteed through PPPs.

Of course, one of the characteristics of Kingdon's 'policy window' notion is that it has a finite time span and is unlikely to stay open forever. So, will the PPP policy preference last? Greve's analysis of this question is illuminating, and is our fifth insight. He suggests that there are several good reasons to expect it will not: PPPs will not ever become a large part of public sector investments as promised; the historical lack of public funding available from which the PPP solution initially arose is not, in many jurisdictions, a problem in reality;[1] those supporting the policy may move onto other things; and the big partnership ideas of flexibility and trust promoted for PPPs may end up being regulated to death. On the other hand, the policy window may indeed remain open if the current professional dialogue continues unabated; policy learning may actually be taking place; PPPs may yet show clear benefits to the public compared with more traditional contracting arrangements; and lastly, the current broadly based coalition may continue its influence and agenda setting with the result that we have only seen the beginning of what is yet to come. Interestingly, Greve argues that the dynamics around the current PPP policy debate mirror in many ways the earlier dynamics around enterprise sales. It will be interesting to see what role is played by citizens in the longer term and how they fare.

The sixth insight concerns the broader notion of private sector development strategy (PSDS). As Cook articulates (Chapter 5), PSDS has had a long history and over the past two decades has played a major role as a component in economic development activities. Over this time, it has been a guiding public policy framework through a mixture of affirmations, actions, goals, aspirations and belief in development potential. The initial emphasis was an appropriate national macroeconomic framework, and a choice between public and private enterprise. Indeed, early World Bank structural adjustment loans were over-whelmingly towards public enterprise reforms (73 per cent) rather than priva-tization, with a large proportion being channelled through development finance institutions. The unveiling in 1989 of a new PSDS symbolized a renewed effort and brought the aims of growth and development under one strategy, so that by 1990 the majority of the World Bank's operations (i.e. 150 of 228) included PSD components. More recently, Cook reports that the Dollar and Kraay (2000) study *Growth is Good for the Poor* provided empirical support from 137 countries to reinforce the consensus which had already evolved: that 'economic growth was central to development, and economic growth was best achieved through the private sector; with government acting as a facilitator to the private sector and ensuring that growth contributes to poverty reduction'. Since then, PSD strategies have again been renewed by development agencies, and the current wave of PSDSs comprise a wide vari-ety of targeted outcomes that aim to create enabling conditions for the private sector; generate business opportunities for the sector; and catalyse private investments.

So, what has changed here, and how effective have PSDS been? Cook reports that few evaluations of PSD programmes have occurred, although there has been broad convergence between agencies on just what ought to be included in a PSD. Importantly, he has previously observed that 'although most strategies refer to the importance of new relationships between the public and private sectors, [and to] competition and the regulatory environment, the models adopted continue to be those principally developed and rooted in the institutional sophistication of the developed economies' (Cook et al., 2004). It looks suspiciously as if international aid ideas continue to be dominated by a 'one size fits all' mentality despite protestations to the contrary.

So, have we learned from the PSDSs of the past? Yes. Notwithstanding the worryingly consistent absence of specific links and channels to poverty and poverty reduction in the newer PSDSs as was the case in the old, new strate-gies do build on earlier experiences in terms of the need to better understand constraints facing private sector operations. Cook thus reports that pilot schemes using output-based aid are aiming to support developmental outcomes while not increasing private sector profitability and have been successful in rural water and sanitation, access to energy and rural telephone connections.

The next insight, the seventh, concerns the role of consultants in the inter-national movement of privatization ideas. There has certainly been a meteoric international rise in the importance of consulting over the past few decades, with international revenues some twenty times bigger than we might expect simply on the basis of growth in line with the consumer price index. And by 2004, the estimated global market value was around $US125 billion. The big four firms (Deloitte Touche Tohmatsu (Deloitte), Ernst & Young (EY), KPMG and PricewaterhouseCoopers (PwC)) are an oligopoly of accounting firms which dominate the world's management consulting market. These four firms employ some 462 500 people worldwide and each has offices in over 140 countries, from Algeria and Angola to Vietnam and Yemen. They have successfully capitalized on three major worldwide movements in both government and business. First, they have acquired expert accounting and financial services central to the needs of growing economies; second, they have provided services in response to the increasing outsourcing of functions considered not core to public and private businesses while also advising on this trend; and third, they have responded to the insatiable desire for wide-ranging management and business reform advice to achieve productivity gains in all sectors. There is now no doubting their strength. With this size and influence, however, has also come criticism. Labels such as the 'consultocracy' or the accusation of being a 'shadow government' are both examples. At the heart of these criticisms rest two primary concerns. The initial concern is that old-style policy processes are now obsolete and policy reform solutions are now sold by consultants rather than being offered up front by elected representatives. To the extent that this is true, consultants may have become a powerful interest group with undue influence underneath less democratic policy development processes. The latter concern is that government accountability to citizens has been reduced through secrecy in contract arrangements, and through the invisibility of the consultant role in democratic policy making in the polity.

So, are policy processes now less democratic, and do we now also face reduced government accountability to citizens? Our review of these questions reveals some complexity in the answer, but no conspiracy. The public–private boundary has been blurring for centuries and consultants have always sought a slice of transactions – whether on enterprise sales or on PPP deals. And governments have used consultants for some time – as well as the other way around. At the international level, there has also been little doubt that their policy influence has been substantial – as phrases like 'policy band-wagoning', 'policy shopping', 'systematically pinching ideas', 'policy pusher' and 'elite networking' all attest. The reputations of some consultants as being jet-setting 'econolobbyists' or 'fly-in, fly-out' consultants has, at one end of the argument, reinforced the judgement that the biggest contribution to developing economies of some consultants has been the provision of hard currency to hotels and taxis rather than policy advice of any veracity. Nonetheless, the effectiveness of aid services ought not be judged by one end of this continuum, but on a broader appreciation of contributions made in what is in reality a difficult intellectual, cultural and geographical environment.

Certainly, the role of consultants in modern governments has been one of a quiet takeover, and even reforming governments in developed economies have been hesitant to highlight the degree to which the day to day role of public administration has been passed over to the business sector. It seems therefore, that consultants have inevitably been the foot-soldiers for the political and public policy directions taken by international reform agencies such as the World Bank and IMF, as well as being front-line players within national public sector reform efforts. In both cases, as has been acknowledged elsewhere, consultants have clearly been one of the biggest winners from privatization family reforms to date (Hodge, 2000). So, whilst trying to avoid the temptation to demonize the consultant role or else romanticize any public sector past, where are the real concerns? The biggest is around the issue of conflicts of interest. The consultant lobby is a powerful new and professional interest group in its own right. As transaction merchants, they favour governments doing something, anything, rather than nothing. Even wasting public money is, to the consultant, better than doing nothing, because transaction costs in public sector planning and reforms are the firm's revenue.[2] Noting the progressive move away from the traditional, conservative neutral stewardship role of the treasury department towards a policy advocacy and implementation role, not one, but multiple conflicts of interest are now present in states. Treasury departments now sell PPPs policies, and take on the multiple and conflicting roles of policy advocate, project promoter, in-house manager, city planner, contract developer, financial steward, project assessor, legislator, contract regulator for subsequent decades and trusted parliamentary adviser. In this instance, advocacy may compromise stewardship several times over and be fatal. Indeed, noting some of the obvious and colourful examples of parallel and serial conflicts of interest at present, this very issue may well be the biggest challenge facing the privatization family as the consulting sector lubricates the future economic engine.

A further major insight, our eighth, is just how regulatory models seem to have spread throughout the globe. As Gilardi, Jordana and Levi-Faur remind us (Chapter 7), 'the era of privatization is also the era of regulation', and so much can be learned about the spread of privatization ideas through the spread of regulatory ideas. The regulatory explosion has indeed been spectacular. In the 17 European and 19 Latin American countries they examine, the number of regulatory agencies grew steadily from a dozen or so to around 50 in the three decades after 1960. But in the single decade of the 1990s, numbers more than tripled up to 174 by 2002. What explains this boom? It appears to have occurred across both the economic sector (including telecoms, electricity, competition and securities and exchange) as well as the social regulatory sector (including food safety, pharmaceutical and environment). Interestingly, their examination of alternative explanations rejects the theory of 'regulatory competition': the notion that states, amidst the global competition for capital, have established attractive investment regimes in which technocratic decision making is removed from the vagaries of political decision making. They also reject the theory of 'regionalization': that with limited human and fiscal resources regions find it 'necessary to rely on regulation as a major tool of governance' and 'develop regulatory capacities on an unprecedented scale'. To them, the diffusion of regulatory agencies was best explained through 'transnational networks of professionals' as major agents of change. These knowledge actors include both the non-state actors and intergovernmental networks of experts. They also observe that networks of regulators – have two masters – both their epistemic community and the particular sovereign state of which they are an autonomous body. And their relative political independence also makes it easier for regulators to follow the policy preferences of their epistemic community. In this way, transnationalization 'increases the power of some experts and agents of the state'. Against a background of 'Western rationality'[3] and supported by Western education systems (especially American universities) and the dominance of the economics profession, it therefore appears that 'these networks have been instrumental in advancing the ideas of market instruments and the work of global markets ... essential for the advance of privatization policies'. These networks appear to have therefore acquired both knowledge power and institutional power given their delegated authority and protection from excessive political control.

Summarizing then, Gilardi, Jordana and Levi-Faur argue that the age of regulatory capitalism has witnessed a boom in regulatory agencies both across sectors (economic and social) and across regions (Europe and Latin America) and 'that this pattern is best explained by the professionalization of the world's elites and their growing interactions in transnational forums'. Networks of expertise have thus been a major driver of regulatory change.

Insight number nine came from the work of Gilligan (Chapter 8), who viewed issues of legitimacy as integral to international systems of regulation and bodies of knowledge. By examining case studies in financial regulation, intellectual property and pharmaceuticals, and using this legitimacy lens, Gilligan revealed how processes of regulation emerge and are sustained. Financial services, for instance, were characterized by a substantial number of multilateral regulatory initiatives over the past three-quarters of a century. Driven through the insatiable desire for trade, these organizations and agreements showed 'a deepening and intensifying influence', in his view. Using the seemingly simple window of 'harmful tax practices' to see how regulatory protocols develop, he observed as well that the OECD's blacklisting of tax havens since 2000 attracted criticism from affected jurisdictions and that this, in the end, led to the recent formation of a Global Forum in order to ensure broader-based legitimacy 'and the capability for differential levels of implementation'. Intellectual property, with an even longer history of regulation going back to medieval Europe and with a more coherent set of national regulatory structures through the Industrial Revolution was followed by regional regulation through bilateral arrangements in the nineteenth century. Indeed, Gilligan notes that 'by 1883 approximately 69 agreements covering IP rights, the majority of which were bilateral, were in force'. Efforts towards international harmonization from the initial Paris and Berne conventions in 1883 and 1886 up to the present time of the Agreement on Trade Related Intellectual Property Rights (TRIPS Agreement) illustrated this complex arena. The economic imperative of multilateral trading regime membership ensured that states signed up to TRIPS. Nonetheless, jurisdictions such as the US have ended up with a complex, multi-tiered framework for IP regulation – indeed under four layers of multilateral, regional, bilateral and domestic regulation, and requiring extensive cooperation. We might also reflect in passing that, as Gilligan notes, the legitimacy of the TRIPS Agreement is yet to be tested. The pharmaceutical sector presented a different case study again. A highly regulated sector with an active regulatory history, this sector remains 'dominated by regional harmonization in preference to global regulatory protocols due to the unwillingness of states to relinquish national authority'. Both the health of citizens and the economic interests of industrial players have figured strongly here. Today, the pharmaceutical industry remains characterized by 'the trade goals of its more powerful transnational conglomerates' in Gilligan's words. Overall, then, unlike the financial sector where thousands of players exist, the pharmaceutical sector has been dominated by a smaller number of large transnational companies behind the workings of national governments. This observation, in conjunction with obvious linkages with the health and well-being of citizens, means that 'struggles for regulatory legitimacy are likely to be even more emotive'. And on this matter, Raustalia and Slaughter (2002) is cited as a reminder that lower levels of legitimacy for a regulatory regime inevitably carry the likelihood of lower levels of compliance.

So, where does all this leave us? What of the future of the privatization family and its spread? And is the new professional power now with international consultants, or overwhelmingly with the 'regulocrats'?

THE FUTURE OF THE PRIVATIZATION FAMILY OF IDEAS

Some factors here are crystal clear. In the first place, the privatization family of policy ideas is now central to all governments in one way or another, albeit that it has changed shape from being simply about selling-off state-owned enterprise to being a more broadly based portfolio of activities including outsourcing and partnerships, as well as the wider PSDS notion for developing economies. Thus, Thatcher's famous privatization tool has evolved into a broader philosophical matter in which more and more governments have openly adopted the capitalist dream. As a consequence, supporting policies in which the business sector increasingly takes over government functions have also been judged on the basis of their contribution to the most important game now in town . . . in the words of the popular old adage, 'It's the economy, stupid!'

The role of the knowledge elite, whether think tanks, consultants, education systems or regulocrats, has indeed been central to this broader understanding of the privatization school of ideas. Such influence has come in many shapes and has covered the fronts of academic publications, the transactions themselves, as well as the direct and explicit advice to governments, and quieter influence behind the scenes. Examples abound: the support of Coopers & Lybrand, for instance, for early books on enterprise sell-offs (Foster 1992); the growth of PricewaterhouseCoopers from consultants on public–private partnerships to academic experts and book authors (Grimsey and Lewis, 2004); the Harvard Institute's roles in Russian privatization investment transactions along with advice, political influence, 'independent' analysis and aid funding; and the less explicit influence of pharmaceutical giants behind the government's skirt, are all examples of these elites.

The dance between government and elites continues, and information undoubtedly flows both ways, but the real trend here is that we are getting closer to a time when government policy will be literally developed by consultants and pushed by executive government onto the citizenry – particularly when, as Parker (2004a) stated, every former regulator general of the UK subsequently became a consultant of one sort or another. Another clear example of the potential for risk here is the remark passed to the editor of this book by a minister in Victoria, Australia, regarding the policy of PPPs. 'Everything I have read about PPPs has been positive', was the reply to a series of diplomatic questions on their efficacy. As a statement of ideology, it was unsurprising. But as a statement by an elected representative to an informed citizen, it was quite remarkable in both its honesty and its naivety. And it was also profoundly worrying in its intellectual bankruptcy.[4] Or perhaps it was simply a reliable indicator of who really had the minister's ear and the narrowness of the policy advice now being sought.

And as governments feel the need to behave more and more like business executives, releasing only the good news as if intent solely on maximizing the chance to continue in office, there is a developing risk that conflicts between their advice behind the scenes and the calculus of the public interest will not be transparent. This 'shadowy influence of capital' (as Kelsey (1993) called it over a decade ago) is in direct conflict with the open pursuit of the public interest and risks corrupting democratic decision making and government resource allocations. Governance under this scenario becomes a series of stage-managed investment announcements in which the event itself is the policy solution.[5] The need to be both far more open and transparent about government's relationships with consultants and the degree to which consultant revenues are tied up in pubic policy ideas are paramount.

As with past policy development processes, there will no doubt continue to be a search for public policy which is evidence based, transparently sourced and publicly debated, and citizen involved, despite the tendency for smaller policy formation groups to dominate smaller but stronger and less open executive governments. Differing perceptions of winners and losers from privatization activities will also exist and winners rather than losers will, if the evidence to date is taken on board, continue to be more influential over governments than the other way around. This of course does present governments with some huge challenges. Governments have already become addicted to the advice of the consulting sector and currently risk being unable to formulate their own policy directions and activities.[6] In the face of powerful interest group coalitions in the future, government may inevitably tend towards simple, consultant-provided solutions. This will also be exacerbated by the desire for easy 'purchasable' policy solutions to complex issues, particularly if any additional costs of such solutions can be borne less visibly by taxpayers over long time periods. Business is happy, and ignorant taxpayers are blissfully none the wiser.

Having made these comments regarding the role of consultants on policy advice, we ought also explicitly acknowledge the other side of the coin. The consultant role in today's privatized state is not only a matter of policy capacity in the sense of ideology. Most regulatory agencies as well as other accountability guardians now require expertise of the highest order. As the state's mechanisms of governance have become fractured and more specialized, so too have the demands grown for specialist technical advice through lawyers, economists, accountants and engineers, for example. Indeed, this need for expertise probably accounts for the largest slice of consultant growth and provides an understandable rationale. But it is just as true that as governments have progressively downsized in response, presumably to growing business demands and either voter pressure or acquiescence, governments have also increased the size of their marketing departments and their capacity to stage-manage events at the expense of the more traditional policy analysis arena and the solid competence to offer 'free and fearless advice' to government.

Likewise, the regulatory fabric will continue to spread as confidence grows in the capacity of new regulatory arrangements to underpin a more dynamic market sector and provide a safety net for private businesses undertaking government functions.

Other factors in our assessment are less clear.

The success of the privatization family of activities still sees a raging debate in every country of the world. It has in large part been superseded by the (hardly surprising) observation that the success of privatization activities is not guaranteed and depends more on contextual issues than it does on a change of ownership of the service provider. In other words, privatization success in reality depends on the veracity of the regulatory state installed along with an enterprise sell-off; the degree of real competition in markets in which outsourcing reforms occur; the veracity of contractual arrangements and the trade-offs and valuations made by governments as they do PPP deals with the business sector; and the strength of underlying governance reforms on which any PSDS reform is founded in a developing economy. And each of these elements will, in turn, require democratic, social and legal legitimacy. Assessments of relative success will continue, and as has been found to date, a wide mix of successes is likely to be found in the future as well. And given that evaluations of regulatory success depend in the end on the degree to which new regulatory regimes lead to desirable long-term corporate behaviour and the deterrence of undesirable service outcomes, rather than any shorter-term administrative assessments or the personal judgements of an individual author, the evaluation of regulatory arrangements is likely to involve a lengthy jury deliberation. But what continues to be most striking here, as Minogue (2001b:36) rightly points out, 'is the degree to which many international institutions and individuals who we would now recognize as leaders in the knowledge elite', are silent on the degree to which evaluation evidence of reform effectiveness has not all been positive whilst they proselytize the privatization family to developing countries. To him, there was a failure 'of those who wish to see NPM reform extended to developing and transitional economies to take account of the very mixed results of these reforms where they have been fully applied'. Supporting these sentiments, Minogue then remarks that although the New Zealand reforms did reduce personnel numbers by a staggering 60 per cent, the NPM literature also points to the lack of hard evidence as to efficiency gains on privatization[7] and contracting-out,[8] the serious loss of public accountability and the democratic deficit and emasculation of local authority. Clearly, evidence has been mixed.[9]

Another continuing aspect of future deliberations will be the question of balance. The regulatory state is now marked by loud criticisms of over-regulation (Business Council of Australia, 2005) and calls to reduce the regulatory burden on business. Paradoxically, however, such calls come in simultaneously as others advocate the need for stronger regulatory action to cover a 'public accountability vacuum' or 'deficit' appearing in the midst of the privatized state (Taggart, 1992; Hodge, 2002; Mulgan, 2003) and to fill obvious flaws to control excesses in corporate behaviour through a global legal tidal wave of Sarbanes-Oxley measures in a post-Enron world. So, where does the balance of assessment really lie here? Whilst we would not suggest for one minute that no jurisdiction on earth has no room to reshape its regulatory arrangements and simplify outdated regulatory requirements, the desire by citizens for continued government actions in a wide range of economic and social arenas has in large part been the driver for more regulation. When cities such as Melbourne proudly boast on one day that they are amongst the worlds 'most liveable cities', and complain of over-regulation on the next, perhaps these are just opposite sides of the same coin? Maybe the stronger regulatory environment is one characteristic of the very community fabric that citizens regard as making the city just that little bit more civilized?

So, are we better off now having experienced the privatization family of reforms? Of all the privatization family debates over the past three decades, this remains one of the most central and contestable. The economic sums suggest to many that there is an aggregate gain.[10] But who exactly is it that is meant by the warm rhetorical '*we*'? In developed countries, whilst the privatization family of reforms has seen mixed reviews, they have also led to a renewed efficiency culture and business awareness, and on balance, have probably served the West well and improved national economies at an aggregate level. In this domain, as well, we have also usually seen a range of strong regulatory regimes to protect the interests of consumers and citizens. Nonetheless, despite the political chest-beating by professional groups who enjoy a slice of reform transactions, the jury is essentially still out on the overall benefit of privatization to citizens here.

In the case of developing economies, the state of knowledge on reform effectiveness is in reality, 'teasingly ambiguous', as Minogue (2001a:18) reminds us. And there is much criticism of central players, such as McCourt's (2001:231) imagery of World Bank reports being 'numerous impressively referenced publications' but with 'oases of fact in a desert of conjecture'. But we ought also remember that the poorly performing governments were initially labelled as an 'unresponsive but invasive state', an 'over-extended state' where government was unable to carry out too many responsibilities and yet support a large bureaucratic elite, and as a 'private interest state' where privileged groups exploited opportunities offered by state activities to enhance their own incomes. So the evaluation here between the reality of imperfect privatization family reform and the imperfect reality of poor previous performance is doubly difficult. As well, it is disappointing that 'those who finance and promote an NPM model so devoted to concepts of results-oriented management and performance measurement appear to have surprisingly little interest in the critical evaluation of the outcomes of their initiatives' Minogue (2001a:18). One is certainly left with more than a tinge of empathy for the conclusion that the privatization reform family has been promoted widely because it serves the self-interest of professional managers and consultants, and that such reforms have been wrapped into neat packages for onward transfer (Minogue, 2001a).[11]

This is a powerful idea. Like the ubiquitous balanced scorecard product in the field of management, ideas underpinning each of the components of the privatization family have inevitably been simplified and commodified. And over time, the complex portfolio of possibilities seems to have become simpler, more sellable, and under a commercial marketing ethos, more certain of its success.

What is also evident is the increasing importance of international systems of regulation governing globalized trade and commerce. As flashpoint demonstrations surrounding meetings of the World Economic Forum show, the legitimacy of international arrangements will continue to be increasingly questioned in a search for fairer, new regimes. Powered by global trade, any regulatory or accountability fissures existing at the local or national level are likely also to be magnified in the international domain. And as these arrangements further evolve, complexity will grow, with multilateral, regional, bilateral and domestic regimes operating more expansively. Additionally, it may be that NGOs play an increased role in brokering future regulatory debates alongside the powerful professional groups of consultants and regulocrats.

CONCLUSIONS

What comes through loud and clear in this book is the notion that the privatization family of reforms has played and will continue to play an important role in both developed and developing country economies. Whether we are discussing enterprise sell-offs, the contracting-out of government services, public–private partnerships or the wider idea of PSDS, the place of privatization in the modern world is assured. There is still much room to learn from the empirical evidence of experience, however, in preference to both the ideological advertising on one side and fierce criticism on the other that these reforms continue to attract. Modest gains are possible, and the overwhelming message for governments is still one of 'buyer beware', in terms of the promised benefits of policies. With almost $US1 trillion of revenues from enterprise sell-offs alone over the 1990s, any privatization business or advisory firm able to gain even a small slice of this pie saw a bag of gold. This business itself has been a boon.

The privatization family of reforms also brought with it the era of regulation. Indeed, a regulatory explosion has occurred, lubricated by transnational networks of professionals serving governments hungry for reform expertise and advice on the optimum path to regulatory capitalism. There is now a pressing need for much of the Western-based reform advice to acknowledge the mixed results of rigorous privatization and regulatory research on reforms in developed as well as developing countries, and be more strongly legitimized within local democratic and cultural contexts. This will require a more open learning approach from all sides, along with improved transparency in government decision making. And in the longer term, we will re-learn that citizens are rightly the ultimate judges of whether governments were serving the community well during the privatization and regulatory family of reforms or whether they passed the wheel over, allowing others to steer our state, at a cost.

NOTES

1. Having said that the matter of public sector funding limitations has been vastly overplayed, we ought to note here that it is nonetheless possible for governments to outlay virtually nothing for PPP infrastructure projects and claim the glory for new facilities whilst getting others to pay. This is indeed what occurs when a government approves a project on the basis that all costs are passed directly onto private citizens through say a toll road!

2. We might reflect on the possibility that to the degree to which this is the case, bureaucratic inefficiencies of past traditional government departments may have simply been replaced by such waste and higher transaction costs.

3. An example of the degree to which the knowledge elite are based in Western, developed countries is given in Cook (2001:224) who notes that the 'Adjustment in Africa' report on his desk at the time of writing had 125 sources in the bibliography, of which some 98 (i.e. 78 per cent) were from either the World Bank or IMF, or were published in either the US or Europe. Indeed, after putting aside academic journals, only one source was actually published in Africa!

4. Hodge and Greve (2005), for example, present multiple case studies and analyses from the UK, US, Europe and Australasia clearly outlining the mixed results which have been surfacing in this domain over the past decade.

5. As the rhetoric of productivity, outputs and market competition has taken over the public service, phrases such as 'the public interest' have progressively been phased out – an interesting observation when the pursuit of the public interest would seem to be the very central purpose of public sector institutions in the same way as private firms unashamedly pursue only the interests of their shareholders.

6. Even consultation forums for privatization activities such as PPPs are now managed by consultants in the state of Victoria, Australia. Advice from the Treasury and Finance officials is that they simply 'do not have the time' to conduct such activities. That particular privatized state has indeed been 'hollowed out'. Former bureaucratic tasks have been replaced by consultant contracts and advisers. Likewise, the Australian Department of Foreign Affairs and Trade's AusAID office now has more consultants being paid at senior levels from its budget than it has senior public servants (Russell, 2003).

7. On the matter of enterprise sell-offs, Minogue (2001b:24) argues that 'in the UK, as in general, evidence for the superiority of private over public enterprise is mixed and inconclusive, the real issue being monopoly and its associated inefficiencies rather than ownership'.

8. On this point, Minogue (2001a:27) argues that whilst the advantages of contracting-out are clear, 'the growing literature generally supplies more negative than positive judgments' and that . . . 'the outcome of contracting reforms is as contested and uneven as their introduction'.

9. These points are not new, and follow numerous previous observations made of privatization family components over decades by authors such as Bovaird (2004), Boyne (2000), Cook and Kirkpatrick (2003), Donahue (1989), Hodge (2000), Martin and Parker (1997), Parker (2004b), Hodge and Greve (2005), Walker and Walker (2000) and Wettenhall (2003).

10. The calculations of Galal et al. (1994) and Abdala (1992) and the discussion of Hodge (2000) are early examples here. The Galal et al. (1994) analysis, for instance, reviewed 12 privatizations in four countries and in 11 out of 12 cases reported increased total welfare: a glowing endorsement of enterprise sales, with overall welfare gains varying between 1.6 per cent to 12.0 per cent for the United Kingdom, and up to between 2.1 per cent to an amazing 155.0 per cent in the case of Chile. But what of the spread of winners and losers? In fact, of the 12 cases analysed from the United Kingdom, Malaysia, Chile and Mexico, no benefits were projected for domestic consumers in three cases, and losses to the consumers were projected in five. In other words, despite the glowing aggregate findings, domestic consumers either did not gain anything or else lost in eight of the twelve cases analysed (Hodge, 2000). The analysis of Abdala (1992) was similarly interesting. For the case of Argentina's ENTel, his analysis showed an overall worldwide gain in welfare of $US1.4 billion. Again, however, massive winners and losers occurred as part of this overall gain. His analysis suggested that despite the overall worldwide welfare gain, Argentina as a country lost by more than this worldwide gain – indeed by an amount of some $US2.2 billion.

11. Not all ideas on the global spread of reforms have favoured such an interpretation, however. For instance, the careful review of Black and Lodge (2005) looked at how regulatory innovation appears to have occurred. Theorizing several models, or worlds, of innovation, they suggest that little can be accounted for by leading individuals or the world of the global polity. Thus, they remark that 'whilst financial regulation international networks provide a forum for information exchange, they were hardly a diffuser of particular professional norms'. Likewise, for a second of their case studies, they observe that although licence auctions 'could in theory be partly a story of the involvement of transnational companies, international consultants and technocratic epistemic communities in the development and implementation of an innovation, it seems rather to be a story of national states responding largely in isolation from one another, in which the outcome of the UK auction (significant revenue) was communicated but little else'. Most accounts of regulatory innovation fell within the state and organizational worlds. Adding some spice to this, they also introduced the notion of a Pavlovian world of innovation in which a knee-jerk reflex regulatory response is required to meet an immediate political crisis – in their case example, the media frenzy following unprovoked attacks on innocent children and the obvious need for the improved control of dangerous dogs.

REFERENCES

Abdala, M.A. (1992), 'Distributional Impact Evaluation of Divestiture in a High Inflation Economy: The Case of Entel Argentina', unpublished PhD thesis, Boston University.

Black, J. and M. Lodge (2005), 'Conclusions', in Julia Black and Martin Lodge (eds), *Regulatory Innovation: A Comparative Analysis*, Cheltenham: Edward Elgar, pp. 181–197.

Bovaird, T. (2004), 'Public–Private Partnerships in Western Europe and the US: New Growths from Old Roots', in Abby Ghobadian, Nicholas O'Regan, David Gallear and Howard Viney (eds), *Private–Public Partnerships: Policy and Experience*, London: Palgrave.

Boyne, G. (2000), 'Public and Private Management: What's the Difference', *Journal of Management Studies*, **39** (1), 97–122.

Business Council of Australia (2005), *Submission to the Taskforce on Reducing the Regulatory Burden of Business*, Melbourne: BCA.

Cook, P. (2001), 'Privatization and Regulation in Developing Countries', in Willy McCourt and Martin Minogue (eds), *The Internationalization of Public Management: Reinventing the Third World State*, Cheltenham: Edward Elgar, pp. 153–173.

Cook, P., C. Kirkpatrick, M. Minogue and D. Parker (eds) (2004), *Leading Issues in Competition, Regulation and Development*, Cheltenham: Edward Elgar.

Cook, P. and C. Kirkpatrick (2003), 'Assessing the Impact of Privatization in Developing Countries', in David Parker and David Saal (eds), *International Handbook on Privatization*, Cheltenham: Edward Elgar, pp. 209–219.

Dollar, D. and A. Kraay (2000), *Growth is Good for the Poor*, Washington, DC: World Bank.

Donahue, J.D. (1989), *The Privatisation Decision: Public Ends, Private Means*, New York: HarperCollins.

Foster, C.D. (1992), *Privatization, Public Ownership and the Regulation of Natural Monopoly*, Oxford: Blackwell.

Galal, A., L. Jones, P. Tandon and I. Vogelsang (1994), *Welfare Consequences of Selling Enterprises: An Empirical Analysis*, Oxford: Oxford University Press.

Grimsey, D. and M. Lewis (2004) *Public–Private Partnerships: The Worldwide Revolution in Infrastructure Provision and Project Finance*, Cheltenham: Edward Elgar.

Guttman, D. (2003), 'Contracting United States Government Work: Organizational and Constitutional Models', *Public Organization Review*, **3** (3), 281–299.

Hodge, G.A. (2002), 'Accountability Lost Amid Privatisation Gains', *The Age*, 6 March, p. 15.

Hodge, G.A. (2000), *Privatisation: An International Review of Performance*, Boulder, CO: Westview Press.

Hodge, G. and C. Greve (eds) (2005), *The Challenge of Public–Private Partnerships: Learning from International Experience*, Cheltenham: Edward Elgar.

Kelsey, J. (1993), *Rolling Back the State: Privatization of Power in Aotearoa/New Zealand*, Auckland: Bridget Williams Books.

Kingdon, J. (1995) *Agendas, Alternatives and Public Policy*, second edition. New York: Longman.

Martin, S. and D. Parker (1997), *The Impact of Privatisation: Ownership and Corporate Performance in the UK*, London: Routledge.

McCourt, W. (2001), 'Moving the Public Management Debate Forward: A Contingency Approach', in Willy McCourt and Martin Minogue (eds), *The Internationalization of Public Management: Reinventing the Third World State*, Cheltenham: Edward Elgar, pp. 220–253.

Minogue, M. (2001a), 'The Internationalisation of New Public Management', in Willy McCourt and Martin Minogue (eds), *The Internationalization of Public Management: Reinventing the Third World State*, Cheltenham: Edward Elgar, pp. 1–19.

Minogue, M. (2001b), 'Should Flawed Models of Public Management be Exported? Issues and Practices', in Willy McCourt and Martin Minogue (eds), *The Internationalization of Public Management: Reinventing the Third World State*, Cheltenham: Edward Elgar, pp. 20–43.

Mulgan, R. (2003), *Holding Power to Account: Accountability in Modern Democracies*, Basingstoke: Palgrave Macmillan.

Parker, D. (2004a), Personal communication, London, September.

Parker, D. (2004b), 'Editorial: Lessons from Privatisation', *Economic Affairs*, **24** (3), 2–8.

Raustalia, K. and A.M. Slaughter (2002), 'International Law, International Relations and Compliance', in W. Carlsnaes, T. Risse, B. Simmons and T. Risse-Kappen (eds), *Handbook of International Relations*, London: Sage, pp. 538–558.

Russell, E.W. (2003), Personal communication, Melbourne, July.

Taggart, M. (1992), 'The Impact of Corporatisation and Privatisation on Administrative Law', *Australian Journal of Public Administration*, **51** (3), 368–373.

Walker, B. and B.C. Walker (2000), *Privatisation: Sell Off or Sell Out? The Australian Experience*, Sydney: ABC Books.

Wettenhall, R.A. (2003), 'The Rhetoric and Reality of Public–Private Partnerships', *Public Organisation Review: A Global Journal*, **3**, 77–107.

Index